PROPHETS

—— OF ——

PSYCHOHERESY I

PROPHETS

— OF —

PSYCHOHERESY I

Martin Bobgan
Deidre Bobgan

EastGate Publishers
Santa Barbara, CA 93110

Quotations taken from *Can You Trust Psychology?* by Gary Collins. Copyright© 1988 by Gary Collins and used by permission of InterVarsity Press, P. O. Box 1400, Downers Grove, IL 60515.
Quotations taken from *Effective Biblical Counseling* by Lawrence J. Crabb, Jr. Copyright © 1977 by the Zondervan Corporation. Used by permission.
Quotations taken from *Understanding People* by Lawrence J. Crabb, Jr. Copyright © 1987 by Lawrence J. Crabb, Jr. Used by permission of Zondervan Publishing House.

PROPHETS OF PSYCHOHERESY I

Published by EastGate Publishers
4137 Primavera Road
Santa Barbara, CA 93110

Library of Congress Catalog Card Number 89-83800
ISBN 0-941717-03-8

Printed in the United States of America.

This book is dedicated to the churches, seminaries and Bible colleges that have a high enough view of Scripture to exclude the pseudoscience of psychotherapies and their underlying psychologies.

We are grateful to Dr. Jay Adams, Dr. Paul Brownback, Ruth Hunt, Dave Maddox, Gary and Carol Milne, Jim Owen, and Dr. Hilton Terrell. Adams, Brownback, Hunt, Maddox, and Owen all critiqued and made helpful suggestions on the Dr. Lawrence Crabb section of this book. Dr. Hilton Terrell helped by commenting on the Drs. Meier and Minirth section. We thank them for their wise counsel.

Gary and Carol Milne have for a long period of time monitored Meier and Minirth's radio program. They have provided us with materials and books, which were the basis for the Meier and Minirth section. In addition, they have called us numerous times to encourage us in this project. We thank them for their help and support.

Comments

by

Jay E. Adams

Ph.D., Professor of Practical Theology, Westminster
Theological Seminary, and Dean of the Institute of Pastoral
Studies, Christian Counseling and Educational Foundation,
as well as author of numerous books on biblical counseling
and practical theology.

Ed Payne

M.D., Professor of Family Medicine, Medical College of
Georgia, and author of *Biblical/Medical Ethics*.

Hilton P. Terrell

Ph. D. (Psychology), M.D. Family Practice,
editor of the *Journal of Biblical Ethics in Medicine*.

Table of Contents

PROPHETS OF PSYCHOHERESY

Throughout this volume we attempt to reveal the source of the wisdom behind the psychologies that are being made palatable and promising to Christians. We do this in hopes that believers who truly love God will turn away from the wisdom of men and once again rely solely on the Lord and His Word in matters of life and conduct. For some readers, this book will be a confirmation of their suspicions. For others it will be an encouragement to be steadfast in the faith. For still others it will be a difficult challenge. And yet others, we fear, will simply take a stronger stand for integration and all it implies.

The title *Prophets of PsychoHeresy* may require some explanation. In this volume we are critiquing writings and teachings of Dr. Gary Collins, Dr. Lawrence Crabb, Jr., Dr. Paul Meier, and Dr. Frank Minirth. We use the word *prophet* according to the dictionary definition which says, "A spokesman for some cause, group, movement, etc."[1] These men are spokesmen for the use of the types of psychology that underlie what is known as psychotherapy or psychological counseling.

As in our other writing, we are attempting to deal with issues and not personalities. And, as we have said in the past, we name people in reference to what they have taught or written. However, we want to make it clear that, while we are critical of their promotion and use of psychological theories and techniques, we are not questioning their faith. The individuals selected for this volume were chosen out of our

3

own interest at the time of writing and based upon their popularity, acceptance, and influence among Christians. Also, there is a certain amount of compatibility that exists among them. In future volumes we hope to critique the work of other individuals.

We have had no public dialogue with any of the individuals in this volume. Opportunity was provided in the past to Collins, Meier, and Minirth for interchange. They all refused. We are still most happy to meet publicly or in the media with any of the individuals we critique. We believe it must be public because we are discussing what these men write and say at the public level. If they had raised these issues privately, we would request to meet with them privately. We believe that open dialogue is the biblical way to address these issues and that the church would benefit from such an interchange.

As in our earlier book, we use the term *psychoheresy* because what we describe is psychological heresy. It is heresy in that it is a departure away from absolute confidence in the biblical truth of God and toward faith in the unproven, unscientific psychological opinions of men.[2]

When we speak of psychology we are **not** referring to the entire discipline of psychology. Instead we are speaking about that part of psychology which deals with the very nature of man, how he should live, and how he should change. This includes psychological counseling, clinical counseling, psychotherapy, and the psychological aspects of psychiatry.

Our position on the matter of psychology and the Bible is more fully stated in our book *PsychoHeresy*. We believe that mental-emotional-behavioral problems of living (nonorganic problems) should be ministered to by biblical encouragement, exhortation, preaching, teaching, and counseling which depends solely upon the truth of God's Word without incorporating the unproven and unscientific psychological opinions of men. Then, if there are biological, medical problems, the person should seek medical rather than psychological assistance.

The opposing position varies from the sole use of psychology without the use of any Scripture to an integration of the two in varying amounts, depending upon the personal judgment of the individual. Integration is the attempt to combine theories, ideas, and opinions from psychotherapy, clinical psychology, counseling psychology, and their underlying psychologies with Scripture. Christian integrationists use psychological opinions about the nature of man, why he does what he does, and how he can change, in ways that seem to them to be compatible with their Christian faith or their view of the Bible. They may quote from the Bible, utilize certain biblical principles, and attempt to stay within what they consider to be Christian or biblical guidelines. Nevertheless, they do not have confidence in the Word of God for all matters of life, conduct, and counseling. Therefore they use the secular psychological theories and techniques in what they would consider to be a Christian way.

Books by Collins, Crabb, Meier, and Minirth present apologetics for the integration of psychology and theology; ours are an apologetic for "solo Scriptura." We believe in the absolute sufficiency of Scripture in all matters of life and conduct (2 Peter 1). Thus we regard our position as being a high view of Scripture; and we refer to the point of view we are criticizing as a high view of psychology.

We admit that our position is a minority position that seems to be shrinking in support as Christians seek to confront the problems of life. Almost everywhere one turns in the church one sees psychology. The psychologizing of Christianity has reached epidemic proportions. We see it everywhere in the church, from psychologized sermons to psychologized persons. However, as we have demonstrated in our earlier books, the psychologizing of the church is not biblically or scientifically justifiable.

We live in an era in which those who profess faith in Jesus Christ have become followers of men just as in the Corinthian church. Therefore, to criticize one of these men is to put oneself in a vulnerable position. How dare anyone say anything about the teachings of such popular, influential leaders? Nevertheless, we believe that it is necessary for Christians to become discerning of what they read and hear.

There is a strong tendency to forget to be a Berean, to neglect thinking for oneself, and to receive teachings without comparison with the Word of God. Rather than examining teaching with the Word of God, many Christians assume that if a particular man, whom they trust, has said something, it must be true. They often base this assumption on reputation, degrees, and institutions. Also, if a man or institution has been known for teaching correct doctrine in the past, the assumption is that current teachings must be orthodox as well. Just because a teacher quotes the Bible and says some very good things does not mean that everything he says is true or biblically sound. Only the Word of God can be entirely trusted.

In our past writing we have often referred to research studies, because if a case can be made for the use of psychology, it must be supported in the research. In addition, we quoted various distinguished individuals, including philosophers of science, Nobel Laureates, and distinguished professors to reveal the strength of the evidence **in opposition** to the credibility of psychology and therefore **in opposition** to the integration stand. Our reason for quoting researchers is because therapists, according to Dr. Bernie Zilbergeld, "tend to forget unsuccessful cases or pretend they weren't failures."[3]

In addition, Zilbergeld adds, "Therapists rarely have systematically collected and controlled information about their own cases from which to draw reliable conclusions about effectiveness."[4] He says, "Very few therapists do any follow up evaluations."[5] Researcher Dr. Dorothy Tennov says, "A recent review of psychotherapy research revealed that in twenty-five years, only fifteen studies had employed a private practice setting."[6]

In an article in **Science '86** magazine titled "Psychabuse," the author compares the results of research with the actual practice of psychotherapists. He gives examples of discrepancies between what therapists do and what scientific research reveals. He refers to these differences as abuses, thus the name of the article. He concludes by saying, "One distressing conclusion that can be drawn from all of these abuses is that psychotherapists don't care much for results or for science."[7]

The point we are making is that private practice therapists generally do not do research and when they do, it is not generally reliable. We stress this point because Christian professional counselors who write books and speak refer to their own personal approaches as if they are successful, when, as a matter of fact, either unreliable research or no research has been conducted to indicate the efficacy of their work. Therefore, it is essential to pay attention to the academic researchers instead of accepting the testimonies of Christian professional counselors, unless backed up by reliable research. That is one reason why we quote research in our work.

We want to make it perfectly clear, however, that we believe the Bible stands on its own. It does not need scientific verification or any kind of research support. Christian presuppositions begin with Scripture, and any information culled from the environment is answerable to Scripture, not vice versa. Therefore, we do not use results of research to prove that the Bible is right, even when they may seem to agree with Scripture. That is totally unnecessary. Scientific investigation is limited by the fact that it is conducted by fallible humans, while the Bible is the inspired Word of God. Furthermore, as Dr. Hilton Terrell points out, "Science is *irrelevant* to essentially religious pronouncements about non-material concepts such as libido."[8] (Emphasis his.)

The Bible records God's revelation to humanity about Himself and about the human condition. It is very clear about its role in revealing the condition of man, why he is the way he is and how he changes. Psychological theories offer a variety of explanations about the same concerns, but they are merely scientific-sounding opinions and speculations.

Paul repudiated the use of such worldly wisdom and depended upon the power of the cross of Christ, the presence of the indwelling Holy Spirit, and the efficacy of the life changing Word of God in all matters of life and holiness. Paul's denunciation of worldly wisdom was no mere quibble over words. He saw the grave danger of trying to mix worldly wisdom (the opinions of men) with the way of the cross. And just as today, it appears foolish to rely solely on the cross, the Word of God and the Holy Spirit in matters of life and conduct, it certainly appeared foolish then. Paul wrote:

> For the preaching of the cross is to them that perish
> foolishness; but unto us which are saved it is the
> power of God. For it is written, I will destroy the
> wisdom of the wise, and will bring to nothing the
> understanding of the prudent. Where is the wise?
> where is the scribe? where is the disputer of this
> world? **hath not God made foolish the wisdom
> of this world?** For after that in the wisdom of God
> the world by wisdom knew not God, it pleased God
> by the foolishness of preaching to save them that
> believe. (1 Corinthians 1:18-21.)

No one can know God through worldly wisdom. Nor can anyone be saved. Yet some will say that the theories of counseling psychology are useful and even necessary for Christians
in their daily lives. But, the theories and philosophies behind
psychotherapy and counseling psychology were all originated
by men who turned their back on God, men who were wise in
their own eyes, but foolish in the eyes of God.

Paul relied on "Christ the power of God, and the wisdom
of God" (1 Corinthians 1:24). He continued his letter:

> Because the foolishness of God is wiser than men;
> and the weakness of God is stronger than men. For
> ye see your calling, brethren, how that not many
> wise men after the flesh, not many mighty, not many
> noble, are called: But God hath chosen the foolish
> things of the world to confound the wise; and God
> hath chosen the weak things of the world to con-
> found the things which are mighty; and base things
> of the world, and things which are despised, hath
> God chosen, yea, and things which are not, to bring
> to nought things that are: That no flesh should glory
> in his presence. But of him are ye in Christ Jesus,
> who of God is made unto us wisdom, and righteous-
> ness, and sanctification, and redemption: That, ac-
> cording as it is written, He that glorieth, let him
> glory in the Lord. (1 Corinthians 1:25-31.)

If indeed Jesus "is made unto us wisdom, and righteousness, and sanctification, and redemption," one wonders why any Christian would desire to look in the ash heap of secular opinions posing as science. What else is necessary for living the Christian life, when His very presence provides all that we require for wisdom, righteousness, sanctification, and redemption? All is provided in Jesus, mediated to us by the Holy Spirit.

One sentence that may get lost in the passage quoted above is this: "That no flesh should glory in his presence." When a believer turns to theories and therapies of worldly wisdom, there is a strong tendency to give at least part of the credit to someone or something other than the Lord. On the other hand, when a believer turns to God and His Word, trusts God to work His good pleasure in his life, and obeys God's Word through the wisdom and power of the indwelling Holy Spirit, the praise, gratitude and glory go to the Lord.

Paul was well-educated and well-acquainted with the wisdom of the Greeks. However, he refused to use anything that would detract from the testimony of God. This is what he said about his determination to teach only the testimony of God:

> And I, brethren, when I came to you, came not with excellency of speech or of wisdom, declaring unto you the testimony of God. For I determined not to know any thing among you, save Jesus Christ, and him crucified. And I was with you in weakness, and in fear, and in much trembling. **And my speech and my preaching was not with enticing words of man's wisdom, but in demonstration of the Spirit and of power: That your faith should not stand in the wisdom of men, but in the power of God.** (1 Corinthians 2:1-5.)

The psychological way unnecessarily brings man's wisdom into the church. Testimonies of the Lord working sovereignly through His Word and His Holy Spirit in the trials of life are becoming more and more scarce, while honor and praise are being given to those who give forth worldly psychological wisdom. Faith is ever so subtly being shifted from the power of God to a combination of God and the wisdom of men. And when it comes to the more serious problems of living, the shift is so great that God is left out almost altogether.

Paul had no use for the wisdom of the world. On the other hand, he understood that wisdom from God comes as a gift. It cannot be reduced to formulas or techniques or anything controlled by human beings.

> Howbeit we speak wisdom among them that are perfect: **yet not the wisdom of this world**, nor of the princes of this world, that come to nought: But **we speak the wisdom of God** in a mystery, even the hidden wisdom, which God ordained before the world unto our glory: Which none of the princes of this world knew: for had they known it, they would not have crucified the Lord of glory.
> (1 Corinthians 2:6-8.)

However, as James reminds us, wisdom only comes to those who trust Him:

> If any of you lack wisdom, let him ask of God, that giveth to all men liberally, and upbraideth not; and it shall be given him. But let him ask in faith, nothing wavering. For he that wavereth is like a wave of the sea driven with the wind and tossed. For let not that man think that he shall receive any thing of the Lord. A double minded man is unstable in all his ways. (James 1:5-8.)

Perhaps the wisdom of God is scarce these days because of the confidence being placed in the wisdom of men. Thus, rather than asking in faith and waiting on God for wisdom, believers are wavering. Or worse yet, Christians are asking psychologists in faith and expecting them to perform miracles. Thus they are caught in a web of double-mindedness, which is a very applicable description of the integration of psychology and the Bible.

The apostles and the early church would be horrified to see what is replacing the pure work of God through His Word and His Holy Spirit throughout the church today. They would wonder if Christians have forgotten the great promises of God and the blessed truths of their present inheritance. They would wonder if the Holy Spirit has been shoved into a corner and ignored in the daily course of Christians' lives. Paul briefly describes the tremendous resources for Christians in contrast to the feeble wisdom of man:

> But as it is written, Eye hath not seen, nor ear heard, neither have entered into the heart of man, the things which God hath prepared for them that love him. But God hath revealed them unto us by his Spirit: for the Spirit searcheth all things, yea, the deep things of God. For what man knoweth the things of a man, save the spirit of man which is in him? even so the things of God knoweth no man, but the Spirit of God. Now we have received, not the spirit of the world, but the spirit which is of God; that we might know the things that are freely given to us of God. **Which things also we speak, not in the words which man's wisdom teacheth, but which the Holy Ghost teacheth**; comparing spiritual things with spiritual. (1 Corinthians 2:9-13.)

Since we have received the Spirit of God, since we have the written Word of God, and since He leads us into wisdom in our daily affairs, it is foolishness to look for answers to the problems of living in the wisdom of men. He gives spiritual discernment. In fact, Paul declares that "we have the mind of Christ."

> But the natural man receiveth not the things of the Spirit of God: for they are foolishness unto him: neither can he know them, because they are spiritually discerned. But he that is spiritual judgeth all things, yet he himself is judged of no man.

> For who hath known the mind of the Lord, that he
> may instruct him? But we have the mind of Christ.
> (2 Corinthians 2:14-16.)

But if we continue to listen to the world's philosophies and psychologies to understand the condition of man, why he is the way he is, and how he is to live, we will lose spiritual discernment. We will drown out the pure doctrine of the Word of God and fail to know the mind of Christ.

When Christians are asked to explain why they turn to psychology, they give a variety of answers. However, the umbrella, "All truth is God's truth," seems to encompass most of the reasons given. The idea underlying this statement is that God is the author of all things and that His truths exist in the world, whether in Scripture or in the natural world. As we address the teachings gleaned from psychology, we need to discern what is being embraced under that umbrella: the wisdom of God or the wisdom of men.

PART ONE

COMMENTS

by Ed Payne

These chapters level another devastating argument against psychologists who are Christians in general and Dr. Gary Collins in particular. The argument is thorough, as it counters psychology on its basis as science, its claim to truth, its integration with Scripture, its being religion, its effectiveness, and its humanism (self-centeredness). While I have some familiarity with the psychological literature, the amount of research **against** psychology is amazing and **from people in their own camps**. It is fascinating that while the federal government is willing to subsidize almost anything today (except conservative Christians), there is insufficient evidence of efficacy for a Senate subcommittee to "justify public support" of psychology (Chapter 5).

I find the supposed attempt at the "integration" of psychology with Scripture to be the most arrogant and serious claim of Collins and others. With all the warnings in Scripture of "being in the world, but not of the world" and the separation of God's truth from all other claims represented as darkness and light, the impossibility of integration of avowedly pagan psychologists with Scripture seems obvious. One begins to wonder whether these promoters of psychology have any biblical discernment.

In fact, discernment seems to be exactly what Christians most want to avoid these days. For all the focus on spiritual gifts over the past decade, how often does any organization seek those with discernment? Evangelists, teachers, seminar leaders, and those with the gift of "helps" are actively sought, but few seek the prophets to discern truth and error. Modern Christians treat those with discernment no better than the prophets of the Old Testament. They are not stoned, but they are effectively isolated from key positions and from most Christian publishers.

With so many concepts contrary to Scripture and all the arguments against psychology, one wonders why it continues to be so widely accepted among conservative Christians. The only conclusion seems to be that psychological concepts appeal to man's sin nature. Why else would Christians choose a way that was contrary to God's way? Indeed, Adam and Eve were enticed away from God by Satan's lie that they would be "like God." Ironically, the concept of "self-esteem" that is advocated by so many Christians in psychology is consistent with this sinful appeal.

Psychologists who are Christians are not primarily at fault. Church leaders must bear the guilt of the invasion of psychology into the church. These are the people who are ordained of God to guard the minds of their sheep. Instead, they have invited wolves into the fold. Christian publishers are guilty as well. The "profit margin" has become the most important consideration for them. In reality Christian publishing ought to be under the authority of the church, so even in this area church leaders are at fault.

No greater issue faces the modern, true church than this Trojan horse of psychology. It has a stranglehold that will not be easily loosened. I applaud the scholarly efforts herein along with the few others who attempt to free the church of the religion of psychology.

PART ONE

CAN YOU REALLY TRUST PSYCHOLOGY?

Dr. Gary R. Collins, a professor of psychology at Trinity Evangelical Divinity School in Deerfield, Illinois, has written *Can You Trust Psychology?* Collins is a prolific writer and anyone who has read his previous books would not be surprised by his answer to the question posed in the title of his book. What is different about the book is that it attempts to answer the Christian critics of psychology. Although the attempt was to give a balanced response, Collins' strong commitment to integrating psychology into Christianity is loud and clear.[1]

Rather than discussing Collins' other books, we will focus on *Can You Trust Psychology?* in which he gives reasons for integrating psychology and the Bible. Collins superficially raised numerous issues in that book, which would take volumes to answer in depth. Therefore, we will concentrate on a limited number of themes, all of which deal with the serious issue of integration.

Collins prefers to lump all of psychology together as he attempts to answer the criticisms aimed at clinical psychology, psychotherapy, psychological counseling, and their underlying theories and therapies. On the other hand, the critics of the integration of psychology and Christianity and the psychologizing of the church have limited their criticism to those psychological theories and therapies which deal with the human condition and the why's and wherefore's of behavior. Therefore, it is important to remember that Collins' arguments are often from the perspective of the broad meaning of psychology. This can be somewhat confusing. He uses details from research psychology when he seeks to give scientific status to the whole field of psychology, which also includes the unscientific, unproven theories which attempt to understand people and change behavior.

1

THE SCIENTIFIC POSTURE

The word *science* has special appeal in the twentieth century. Many believe that if something is scientific it must be factual and true. In fact, any human endeavor that can be labeled "science" or "scientific" gains immediate merit in the Western world. Therefore it is understandable that those people who wish to integrate psychology with Christianity assign a scientific status to this type of psychology. The appeal of science has drawn many Christians into a maze of psychological opinion accepted as fact. Since science bears this high stamp of approval, it serves as a Shibboleth for psychological theories to gain entrance into the church. Therefore, we must determine the scientific status of psychology.

Collins continually refers to the kind of psychology that is to be integrated with Christianity as *science*. However, in considering the question, "Is Psychology Really a Science?," Collins lists some characteristics of "What all good science attempts to accomplish."[1] He says that scientists "observe data," "classify data," "explain data," and finally "predict and even control how their subject matter will respond in the future."[2]

What does Collins mean when he says that scientists "observe data"? Does he mean visual observation of behavior or does he include other ways of gathering information? Most of what psychological studies call "observation" is not visual or objective, but rather verbal and subjective forms of personal revelation. In other words, rather than gaining their data through observation, they gain it through verbal means, such as interviews, conversations, and questionnaires. Thus, a subject reveals his own perceptions to a listener or reader rather than performing an act that can be observed. Self-reporting or descriptions of others cannot be fully objective. Therefore, the practice of observation—especially as related to the psychologies that underlie psychotherapies or psychological counseling—is generally the practice of gathering subjective information. This does not mean that such information lacks all accuracy. However, there is a great possibility for inaccuracy in the very basics of data gathering in this field.

The second activity he lists is "classify data," but he does not mention that classifying data can be as objective as classifying blood types and as subjective as classifying personality or astrological types. The third activity, "explain data," gets even stickier, especially in the area of clinical psychology, psychotherapy, psychological counseling and the psychologies that underlie these activities. Is the psychologist going to explain the data according to a Freudian, Jungian, Skinnerian, Adlerian, Maslovian, or Rogerian point of view? What theoretical, philosophical influences will determine how the data is explained? Will it be psychoanalytical, behavioral, humanistic, or transpersonal?

When we reach Collins' requirement for science to "predict and even control," we come to one of the primary well-known failures of psychotherapy as a science. In physics and chemistry the scientist can predict what will happen under given circumstances. He can even talk about the probability of certain events occurring. However, in psychotherapy the system breaks down at the level of prediction. It is not known why some people get better and some worse; nor can one even predict which people will get better and which ones will deteriorate.

Much research on clinical judgment and decision-making reveals that the experts substantially lack the ability to predict. Einhorn and Hogarth say that "it is apparent that neither the extent of professional training and experience nor the amount of information available to clinicians necessarily increases predictive accuracy."[3] It is shocking that in spite of the great fallibility of professional judgment people seem to have unshakable confidence in it.

The American Psychiatric Association admits that psychiatrists cannot predict future dangerous activities of their patients. In a court case involving a person who committed murder shortly after having seen a psychiatrist, the APA presented an *amicus curiae* brief, which stated that research studies show that psychiatrists are unable to predict future potential dangerous behavior of a patient.[4] To circumvent their inability to predict behavior, some have called psychotherapy a "post-dictive science." One psychologist admits, "Since the days of Freud, we have had to rely on post-dictive theories—that is, we have used our theoretical systems to explain or rationalize what has gone on before."[5]

Psychotherapists are unable to predict the future mental-emotional health of their clients with any confidence. They can merely look into a person's past and guess why he is the way he is today. However, psychotherapy should not even be labeled "post-dictive," because the explanation of behavior and its relationship to the past is subjective and interpretive rather than objective and reliable.

Collins varies his requirements for whether a discipline is or is not a science. When he discusses parapsychology he says:

> Science must be able to observe facts carefully and accurately, find cause-effect relationships and explain events in accordance with naturalistic laws. Parapsychological research has trouble complying with these requirements.[6]

As we shall show, psychological theories regarding the nature of man, why he behaves the way he does, and how he changes have trouble complying with these requirements as well. And the warning he sounds about psychic phenomena applies equally to those psychological theories and therapies:

> The human mind has a remarkable ability to let
> preconceived notions bias the way in which
> information is interpreted and remembered.[7]

On the other hand he is more generous in his requirements
for psychology to be considered a science:

> If by *science* we mean only the use of rigorous,
> empirical and experimental methods, then it must
> be concluded that the broad field of psychology is
> not a science. . . . If, in contrast, we think of science
> as a careful, systematic observation and analysis of
> data—including data coming from outside the
> laboratory, from the humanities and from divine
> revelation—then psychology can be considered a
> science.[8]

Such a definition of science opens the door to all forms of
study, whether they be objective or subjective, or whether
they be fact or opinion.

Although psychological theories and their therapies have
indeed   adopted the scientific posture, they have not been
able to meet the scientific requirements. In a herculean
attempt to evaluate the status of psychology, the American
Psychological Association appointed Dr. Sigmund Koch to
plan and direct an extensive study involving eighty eminent
scholars. After assessing the facts, theories, and methods of
psychology, they published their results in a seven volume
series entitled *Psychology: A Study of a Science.*[9] Koch's
words bluntly address the delusion under which our society
has been suffering in reference to psychology as a science:

> The *hope* of a psychological science became indistin-
> guishable from the *fact* of psychological   science.
> The entire subsequent history of psychology can be
> seen as a ritualistic endeavor to emulate the forms
> of science in order to sustain the delusion that it al-

ready *is* a science.[10] (Emphasis his.)

Koch also says: "Throughout psychology's history as 'science,' the *hard* knowledge it has deposited has been uniformly negative."[11] (Emphasis his.)

In a book titled *The Sorcerer's Apprentice*, psychology professor Mary Stewart Van Leeuwen demonstrates "that the apprenticeship of psychology to natural science . . . does not work."[12] Psychiatrist Lee Coleman in his book about psychiatry, *The Reign of Error*, argues that "psychiatry does not deserve the legal power it has been given" and contends that "psychiatry is not a science."[13] He says:

> I have testified in over one hundred and thirty criminal and civil trials around the country, countering the authority of psychiatrists or psychologists hired by one side or the other. In each case I try to educate the judge or jury about why the opinions produced by these professionals have no scientific merit.[14]

In spite of the fact that psychotherapy as science has been seriously questioned over the past thirty-five years, both Christian and non-Christian psychotherapists persistently claim that they are operating under scientific principles and continue to consider themselves solidly scientific. Research psychiatrist Jerome Frank says that most psychotherapists "share the American faith in science. They appeal to science to validate their methods just as religious healers appeal to God."[15]

Dr. Karl Popper, considered by many to be the greatest twentieth-century philosopher of science, has examined psychological theories having to do with understanding and treating human behavior. He says that these theories, "though posing as sciences, had in fact more in common with primitive myths than with science; that they resembled astrology rather than astronomy." He says, "These theories describe some facts but in the manner of myths. They contain most interesting psychological suggestions, but not in testable form."[16] Psychologist Carol Tavris says:

> Now the irony is that many people who are not
> fooled by astrology for one minute subject them-
> selves to therapy for years, where the same errors
> of logic and interpretation often occur.[17]

Research psychiatrist Jerome Frank also equates psychotherapies with myths because "they are not subject to disproof."[18]
One can develop a theory for explaining all human behavior
and then interpret all behavior in the light of that explanation. This not only applies to psychology but to graphology,
astrology, and other such "ologies" as well.

For an area of study to qualify as a science, there must be
the possibility of not only refuting theories but also predict-
ing future events, reproducing results obtained, and controlling what is observed. Lewis Thomas says, "Science requires,
among other things, a statistically significant number of re-
producible observations and, above all, controls."[19]

When one moves from the natural sciences to the "behavioral sciences," there is also a move away from refutability,
predictability, reproducibility, and controllability. Furthermore, the cause and effect relationship, so evident in the
natural sciences, is ambiguous or absent in the "behavioral
sciences." Instead of causation (cause and effect), psychotherapy rests heavily upon covariation (events which appear
together which may not necessarily be related).

Because of the subjectivity of psychotherapy, there is a
great temptation to assume that when two events occur
together (covariation) one must have caused the other. This
is also the basis of much superstition. For example, if one
walks under a ladder and then has "bad luck," a cause and
effect relationship is assumed and one then avoids walking
under ladders for fear of "bad luck." This type of
superstitious relationship occurs often in the "behavioral
sciences." And the superstitious nonscientific illusions of
psychotherapy are many.

Scientific Facade.

If the type of psychology we are discussing does not meet the rigors of scientific inquiry and yet continues to claim scientific status, we must wonder if it is indeed pseudoscience. The dictionary definition of *pseudoscience* certainly seems to fit: "a system of theories, assumptions, and methods erroneously regarded as scientific."[20] Pseudoscience or pseudoscientism uses the scientific label to protect and promote opinions which are neither provable nor refutable.

Numerous critics in the field recognize the pseudoscientific nature of psychotherapy. In his book *The Powers of Psychiatry*, psychiatrist-lawyer Jonas Robitscher, says this about psychiatrists in general:

> His advice is followed because he is a psychiatrist, even though the scientific validity of his advice and recommendations has never been firmly established.[21]

He further states, "The infuriating quality of psychiatrists is . . . their insistence that they are scientific and correct and that their detractors, therefore, must be wrong."[22] Research psychiatrist E. Fuller Torrey's words are even more blunt:

> The techniques used by Western psychiatrists are, with few exceptions, on exactly the same scientific plane as the techniques used by witch doctors.[23]

Torrey also says, "If anything, psychiatric training may confer greater ability to rationalize subjective conviction as scientific fact."[24]

Walter Reich refers to "the sudden recognition among psychiatrists that, even as a *clinical* enterprise, psychoanalysis and the approaches derived from it are neither scientific nor effective."[25] Reich warns of "the dangers of ideological zeal in psychiatry, the profession's preference for wishful thinking to scientific knowledge, and the backlash that is provoked, perhaps inevitably, when the zeal devours the ideology and the wish banishes the science."[26]

Psychotherapy escapes the rigors of science because the mind is not equal to the brain and man is not a machine. Psychotherapy deals with individuals who are unique and make personal choices. Interaction in a therapeutic setting involves the individuality and volition of both the therapist and the person being counseled. Additionally, variables of time and changing circumstances in the lives and values of both therapist and counselee may have more to do with change than the therapy itself. Scientific endeavor is extremely useful in studying physical phenomena, but is at a loss in studying the psyche, because the deep thoughts and motivations of humanity escape the scientific method. Instead, the study is more the business of philosophers and theologians.

Dave Hunt addresses this issue in his book *Beyond Seduction*:

> True faith and true science are not rivals, but deal with different realms. . . . To mix faith with science is to destroy both. . . . The God who created us in His image exists beyond the scope of scientific laws. Therefore, human personality and experience, which come from God and not from nature, must forever defy scientific analysis. No wonder psychotherapy, which pretends to deal "scientifically" with human behavior and personality, has failed so miserably! No human being has the power to define from within himself, much less dictate to others, what constitutes right or wrong behavior. Only God can set such standards, and if there is no Creator God, then morality is nonexistent. This is why psychology's "scientific" standards for "normal" behavior are arbitrary, changeable, meaningless, and inevitably amoral.[27]

The actual foundations of psychotherapy are not science, but rather various philosophical world views, especially those of   determinism, secular humanism, behaviorism, existentialism, and even evolutionism. With its *isms* within *isms*, psychotherapy   penetrates   every   area   of   modern thought. Its influence has not been confined to the therapist's office, for its varied explanations of human behavior and contradictory ideas for change have permeated both society and the church. And, unfortunately the major emphasis in psychology that is generally taught at most seminaries (such as in pastoral counseling classes) is that part of psychology which is the least scientific.

To support his position that this type of psychology is science, Collins fails to mention one philosopher of science, one Nobel Laureate, or one distinguished professor who supports his subjectively held personal view, which is propagated by fiat rather than fact. Yet he continues to refer to such theories as "scientific conclusions."[28]

2

TRUTH OR CONFUSION?

Collins says, "Based on what we know thus far, it is . . . irresponsible to dismiss psychotherapy as a pseudoscience riddled with contradictions and confusion. Such a conclusion is clear bias, not supported by research."[1] In another place, he refers to "the science of human behavior."[2]

In spite of Collins' label of "irresponsible" for those who "dismiss psychotherapy as a pseudoscience riddled with contradictions and confusion," any person familiar with the research must admit that psychotherapy is rampant with conflicting explanations of man and his behavior. Psychologist Roger Mills, in his article "Psychology Goes Insane, Botches Role as Science," says:

> The field of psychology today is literally a mess. There are as many techniques, methods and theories around as there are researchers and therapists. I have personally seen therapists convince their clients that all of their problems come from their mothers, the stars, their bio-chemical make-up, their diet, their life-style and even the "kharma" from their past lives.[3]

Instead of knowledge being added to knowledge with more recent discoveries resting upon a body of solid information,

one system contradicts or disenfranchises another, one set of
opinions is exchanged for another, and one set of techniques
is replaced by another.

As culture and life styles change, so does psychotherapy.
With over 250 separate systems, each claiming superiority
over the rest, it is hard to view so many diverse opinions as
being scientific or even factual. The entire field is amassed
in confusion and crowded with pseudo-knowledge and
pseudo-theories resulting in pseudo-science.

The contradictions are not simply minor variations. The
contradictions within this kind of psychology are both
pervasive and extensive. At a gathering of more than 7000
psychiatrists, psychologists, and social workers, described by
its organizer as "the Woodstock of psychotherapy," well-
known and highly respected behavioral psychologist Dr.
Joseph Wolpe confessed that "an outside observer would be
surprised to learn that this is what the evolution of
psychotherapy has come to—a Babel of conflicting voices."[4]
Whereas, the question used to be, "What hath Athens to do
with Jerusalem?" the question we must now raise is, "What
hath Babel to do with the Bible?"

If psychotherapy had succeeded as a science, then there
would be some consensus in the field regarding mental-
emotional-behavioral problems and how to treat them.
Instead and contrary to Collins' objections, the field is filled
with many contradictory theories and techniques, all of
which communicate confusion rather than anything
approximating scientific order.

More Confusion.

Collins engages in a number of confusions that are
typical among Christians who are enamored of psychological
counseling and its underlying psychologies. He says, "In
mathematics, medicine, physics, geography, marine biology
and a host of other areas there is much truth that is not
mentioned in the Bible."[5] Collins uses this statement to add
to his continual analogy of science and psychology. It is
understandable that real science is useful in revealing the

physical universe to us. The Bible is not a physics book nor a chemistry book, but rather a book about God and man. It is the only book that contains uncontaminated truth about man, whereas psychology provides only opinions.

Collins continues this error in logic when he equates using psychology with using modern technology, such as the radio and antibiotics. He argues that Jesus and Paul didn't use modern technology, not because it was wrong, but because it was not available, with the implication that the only reason Jesus and Paul did not avail themselves of psychology is because it was not available then.[6] Elsewhere, however, Collins admits that Jesus and Paul would not have used psychology even if it had been available. Of Jesus he says:

> If psychology had been taught at the universities when he walked on the earth, Jesus probably would not have taken a course because he didn't have to. His knowledge of human behavior was infinite and perfect.[7]

Jesus' knowledge is still infinite and perfect. That is why a biblical counselor will rely on Jesus dwelling in him and guiding the counseling process through His Word. In reference to Paul, Collins admits:

> Paul, in contrast, did not have Jesus' infinite understanding, but he was a well-educated intellectual who understood many of the world's philosophies. He rejected the notion that these could give ultimate answers to human questions. Instead he built many of his arguments on Scripture and insisted that the scholars of his time repent. Surely the apostle would have presented a similar message to psychological scholars if they had existed when Paul was alive.[8]

And, indeed, Paul would have opposed the inclusion of psychological explanations of man. Psychology evolved out of philosophy and Paul warn against using the vain

philosophies of men. (Colossians 2:8.) Nevertheless, in spite
of this admission, Collins asks:

> Does it follow, however, that the modern disciple of
> Christ and reader of Paul's epistles should throw
> away psychology books and reject psychology
> because it was not used centuries ago?[9]

We would have to answer a strong **yes**, because they did not
use it centuries ago for the same reasons they would not use
it now. Are we to change the intent of Scripture simply
because we are living in a different century?

Confusion between Science and Opinion.

Collins attempts to justify psychology as if it were a
science with proven, objective, verifiable evidence (which it
grossly lacks) by arguing, *"Even though the Bible is all true,
it does not follow that all truth is in the Bible."*[10] (Emphasis
his.) He then cites the use of mathematics, medicine, and
physics to justify the use of psychology as if the Bible were
not explicitly written to tell us who we are and how to live.

The Bible was not written as a science text on physical
aspects of the universe. Rather, it was written for the
express purpose of revealing to man what he needed to know
about living in relationship to God and to others. Within that
revelation comes the knowledge of the fall, the sinful
condition of unredeemed man, God's provision for salvation,
and how a redeemed person is to live in relationship to God
and man through the new life in Jesus. Between the Bible's
covers lie "exceeding great and precious promises, that by
these ye might be partakers of the divine nature" (2 Peter
1:4). The Word of God is revealed truth about mankind, with
no error or bias.

The confusion between what is observed in science and
what is done in psychology continues as Collins declares:

> Some critics of psychology seem to argue, however,

that God has not allowed human beings to discover any truths about interpersonal relations, mental health, counseling techniques, mental disorders, personal decision making or any other issues related to stress management and daily living. Such a view maintains that God has allowed human beings to discover truth in almost every field of human study except psychology.[11]

The problem with such a statement is two-fold. First, accurate observation and reporting may indeed be helpful. However much of what is reported is subjective, rather than objective, and is therefore unreliable, especially in that part of psychology which we are discussing here. And what may be accurate in observation loses any scientific objectivity by the time it is explained and theorized into over 250 different systems of psychotherapy.

Confusion of Psychotherapy with Medicine.

Collins says of the Christian counselor,

When such a person does counseling, he or she may use techniques that some consider secular—just as the Christian physician uses "secular" medical techniques, the Christian banker uses "secular" banking methods, and the Christian legislator uses "secular" approaches to lawmaking.[12]

Collins constantly creates a parallel between the psychological and the medical. However, one is in the realm of science (medical) and the other is not. Equating the practice of medicine with the practice of psychology shows little sensitivity to the gross errors involved in this mistaken logic. The error is compounded throughout Collins' book.[13]

By comparing the practice of psychological counseling with medicine, psychologists often use the medical model to justify the use of psychotherapy. By using the medical model, many assume that "mental illness" can be thought of and talked about in the same manner and terms as medical illness. After all, both are called "illnesses." However, in the medical model physical symptoms are caused by some pathogenic agent, such as viruses. Remove the pathogenic agent and the symptom goes as well. Or, a person may have a broken leg; set the leg according to learned techniques and the leg will heal. One tends to have confidence in this model because it has worked well in treating physical ailments. With the easy transfer of the model from the medical world to the psychotherapeutic world, many people believe that mental problems are the same as physical problems.

Applying the medical model to psychotherapy originated with the relationship between psychiatry and medicine. Since psychiatrists are medical doctors and since psychiatry is a medical specialty, it seemed to follow that the medical model applied to psychiatry just as it did to medicine. Furthermore, psychiatry is draped with such medical trimmings as offices in medical clinics, hospitalization of patients, diagnostic services, prescription drugs, and therapeutic treatment. The very word *therapy* implies medical treatment. Further expansion of the use of the medical model to all psychological counseling was easy after that.

The practice of medicine deals with the physical, biological aspects of a person; psychotherapy deals with the spiritual, social, mental, and emotional aspects. Whereas medical doctors attempt to heal the body, psychotherapists attempt to alleviate or cure emotional, mental, and even spiritual suffering and to establish new patterns of personal and social behavior. In spite of such differences, the medical model continues to be called upon to support the activities of the psychotherapist.

Additionally, the medical model supports the idea that every person with social or mental problems is ill. When people are labeled "mentally ill," problems of living are categorized under the key term *mental illness*. Dr. Thomas Szasz explains it this way: "If we now classify certain forms of personal conduct as illness, it is because most people believe that the best way to deal with them is by responding to them as if they were medical diseases."[14]

Those who believe this do so because they have been influenced by the medical model of human behavior and are confused by the terminology. They think that if one can have a sick body, it must follow that one can have a sick mind. But, is the mind part of the body? Or can we equate the mind with the body? The authors of the *Madness Establishment* say, "Unlike many medical diseases that have scientifically verifiable etiologies and prescribed methods of treatment, most of the 'mental illnesses' have neither scientifically established causes nor treatments of proven efficacy."[15]

Myth of Mental Illness.

In discussing the topic "Is Mental Illness a Myth?" Collins says:

> Have you ever felt trapped by some habit you couldn't shake—perpetual procrastination, nail biting, overeating, masturbation, lustful thoughts, worry, overusing credit cards or others? We might try to dismiss these as myths that are of no consequence or as "nothing but spiritual issues."[16]

We know of no one who would call any of the above habits "myths." Collins mentions Dr. Thomas Szasz and his book *The Myth of Mental Illness*. The problem which Collins seems to have missed is that the above are wrongly referred to as "mental illness." That is the point that Szasz is making in his book! Contrary to what Collins would have us believe, "Perpetual procrastination, nail biting, overeating, masturbation, lustful thoughts, worry, overusing credit cards" are **not** mental illnesses. And that's no myth!

Collins gives an example of a friend who "flunked out" of college. Collins says the problem "appears to have a psychological root."[17] The remedy? The man never learned time management or study skills. This displays a confusion on the part of many psychologists between psychological problems and educational problems. Time management skills and study skills are used by educators to help students. This is not therapy; it is education. Some psychologists claim the field of education and broaden the confusion that already exists.

Psychotherapy deals with thoughts, emotions, and behavior, but not with the brain itself. Psychotherapy does not deal with the biology of the brain, but with the psychology of the mind and with the social behavior of the individual. In medicine we understand what a diseased body is, but what is the parallel in psychotherapy? It is obvious that in psychotherapy mental illness does not mean brain disease. If brain disease were the case, the person would be a *medical* patient, not a *mental* patient. Szasz very sharply refers to the "psychiatric impostor" who "supports a common, culturally shared desire to equate and confuse brain and mind, nerves and nervousness."[18]

It is necessary to understand this distinction to appreciate the difference. Although the brain is a physical entity and may require physical/chemical treatment, the mind and the soul are nonphysical entities. Whereas the former can be studied through scientific investigation and can become physically ill; matters of the psyche and the soul are studied through philosophy and theology. And, indeed, those aspects of psychology which attempt to investigate and understand the mind and the soul resemble religion more than science. We suggest that one examine the differences between incisions and decisions and between tissues and issues. This will get at the difference that many Christian psychologists fail to recognize.

Confusion of Body, Soul, and Spirit.

Collins says, "There is abundant evidence that all human problems have three components: physical, psychological and spiritual."[19] We as Christians know that man is physical and spiritual. However, what is the psychological part of man? Is psychological a third part of man somewhere between the physical and spiritual? This third part of man has been spoken of by philosophers and scientists. Dr. Barbara Brown, who is an experimental physiologist and researcher, discusses this third part of man in her book *Supermind*. She refers to this third part of man not as psychological, but as mind. She says, "When science speaks of mind, it means brain; when the average person talks about the mind, he really means the mind."[20]

Does Collins' *psychological* mean brain or mind or some interaction between the two? If Collins means *brain*, then it becomes a medical, biological, or physiological problem. If by *psychological* Collins means mind. Then what is mind? Dr. Brown has come to the conclusion that mind is more than brain. She says:

> I believe that the scientific consensus that mind is only mechanical brain is dead wrong. . . the research data of the sciences themselves point much more strongly toward the existence of a mind-more-than-brain than they do toward mere mechanical brain action.[21]

Does Collins mean by *psychological* a "mind-more-than-brain"? If so, what is the difference between the "mind-more-than-brain" and the *spiritual* to which he refers? Sir John Eccles, winner of the Nobel prize for his research on the brain once referred to the brain as "a machine that a 'ghost' can operate."[22]

Sir John Eccles and Sir Karl Popper, and other great thinkers of our time as well as others from the past have attempted to grapple with explaining the mind of man. The opinions vary from mind is brain to mind is more than brain. In other words, this third part of man is not simply resolved by naming it "psychological" or "mind."

The Bible refers to the soul of man. The words *psychological* and *psychology* are derived from the Greek word *psyche*, which means soul. It is the invisible aspect of man which cannot be observed. The study of the soul is thus a metaphysical endeavor. Furthermore, any attempt to study or know about the intangible part of man is limited by subjectivity and conjecture. Psychological counseling therefore is religious and/or metaphysical rather than scientific and/or medical. Thus psychology has intruded upon the very same matters of the soul which the Bible addresses and for which the Bible should be the sole guide.

Regardless of the terminology used or the remedies offered, we eventually need to look to the source of these solutions. There are also many other descriptions and remedies for man outside of psychology. There are sociological, philosophical, and literary descriptions and remedies. Each of them may be just as valid as the psychological descriptions and solutions. And each of them could, for the same justifications that underlie psychology, be licensed professions. But, what is the source of these? The source for all of them is the opinions of men. This type of psychology is not science; it offers only the many conflicting opinions of men. In contrast, the Bible provides the truth of God.

Collins' view is simply that "we can view human beings from a spiritual, psychological or physical perspective. Each gives a slightly different viewpoint. Each is partially right, but none give the complete picture."[23] Why he limits it to these three is not clear. However, what is clear is that he has confidence in psychology as being partially right (and from the above statement, his confidence in the spiritual perspective in the Scripture must also be partial). Which psychology is partially right and why Scripture is not entirely right is not clear. We can only infer it from the example given of depression in his following statement:

> Depression, for example, may have a strictly physical cause; it may be a biochemical reaction to illness or some other body malfunction. Other depression may come as a reaction to stress such as the loss of a loved one or failure in a job. As we have seen earlier, depression can also come from sin. The complexity of depressive reactions shows the inaccuracy of concluding that psychological problems are nothing but spiritual problems.[24]

Collins obviously believes that "reaction to stress" is a

psychological and not a spiritual problem. Since he uses the example of depression we will pursue this. In addition to physical causes of depression, there are various psychological explanations. These explanations have competed with one another for years with none being victorious over the others. There are literally thousands of Christian psychologists who follow many conflicting and contradictory approaches. The fact that there are so many systems based upon so many opinions of their founders ought to be reason enough to avoid them.

Collins' choice of depression as an example is a good one because depression is one of the most often mentioned problems by individuals who seek help. One of the many popular writers who is followed by many Christian psychologists is Dr. Aaron T. Beck. Beck has described what he calls the "cognitive triad of depression." He says that "depressed patients typically have a negative view of themselves, of their environment, and of the future."[25] Beck goes on to describe the hopeless view that these individuals have and how to help them.

The method used by Beck to help depressed people is a common psychological approach. Many Christian psychologists use this psychological approach. Unfortunately their psychological training and commitment often blinds them to the spiritual implication of each part of the "cognitive triad" formula. While Collins may disagree, this is definitely a spiritual, not a psychological problem. The "negative view of themselves, of their environment, and of the future" can all be addressed either psychologically or spiritually. However, should one use the truth of God or the multitude of the the opinions of men?

Either 2 Peter 1:3-4 is true or it is not.

> According as his Divine power hath given unto us all things that pertain unto life and godliness, through the knowledge of him that hath called us to glory and virtue:
>
> Whereby are given unto us exceeding great and precious promises: that by these ye might be

partakers of the divine nature, having escaped the
corruption that is in the world through lust.

To use psychology, which is based upon the opinions of men,
rather than the Bible, which is the truth of God, communicates a highly unwarranted view of psychology and a less
than high view of Scripture. The vast amount of confusion in
the field of psychological theories and therapies hardly
indicates clarity, vision and truth. Confusion is darkness,
while the Gospel brings light, clarity, and life. "For God is
not the author of confusion, but of peace." (1 Corinthians
14:33.)

3

PSYCHOLOGICAL CULTS

Psychology, with its false facade of respectability, science, and medicine, has already enticed many Christians. Under the guise of so-called Christian psychology, the teachings of Sigmund Freud, Carl Jung, Carl Rogers, Abraham Maslow, Eric Fromm, Alfred Adler, Albert Ellis, and many other non-believers and anti-Christians have corrupted the faith once delivered to the saints. Because of the false scientific cloak of psychology, many Christians do not see that its major theories (of why people are the way they are and how they can change) are simply faith systems.

Psychology and Religion.

When Collins says, "Some have elevated psychology to the status of a new religion,"[1] he does not seem to realize that this type of psychology has not been elevated to "the status of a new religion"; it already is religion. In his book *Psychology As Religion: the Cult of Self Worship*, Dr. Paul Vitz extensively addresses the issue of the basic religious nature of psychology.[2] He especially delves into the problems of humanistic psychology. However, psychoanalysis and behavior therapy are also religious in nature. Both attempt to understand man and to tell him how he should live and change.

Psychotherapy and its psychologies involve rituals, values, and morals. The focus is on the soul (*psyche*) and even the spirit of man. Therapists often deal with religious questions and yearnings from an anti-biblical point of view, and they incorporate a deity and priesthood of some kind or another. While Collins continually claims that psychology is science, he quotes Everett Worthington, Jr. , who says that one study indicated that "psychotherapy may have its greatest effect on attitudes of a philosophical nature dealing with ethics and religion."[3] The implications of this statement are extremely important. Psychotherapy is not science, but religion and philosophy. Even when combined with Christianity, basic unbiblical presuppositions maintain subtle influence on the counseling and on the person receiving counsel.

Values.

Collins' chapter title "Should a Christian Ever Go to a Non-Christian Counselor?" illustrates that counseling is by nature value-laden. In this chapter he tells about a lady who called him about her teenage son who "professed to be a Christian and attended church regularly," but was "heavily involved with drugs."[4] The values of both the therapist and the client come into play as can be seen by the family decision and Collins' response. Collins says,

> When all things were considered this Christian family chose to admit the young man to a secular residential treatment program. I don't think their decision was wrong.[5]

The very questions of why the young man would want to be free of drugs, how he will accomplish that, and what he will do with his life following recovery are all value issues. The decision to "admit the young man to a secular residential treatment program" is wrong not only from a biblical perspective—sending a Christian to a secular program to deal with spiritual issues—but it is wrong from a research perspective.

In spite of the fact that in the same chapter Collins says, "Sometimes the problem has little or nothing to do with values,"[6] values play a highly significant role in all counseling situations. In fact, **there is a world view with a set of values within every theory having to do with psychotherapy**. A person's views of life and his values will influence his life and behavior.

A counselor's philosophical view of life and his concept of man and the world will affect every aspect of his counseling. Many researchers agree that one cannot counsel without a value system. Research psychologist Dr. Allen Bergin contends:

> Values are an inevitable and pervasive part of psychotherapy.[7]

> There is an ideology in everyone's therapy.

> Techniques thus become a medium for mediating the value influence intended by the therapist.

> A value free approach is impossible.[8]

Bergin warns that sometimes the therapist or counselor assumes that what he does "is professional without recognizing that [he is] purveying under the guise of professionalism and science [his] own personal value [system]."[9] Elsewhere he says, "It will not do for therapists to hide their prejudices behind a screen of scientific jargon."[10] Dr. Hans Strupp says, "There can be no doubt that the therapist's moral and ethical values are always 'in the picture.'"[11] Dr. Perry London believes that avoidance of values is impossible. "Every aspect of psychotherapy presupposes some implicit moral doctrine."[12] Further, "Moral considerations may dictate, in large part, how the therapist defines his client's needs, how he operates in the therapeutic situation, how he defines 'treatment,' and 'cure,' and even 'reality.'"[13] Morse and Watson conclude, "Thus values and moral judgments will always play a role in therapy, no matter how much the therapist attempts to push them to the background."[14]

Because morals and values play such a crucial role in counseling, it is quite important for the counselor and the counselee to share the same basic view of man and similar values. The counselee should at least be aware of a counselor's view of life and his values when he seeks counseling. If the counselee would like to adopt the same view and values as the counselor there would be no conflict. However, if there is conflict or confusion in this area, the counselee should find another counselor.

Even Collins says, "Counselees are more likely to get better and to experience personal growth when their values are similar to those of the therapist."[15] More significantly, the religious and moral values of a therapist will often affect those of the counselee. This has deep implications when secular therapies are used by Christians, because all therapies are value-laden and culture-bound. Nevertheless Collins sees the value of Christians incorporating therapies of non-Christians with different values into their own practices. Surely those secular values seep through and affect his counseling.

Counseling Nonbelievers.

Because of the inherent religious nature of psychological counseling, the question of counseling non-Christians must be addressed. And the question must involve both whether to counsel and what to counsel. In attempting to address this question, Collins quotes an example of a man who says,

> I tell the person who comes for help that I don't even want to hear about the problem until we deal with a basic spiritual question: Have you been born again? If the counselee is a believer, we go on to the problem. If not, I present the gospel and state that I don't help people unless and until they have committed themselves to Jesus Christ.[16]

Collins wonders "how many people had been turned away by his insensitive and rigid approach."[17]

There are really two issues here rather than one. The two issues addressed and confused as one by this example are the individual's theological position and his means of expressing it. One can criticize the way the man expressed himself and thereby avoid the real issue. Although this man's description sounds abrupt, he realized that the primary goal of counseling unbelievers is for them to be saved and born anew of the Spirit by faith in Christ. "For what shall it profit a man, if he shall gain the whole world, and lose his own soul?" (Mark 8:36.) Jesus ministered to the people for a greater purpose than any temporal needs or desires. In reality, the man in Collins' example may be leading many to Christ and fulfilling the Great Commission in a way that few counselors do.

Collins goes on to say, "Bringing people to Christ is the essence of the Great Commission (Matthew 28:19-20), but from this it does not follow that Christian counselors should offer help only to believers."[18] However, "bringing people to Christ" is offering help to the nonbeliever at his greatest point of need. Furthermore, if a nonbeliever finds his help through secular theories and therapies rather than through Jesus, he may remain in the flesh and never really know what it is to walk in the Spirit.

Collins raises two points from Scripture to support his position. The first point he makes is that "Jesus helped non-believers."[19] To prove this point, he says "Jesus was willing to reach out and help nonbelievers. Shouldn't his followers do the same?" Jesus primarily ministered to the Jews. Whenever he ministered to non-Jews it was on the basis of their faith. In fact, even when He ministered grace and healing to the Jews faith was involved. Jesus is indeed our example. Not only is He our example; He is the very One who does minister in counseling that seeks to glorify Him and encourage faith in Him. Therefore, we must follow Him—all the way.

Thus, we must ask ourselves, "What was Jesus' purpose in ministering to wayward Jews, the Roman centurion, the

Syro-Phoenician woman, and the Samaritans?" His purpose
was to bring people to God. Jesus' speaking, healing, counseling, driving out demons and teaching were all to bring people
into a right relationship with God. Yes, Jesus was willing to
reach out and help those who were not walking with God, but
for the sole purpose of bringing them to God. The entire ministry of Jesus is a testimony against the very thing that
Collins is trying to justify. Can you imagine Jesus being
"willing to reach out and help nonbelievers" without revealing
the Father?

Collins goes on to say:

> Jesus spent time with sinners, healed a Roman
> centurion's slave, counseled a hated tax collector,
> drove demons out of a heathen pig rancher, and
> freely taught anyone who would listen. Jesus was
> willing to reach out and help nonbelievers.[20]

Let's examine the examples Collins gives.

"Jesus spent time with sinners." He knew they needed
to know the Lord. Therefore He did not waste time by giving
them the opinions of men to help solve their problems of
living. Instead He ministered the truth and grace of God to
them. (Luke 5:27-32.)

Jesus "healed a Roman centurion's slave." The centurion
obviously knew who Jesus was and demonstrated greater
faith than the Jews. Therefore there was no need for evange-
lism. In fact, Jesus recognized the faith and said, "I have not
found so great faith, no, not in Israel." (Luke 7:9.)

Jesus "counseled a hated tax collector." Jesus tells us his
purpose of going to Matthew's house, "I am not come to call
the righteous, but sinners to repentance." (Matthew 9:13.)
Jesus also told Zaccheus, "For the Son of man is come to seek
and to save that which was lost." (Luke 19:10.)

Jesus "drove demons out of a heathen pig rancher." Even
the demons recognized who Jesus was for they said, "What
have we to do with thee, Jesus thou Son of God?" (Matthew
8:29.)

Jesus "freely taught anyone who would listen." And in-

deed, Jesus did teach. But, He did not teach the ways of men.
He taught and demonstrated the ways of God. He did not
offer the counsel of men, but the counsel of God. He did not
borrow from the world, but went against the mind-set of the
world. He had a greater purpose than to dress up the flesh or
to instruct the flesh how to live more successfully and how to
feel better about oneself. Jesus knew that the flesh was of no
avail and said to Nicodemus,

> Verily, verily, I say unto thee, except a man be born
> of water and of the Spirit, he cannot enter into the
> kingdom of God. That which is born of the flesh is
> flesh; and that which is born of the Spirit is spirit.
> marvel not that I said unto thee, Ye must be born
> again. (John 3:5-7.)

Even when Jesus ministered to nonbelievers, he ministered
according to the ways of God and not according to the current,
popular wisdom of men.   In each and every case He was
revealing God to them and **not** teaching the ideas of men.

Collins' second point is that "The Scriptures do not instruct us to limit our helping to believers."[21] To prove his
point he quotes Galatians 6:9-10, which includes Paul's admonition, "Therefore as we have opportunity let us do good to all
people, especially to those who belong to the family of believers." In the context of all Scripture, why would Christians do
good to all people? For at least two reasons: First, to show
forth Christ in their lives, and second, to win them to Christ.
What would show forth Christ more, their example of Christ
in them or a discussion based on someone's psychological
opinion? What is lacking in Collins' argument is an example
from Scripture where Jesus or the disciples ministered the
opinions of men rather than God's truth, or where they failed
to use the circumstance to follow the Great Commission.

The biblical counselor must present the claims of Christ.
For the psychologist to present the claims of Christ at the
financial expense of a client, though they are more valuable
than gold, could be unethical and not consistent with his professional role as a psychologist. In other words, to proselyte at

the expense of a client during time that he has paid for psychological services would be taking undue advantage of him. It is often difficult for a Christian to see this, because we know that the Bible is true. However, imagine going to a psychologist, expecting psychotherapy and being proselyted according to the Buddhist religion during time that costs fifty-plus dollars an hour.

The man in Collins' example certainly had a desire to bring people to Christ. His way of expressing it may seem "insensitive and rigid," but he certainly had the right idea. Furthermore, one cannot tell from his words the manner or tone of voice he used. Perhaps he has not only led many to Christ, but has effectively discipled them according to the ways of the Lord rather than through the "insights" borrowed from Freud et al.

The Gods of Psychology.

Not only are morals and values involved, but this kind of psychology has its own gods, priesthood, and means of salvation. These are most obvious in the transpersonal psychologies, which include various combinations of Eastern religions, shamanism, astrology, and other occult practices. To miss the fact that much psychology is influenced by Eastern ideas is to have a very shallow understanding of the relationship between Eastern religion and Western psychology. Dr. Daniel Goleman, former editor of *Psychology Today*, has written a book titled *The Meditative Mind*, which addresses this very issue.[22]

Collins says, "It would be unfair to blame this rise of humanistic heresy solely on the works of psychoanalysts and psychologists."[23] Nevertheless, the religious nature of psychotherapy and the underlying psychologies can easily be seen in their support and clear identification with the religion of secular humanism, which has fed into the new age mentality. New agers embrace these psychological systems and see them as giving people what they need to save themselves and their society.   In his article "What is the New Age?" in the publication *Guide to New Age Living*, Jonathan Adolph says:

> Perhaps the most influential ideas to shape contemporary new age thinking were those that grew out of humanistic psychology and the human potential movement of the '60s and '70s. The fundamental optimism of new age thinking, for example, can be traced to psychologists such as Carl Rogers and Abraham Maslow, who postulated that when basic needs are met, people will strive to develop themselves and find meaning in their life, a concept Maslow called self-actualization.[24]

Humanistic psychology is basic to new age thought. Such thinking strips Jesus of His unique personhood and godhood and bestows divine potential upon mere humans. With such divine potential, humans are considered to be capable of redeeming society through their own personal transformation, which comes from a divine spark which supposedly resides within each person.

Humanistic psychology has embraced transpersonal psychology, occultism, and Eastern religion. The move from humanistic to transpersonal psychological theories is no surprise to the initiates. Abraham Maslow, one of the founders of humanistic psychology, predicted that humanistic psychology would be an important stepping stone to transpersonal psychology. In his book *Toward a Psychology of Being*, which was published in 1968, he wrote:

> I consider Humanistic, Third Force Psychology to be transitional. A preparation for a still higher fourth force psychology, transpersonal, transhuman, centered in the cosmos rather than in human needs and interest, going beyond humanness, identity, self-actualization and the like.[25]

Although he seems to be referring to some kind of god, he certainly was not talking about the God of the Bible. Instead, his self-actualization was just a step away from pantheism and self-deification.

Psychological ideologies combined with paganism are the heartbeat that throbs beneath the scientific facade of psychotherapy. And that heartbeat has begun to throb in the church. On the heels of that heartbeat is the hoofbeat of the white horse in Revelation 6. The rider, wearing a crown and carrying a bow, deceives the nations with the appearance of goodness and purity. He is the deceiver who shoots his arrows into the minds of men and conquers them through false ideologies and psychologies combined with idolatry and paganism.

The psychological cults have been erected with the wood, hay, and stubble of the opinions of men. Beneath a veneer of pious platitudes they hide their true foundations of evolutionism, determinism, agnosticism, atheism, secular humanism, transcendentalism, pseudoscientism, mesmerism, and other anti-Christian "isms." These religions include the psychoanalytic, the behavioristic, the humanistic, and the transpersonal psychologies mixed and blended with whatever beliefs and practices may appeal to an individual. Their catalog of choices is ever expanding, and psychological evangelists hawk many other gospels.

These psychological religions are not only in the world; they are blatantly standing in the church and offering numerous combinations of theories and therapies. They are readily accessible to Christians, especially when they are whitewashed with Bible verses and given top billing in Christian bookstores and on Christian media. Rather than guiding people to the strait gate and along the narrow way, too many Christian pastors, leaders, and professors are pointing to the wide gate made up of over 250 different psychological systems combined in thousands of ways. Rather than calling the people to come out of the world and to be separate, they have brought the worldly psychologies right into the church. Rather than open altars, there are wide gates. And, it is almost impossible to avoid the wide gate and the broad way—especially when disguised as the strait gate and the narrow way.

4

INTEGRATION OR SEPARATION?

Those who attempt to integrate psychology and Christianity hope to bring together the best of both. Their faith rests in a combination of one or more of the many psychological systems of men's minds along with some form of Christianity. Collins says that Christian therapists have goals that are different from secular therapists.[1] Nevertheless they use theories and methods borrowed directly from approaches devised by secular psychologists whose systems have underlying presuppositions that are antithetical to the Bible.

Collins admits that Christians cannot trust all of psychology. However, in answer to his title *Can You trust Psychology?* Collins says, "It all depends on the psychology and the psychologist."[2] Then he gives his criteria of acceptance. He says:

> When a psychologist seeks to be guided by the Holy Spirit, is committed to serving Christ faithfully, is growing in his or her knowledge of the Scriptures, is well aware of the facts and conclusions of psychology, and is willing to evaluate psychological ideas in the light of biblical teaching—then you can trust the psychologist, even though he or she at times will

49

> make mistakes, as we all do. If the psychology or
> psychological technique is not at odds with scrip-
> tural teaching, then it is likely to be trustworthy,
> especially if it also is supported by scientific data.[3]

This is a constantly recurring theme throughout his entire
book.

Now let us try to apply this criteria. At the present time
there are over 250 competing and often contradictory therapies and over 10,000 not-always-compatible techniques. To
determine methodological systems used by Christians who
practice psychotherapy, we conducted a survey with the
Christian Association for Psychological Studies (CAPS), a
national Christian organization composed of numerous
practicing therapists. In our survey we used a simple
questionnaire in which we asked the psychotherapists to list
in order the psychotherapeutic approaches that most
influenced their private practices. We listed only ten
approaches, but provided blank spaces at the bottom of the
sheet for adding others before final ranking. The results indicated that Client-Centered Therapy (Rogers) and Reality
Therapy (Glasser) were the two top choices, and that
psychoanalysis (Freud) and Rational Emotive Therapy (Ellis)
followed closely behind.

One especially interesting result from the survey is that
many of the psychotherapists listed a variety of approaches at
the end of the form as well as checking and ranking many of
the approaches listed. Their doing so indicates that they have
a highly eclectic approach to counseling. In our conclusion we
had this to say:

> If this survey constitutes a representative sample, it
> is probably fair to say that there is not just one
> Christian psychotherapeutic way. There is a great
> variety in the approaches influencing the clinical
> practices of CAPS members. This survey seems to
> demonstrate that, while some psychotherapies are
> more influential than others in the practice of
> Christian counseling, in general the Christian

psychotherapist is both independent and eclectic in his approach to counseling. [4]

Each Christian practicing psychotherapy has his own conglomeration of approaches. That is not surprising. Researcher Dr. Morris Parlof observes, "Most psychotherapists are eclectic either by intent or default."[5]

If one were to ask the numerous Christian psychologists if they met Collins' criteria, we would venture to guess that they would say that they do. But then we have to ask why it is that the numerous Christian psychologists who would say that they meet Collins' criteria come to contradictory conclusions about what therapeutic systems to use and which techniques to apply. There must be a lot of prooftexting going on, to say the least.

Collins makes the constant point that there is a variety of approaches to Christian counseling, which is true. However, the basis for biblical counseling is the truth revealed by God, while the basis for psychological counseling is the opinions of men. No matter how much one attempts to biblicize psychology or proceed to use psychology because it does not **seem** to contradict Scripture (which is apparently okay with Collins), it is still the opinions of men. Even after supposedly finding a certain psychology in Scripture or failing to find it in Scripture, it is still made up of the opinions of men. We cannot think of one of the over 250 approaches to psychotherapy or one of its underlying psychologies that cannot somehow be rationalized biblically. But rationalizing it biblically does not make it biblical. It is still the opinions of men.

For example, Carl Rogers is probably the name best known among Christian psychologists. In the CAP's survey of Christian psychologists mentioned earlier, Rogers was listed in first place. Rogers said once that his crowning discovery after a lifetime of counseling is that of love.[6] However, love for Rogers means "love between persons." But what does Rogers mean by "love between persons"? First of all, Rogers is only speaking about human love. While human love is an admirable virtue, it does not compare with divine love. Human love without the divine is merely another form of self-love. Divine love, on the other hand, encompasses all the qualities listed in 1 Corinthians 13. Second, Rogers is only speaking of love between persons. He ignores the great commandment to "love the Lord thy God." Third, he never mentions God's love for man, which is demonstrated throughout the Bible.

Rogers' crowning discovery is a limited human love between persons, which excludes the love of God and the love for God. In excluding God, Rogers sets up the me, myself, and I as the evaluator and prioritizer of all experiences. The self, rather than God, becomes the center of the universe, and love apart from God becomes only a self-rewarding activity. In leaving out God, Rogers ends up with a "love between persons," which is hardly more than a feeble extension of self love. The important ideas about love did not originate with Rogers. They have always existed. Rogers merely found out something about the importance of love, but ignored the depth of God's love.

One Christian psychologist will depend upon Rogers' nondirective approach, another on the Freudian unconscious determinants of behavior, another on Glasser's reality, responsibility and right-and-wrong, and another on Ellis's Rational Emotive Therapy. And, numerous other Christian psychologists, all "willing to evaluate ideas in the light of biblical teaching," will use other mutually conflicting systems and multifarious contradictory techniques.

To confuse matters even more, think about the fact that the Christian *critics* of psychology also claim to meet Collins' criteria. We will substitute in Collins' criteria the words "critic of psychology" for the word "psychologist" as follows: "When a [critic of psychology] seeks to be guided by the Holy Spirit, is committed to serving Christ faithfully, is growing in his or her knowledge of the Scriptures, is well aware of the facts and conclusions of psychology, and is willing to evaluate psychological ideas in the light of biblical teaching—then you can trust the [critic of psychology], even though he or she at times will make mistakes, as we all do."[7] Or, is Collins suggesting that the critics are not "guided by the Holy Spirit," etc.?

What is a Christian to do? The psychologists claim to be following God; the critics claim to be following God. The psychologists who claim to follow God often use contradictory systems; the critics of psychology also end up, at times, using different systems. However, the critics of psychology use the Bible as their first source, while the psychologists use psychology as their first source.

Collins says, "If you don't know your psychology, find a committed believer who can help you decipher what is valid and what may be counterfeit."[8] But here again, what's a Christian to do? The Christian critics of psychology say that the over 250 competing and often contradictory systems are all counterfeit. The Christian psychologists claim that the therapies they use are authentic and in harmony with Scripture. Once more, the critics of psychology who recommend biblical approaches go first to the Bible, while the psychologists begin with psychology.

It is interesting to note that the originators of the psychological systems, which are taught and used by Christians, were not believers. The originators of these often competing systems did not begin with Scripture; nor did they ever compare what they concluded with Scripture. They devised their systems out of their own fallen opinions about man.

In her article "Theory as Self-Portrait and the Ideal of Objectivity," Dr. Linda Riebel clearly shows that "theories of human nature reflect the theorist's personality as he or she externalizes it or projects it onto humanity at large." She says that "the theory of human nature is a self-portrait of the theorist . . . emphasizing what the theorist needs," and that theories of personality and psychotherapy "cannot transcend the individual personality engaged in that act."[9]

Dr. Harvey Mindess has written a book titled *Makers of Psychology: The Personal Factor*. The thesis of his book can be seen in the following quotes:

> It is my intention to show how the leaders of the field portray humanity in their own image and how each one's theories and techniques are a means of

validating his own identity.[10]

The only target I wish to attack is the delusion that psychologists' judgments are objective, their pronouncements unbiased, their methods based more upon external evidence than personal need. Even the greatest geniuses are human beings, limited by the time and place of their existence and, above all, limited by their personal characteristics. Their outlooks are shaped by who they are. There is no shame in that, but it is a crime against truth to deny it.[11]

The field as a whole, taking direction as it does from the standpoints of its leaders—which, as I will demonstrate, are *always* personally motivated—may be regarded as a set of distorting mirrors, each one reflecting human nature in a somewhat lopsided way, with no guarantee that all of them put together add up to a rounded portrait.[12] (Emphasis his.)

The enigma of human nature, we may say, is like a giant Rorschach blot onto which each personality theorist projects his own personality characteristics.[13]

The conclusions we should reach about the field as a whole, however, must begin with a recognition of the subjective element in all personality theories, the limited applicability of all therapeutic techniques, and proceed to the relativity of psychological truth.[14]

This is truly a case of the opinions of nonbelieving psychologists being used by Christian psychologists on the basis of whether or not they seem Scriptural. Is it not strange that these conflicting personal opinions by these non-Christians are to be evaluated on the basis of the testimony of Christians who claim to fulfill Collins' criteria?

Collins says, "If the psychology or psychological technique is not at odds with scriptural teaching, then it is likely to be trustworthy, especially if it also is supported by scientific data."[15] The criteria of "not at odds with scriptural teaching" as a means of being "trustworthy" is strange. Apparently the psychologist who meets Collins' criteria up to this point only needs to make sure that the psychology used is "not at odds with scriptural teaching." The intent and purpose of Scripture is not to be either a support or framework for worldly wisdom in the area of who man is and how he should live. Of course all must be evaluated in terms of Scripture, but that does not mean that a theory or opinion that is not in Scripture is therefore "not at odds with scriptural teaching" simply because it is not mentioned. Anyone who seeks to evaluate the wisdom of men in the light of Scripture must immerse himself more in the Bible than in the wisdom of men. There should be a biblical bias rather than a psychological bias.

How about using another criteria, such as "Only if it is not at odds with other psychological systems?" (Of course that would eliminate all of them.) Or, "only if it is not addressing problems already addressed in Scripture?" The "not at odds with scriptural teaching" criteria is open to individual interpretation and this is why so many Christian psychologists have so many different, often-contradictory systems that they use. In addition, does this criteria for psychology not open Pandora's box? For examples, graphology, use of the Hindu chakras, hypnosis, and levitation could all be rationalized to be "not at odds with scriptural teachings" by some Christians (not us!). But should a Christian use them? The last part of the sentence "especially if it also is supported by scientific data" should, in all fairness, read "*only* if it also is supported by scientific data." Else, why would one want to use an unproven and unsupported psychology or psychological technique?

Collins says, "Some psychological conclusions cannot be trusted and must not be accepted." [16] However, Collins nowhere distinguishes between what can and what cannot be trusted. Nor has he instructed the reader as to what "cannot be trusted" and "must not be accepted." For example, if a number of Christian psychologists who meet Collins' criteria and are claiming "to be guided by the Holy Spirit" come to obviously contradictory conclusions as they often do, which one or ones "cannot be trusted and must not be accepted"?

Partially quoting us, Collins says, "One recent Christian book makes the valid criticism that some secular therapists are 'long on promises, but short on independent scientific research.' These systems are based on therapists' 'own say-so and not upon independent research and followup.'"[17] He goes on to say,

> The Christian authors of this book apparently fail to see that the same criticism applies to their own approach to counseling. Because they are built on biblical teachings, Christian approaches rarely get tested but are assumed to be right—even when they disagree with other biblically based methods of counseling.[18]

Collins is right about Christian approaches rarely being tested. He must include in this concern the vast array of integration approaches as well. Most of the research studies on counseling are conducted at universities with staff therapists rather than with private-practice therapists. We would like to know if there are any carefully conducted, controlled studies of discretely defined integration approaches. Since Christian integrationists believe they are using science, they should submit to scientific investigation.

Collins says, "But if we are to be consistent and fair, we must test our approaches carefully and with the same rigor that we demand of the psychotherapists whose theories we so quickly criticize."[19] He evidently does not realize that if a person is claiming scientific validity and that what he is doing is based on science, he must be open to being tested. If, on the other hand, psychotherapists admitted that they are promoting the opinions of men and practicing religion rather than science, we would not require proof any more than we require proof for the efficacy of Buddhism or the Moslem faith.

Biblical counseling is based on faith, rather than science. We make no other claim than that which the Word of God declares. Collins demands proof for the practices of biblical counselors, but God's truth is true whether biblical counselors apply it rightly or not. But, man's opinions (psychology) are just that until they become scientifically formed, tested, and proven. In addition, would Collins ask for proof that the Bible is effective in the lives of believers just because there are various Christian denominations? We need to keep in mind that in psychological counseling we are dealing with a questionable source (Carl Rogers, William Glasser, Sigmund Freud, Albert Ellis, et al); in biblical counseling we are dealing with truth (the Bible).

Collins refers to "our current pressure-filled age"[20] as the justification for the amalgamation of clinical and counseling psychology. What he neglects to mention is that many of the modern principles of stress management originated in ancient occult practices of visualization and self-hypnosis. Apparently the Bible was sufficient to answer the problems of the early church but is not sufficient for our present complex society.

Collins lists several kinds of problems that people bring to counselors which he contends "are never discussed in the Bible."[21] He says, "It could be difficult to find scriptural principles to guide in all the sample problems we have listed."[22] His first examples of problems brought to a counselor have to do with decision making:

> "I've been accepted by two Christian colleges. I can't decide which one to attend."

> "Should I get married now, or wait until I am well launched on my career?"[23]

Aren't these matters of seeking God's will through prayer as well as through gathering necessary information (i. e. about what the colleges offer, their possible influence on the person, the demands of the job or career, etc.) and thinking through

godly priorities? Would not the principle of "Seek ye first the
kingdom of God" be essential in these considerations? There
is no need for psychological theories and therapies to assist a
person with such questions.

How can a psychologist help any more than a person who
is walking with the Lord and who is gifted in godly counsel
with the next problems Collins lists?

> "I know God has forgiven me for my past sins, but
> what do I do now that I'm pregnant?"

> "How can I stop eating so much?"

> "I am really depressed. The doctor says there is
> nothing physically causing this, and I can't think of
> any sin in my life that might be pulling me down.
> What should I do?"[24]

Often people think that if there is not a specific verse or
formula that the Bible does not speak to an issue. We must
always remember that the Lord works together with His
Word , with His Holy Spirit, and with members of the body of
Christ. The Lord does give victory in these areas. And even
when sin is not involved, there may be a misunderstanding of
who the Lord is and/or a lack of knowledge concerning His
purposes in an individual's life.

Collins' next example, "Can you help me? I've got
AIDS,"[25] shows a lack of understanding of the Gospel
message of hope and of the purpose of the body of Christ to
bear one another's burdens. Psychological theories and
therapies cannot give him true hope or eternal life. Nor can
they give the kind of love that goes beyond words.

The examples continue. However, in each instance,
except for the one which is an educational, school problem of
failing math, these are matters which have to do with life and
faith. Each is one that can motivate a person to move closer
to God and find Him sufficient, or that can tempt a person to
move away from God and to look for answers in the world.
Psychological theories and therapies could very well lead a

person further out of the will of God. The point is not which way works. The point must be: Which way pleases the Father? Nevertheless, because Collins continues to believe that psychological theories are based on scientific discovery and are therefore gifts from God, he insists:

> Surely there are times, many times, when a sensitive, psychologically trained, committed Christian counselor can help people through psychological techniques and with psychological insights that God has allowed us to discover, but that he has not chosen to reveal in the Bible.[26]

Since all of the psychologies have been contrived by non-Christians, it is strange that God has given those "psychological insights" to them, especially in light of Paul's letter to the Corinthians where he says:

> I will destroy the wisdom of the wise, and will bring to nothing the understanding of the prudent. Where is the wise? where is the scribe? where is the disputer of this world? hath not God made foolish the wisdom of this world? . . . the foolishness of God is wiser than men . . . . But God hath chosen the foolish things of the world to confound the wise . . . . That no flesh should glory in his presence. But of him are ye in Christ Jesus, who of God is made unto us wisdom, and righteousness, and sanctification, and redemption. (1 Corinthians 1:19, 20, 25,29, 30.)

> But the natural man receiveth not the things of the Spirit of God: for they are foolishness unto him: neither can he know them, because they are spiritually discerned. But he that is spiritual judgeth all things, yet he himself is judged of no man. For who hath known the mind of the Lord, that he may instruct him? But we have the mind of Christ. (1 Corinthians 2:14-16.)

And, since there are so many often conflicting "psychological insights" used by professing Christians with no real agreement or research evidence for support, it certainly raises a whole lot of questions about Collins' position.

Are the "psychological insights" used by Collins any better than those used by other professing Christians, such as psychiatrist M. Scott Peck, pastor-turned-psychologist H. Norman Wright, psychologist Lawrence Crabb, psychiatrists Paul Meier and Frank Minirth, Morton Kelsey or any one of a number of other professing Christians? But which one of the many systems used by professing Christians from the Freudian Oedipus Complex to the Jungian Archetypes are "psychological insights that God allowed us to discover, but that he has not chosen to reveal in the Bible"? There are many Christians who practice psychological therapy who still believe in the Oedipus complex.

Collins answers the question, "Can Secular Psychology and Christianity Be Integrated?" in the affirmative. Collins says,

> For the Christian psychologist, integration involves a recognition of the ultimate authority of the Bible, a willingness to learn what God has allowed humans to discover though psychology and other fields of knowledge, and a desire to determine how both scriptural truths and psychological data can enable us better to understand and help people.[27]

Collins evidently trusts more in a Christian psychologist's understanding of the Bible than a theologian's in this regard, for he says that criticisms of professional therapy "could be dismissed had they come from a journalist or a theologian writing as an outsider."[28] How can a theologian be an "outsider" when psychotherapy and counseling psychologies deal with the soul of man? How can he be an "outsider" when so-called integration involves the Bible? Collins says, "Psychological conclusions that contradict biblical principles certainly cannot be integrated with Christianity."[29] Yet, who would know better than a biblical scholar and theologian indwelt by Christ? One does not have to be a psychologist to see the contradictions.

Collins then goes on to restate his constant theme, "It is important, therefore, that integration be done carefully, selectively, tentatively and by individuals who seek to be led by the Holy Spirit."[30] We receive much information from individuals who have been therapized by Christian professionals, from Christian therapists who have left the profession, and from numerous others about whether or not Collins' theme is played out in practice. In addition, the Christian practitioners who participated in our survey of CAPS, described earlier, would certainly believe that they are being led by the Holy Spirit, in spite of the fact that they follow a widely divergent variety of theories and practices. There is about as much agreement among them as among their secular counterparts. In fact, some who claim to be led by the Holy Spirit use techniques from est, the Forum, LIFESPRING, and even from Eastern therapies with their emphasis on visualization and spirit guides.

Collins is correct when he says, "There are no formulas."[31] There are also no consistent and dependable differences between professing Christian therapists and secular therapists. The picture of Holy-Spirit-led therapists coming to conclusions and having practices much different from their secular counterparts is a false one. In fact, at one of the CAPS meetings the following statement was made:

> We are often asked if we are "Christian psycholo-gists" and find it difficult to answer since we don't know what the question implies. We are Christians who are psychologists but at the present time there is no acceptable Christian psychology that is markedly different from non-Christian psychology. It is difficult to imply that we function in a manner that is   fundamentally distinct from our non-Christian colleagues . . . as   yet there is not an acceptable theory, mode of research or   treatment methodology that is distinctly Christian.[32]

Collins believes that "Integration is not always avoidable." He says, "It would be convenient if all counseling could be divided neatly into 'the psychological way' and 'the spiritual way' with no overlapping goals, methods or assumptions."[33] He then adds,

> Even those who try to dichotomize counseling into psychological versus biblical approaches have to admit that there is overlap. Listening, talking, confessing, accepting, thinking and understanding are neither purely psychological nor exclusively biblical activities. [34]

Again we would disagree with him. To us anyone who bases his counseling in the Word of God is using the spiritual way; and anyone who is using the psychological opinions of men is using the psychological way. The fact that both kinds of counseling use listening, talking, and so forth is not the point The point is upon what foundation is their listening, talking, etc. based?

Collins continues, "Even love, hope, compassion, forgiveness, caring, kindness, confrontation and a host of other concepts are shared by theologians and psychologists."[35] When he wants to make a case for similarities so that he can accuse biblical counselors of integration, he admits that biblical counselors are caring and compassionate. However, in other places he constructs a straw-man biblical counselor who is rigid, uncaring, and limited in his understanding of people and problems. The problem seems to lie in the assumption that if anyone can relate to people or understand them he is using psychology, for he says:

> The person who wants to understand and help others cannot avoid at least some overlap and integration of psychological and Christian principles.[36]

This begs the question, "Could anyone understand and help anyone before the so-called science of psychology?" What Collins and others who want to justify the intentional use of psychology do not seem to grasp is that the Bible provides greater depth and breadth for understanding and helping people. The great difference between biblical/spiritual counselors and those who integrate with psychology is whether the reliance is on the Word of God and the work of the Holy Spirit **or** on a combination of the opinions of men and elements of the Christian faith.

Collins claims, "The various secular and Christian approaches overlap and use many of the same techniques."[37] He blurs the differences between biblical and psychological counseling by continually referring to similarities that are not real similarities and overlaps that are not real overlaps. It's like an atheist friend of ours who says that all world religions are the same because they all use prayer and worship a deity.

Collins persists in the error of looking at superficialities rather than substance. The argument is something like this: Medical doctors speak to their patients and psychologists speak to their patients. Therefore there is an overlap between medical and psychological practices and it cannot be avoided. However, friends talk to one another. If we follow the logic, that means they are practicing medicine and psychology.

As a further example of this confusion, Collins says of the two approaches, "Both emphasize listening."[38] Listening in biblical counseling is about as similar to psychological counseling as Christian prayer is to Hindu prayer. It would be difficult to think of one profession which deals with people that does not emphasize listening. Doctors do it, teachers do it, lawyers do it, salespersons do it and lots of others. But that doesn't mean those professions are all alike. Superficial similarities do not cause equalities by any means.

Collins says:

> I once read a humorous and overstated story about a man who refused to wear gloves, celebrate Christmas or use toothpaste because secular humanists did all of these. We couldn't survive if we avoided everything used by nonbelievers. In the same way, we couldn't counsel if we rejected all helping methods used by non-Christians.[39]

While biblical counselors and psychological counselors may seem to do the same things, such as talk and listen, the basis is different. The biblical counselor's source is Scripture, not psychology. Whatever seems to be the same is accidental, not intentional. If the biblical way seems to involve similar activities, it should never be because it was borrowed or learned from the psychological world. When these activities are conducted to conform to a psychological model of man and a psychological methodology of change, they become identifiable tools of that therapy. Conversation influenced by the psychological way cannot fully fulfill biblical goals of walking in the spirit rather than according to the flesh.

On the other hand, there may be some overlap when a psychologically trained counselor is also trying to counsel according to the Bible. Collins' description of a Christian counselor[40] would definitely describe certain aspects of biblical counseling. However, any true overlap would be because a psychologist is attempting to use some of the biblical way along with the psychological way.

Although a biblical counselor may avail himself of any scientifically established data, he would be careful not to dip into the theoretical systems which attempt to explain why man is the way he is and how he should and can change. Though there may be elements of truth, they are too bound to the ungodly systems to be used. And, those isolated elements which superficially appear to agree with Scripture are based upon philosophies which deny the Lordship of Christ.

A more extreme example of the integrationist position is found in Dr. John Carter and Dr. Bruce Narramore of Rosemead Graduate School of Psychology, who say in their book *The Integration of Psychology and Theology*, "Both the Bible and psychology have a great deal of subject matter in common. Both study the attitudes and behavior of the human race."[41] This in essence equates the Bible and psychology as both being a "study . . . of the human race." However, the Bible is not merely a "study . . . of the human race"; it is the **truth** about the human race! In fact, the Bible is the only fully dependable, trustworthy **truth** about man; while psychology is merely the **opinions** of men about man.

Furthermore, psychology consists of the **opinions** of godless men about man.

Think of all the psychological theorists, such as Freud, Jung, Adler, Rogers, Ellis, et cetera. Do you know of any major psychological theorist who is a Christian? In contrast to this, the Bible provides the complete and only unchanging explanations and answers from God about men; whereas psychology is a constantly changing chameleon-like catechism of cure. Dr. Charles Tart, a prolific speaker and writer in the field of psychology, admits that the prevailing popular psychotherapeutic systems merely reflect the current culture.[42] We know that the truths of Scripture are eternal. but, which psychological "truths" are eternal?

The results of a study of 177 articles having to do with integration indicated that most Christians practicing psychology do **not** use theology as a filter to retain only that which is biblical.[43] Approximately one third use a form of integration which stresses compatibility. This is much like Collins' idea of overlap. However, the researchers are quick to add:

> Psychological and theological facts may appear on the surface to be saying the same thing, but a more comprehensive understanding of each may prove that there are significant differences between the secular and Christian concepts identified as parallel.[44]

The predominant mode was that of "active reconstruction and relabeling," either by "reinterpreting psychological facts from the perspective of theological facts" or "reinterpreting theological facts from the perspective of psychological facts."[45]

The integration approach, while complimentary of psychology, often ends up being derogatory of the Bible. As we have shown, it gives psychology a status not confirmed by philosophers of science and other experts on the subject. Thereby it denigrates the Bible in a subtle and almost unnoticed way. According to a study conducted by E. E. Griffith, the psychological counseling done by those who describe themselves as operating within a Christian framework actually consists mostly of secularly derived techniques.[46]

Collins concludes his chapter by saying, "But it is confusing, potentially harmful and invalid to propose that there is one psychological way that deals with the 'cure of minds,' one spiritual way that deals with the 'cure of souls,' and no overlap."[47] More confusing and potentially **spiritually** harmful is the focusing on superficial similarities in order to establish equalities. Biblical counseling is deeper and more complex than that.

After all of his arguments in support of integration, Collins' final conclusion about integration is quite puzzling. He says, "It is too early to answer decisively if psychology and Christianity can be integrated."[48] This begs the question: If the conclusion of Collins is correct, then why does he recommend integration?

5

EFFECTIVENESS

Does psychotherapy or psychological counseling really help people? Given the numbers of Christians seeking psychological help and the numbers of Christians who have chosen psychological counseling as a profession and the numbers of pastors who refer people to professional psychologists, the answer must be "yes." But is it? Or perhaps a better question is this: Does anyone really know if psychological counseling works?

Three eminent researchers in the field of outcomes in psychotherapy declare that "the urgent question being pressed by the public—Does psychotherapy work?—goes unanswered."[1] The American Psychiatric Association published *Psychotherapy Research: Methodological and Efficacy Issues*, which indicates that a definite answer to the question, "Is psychotherapy effective?" may be unattainable. The authors conclude, "Unequivocal conclusions about causal connections between treatment and outcome may never be possible in psychotherapy research."[2]

In a review of that book, *Brain-Mind Bulletin* says, "Research often fails to demonstrate an unequivocal advantage from psychotherapy." Here is an interesting example from the book:

. . . an experiment at the All-India Institute of

Mental Health in Bangalore found that Western-trained psychiatrists and native healers had a comparable recovery rate. The most notable difference was that the so-called "witch doctors" released their patients sooner.[3]

Researcher Dr. Allen Bergin, whom Collins quotes in support of psychological therapy, also admits that it is very hard to prove things in psychotherapy.[4] Psychological researcher Dr. Judd Marmor says that there is a "paucity of sound research in this area" because of the difficulties involved.[5] Two other writers indicate that "the paucity of 'outcome' data leaves the profession vulnerable to the familiar charge that it is not a science at all, but rather a 'belief system' that depends on an act of faith between the troubled patient and a supportive therapist."[6]

In presenting his case for the effectiveness of psychotherapy, Collins quotes Bergin's comments about some earlier work done by Dr. Hans Eysenck. Bergin is a well-known psychologist and co-editor with Dr. Sol Garfield of the *Handbook of Psychotherapy and Behavior Change.*[7] Eysenck is regarded as one of the world's leading psychologists. After examining over 8000 cases, Eysenck concluded that:

> . . . roughly two-thirds of a group of neurotic patients will recover or improve to a marked extent within about two years of the onset of their illness, whether they are treated by means of psychotherapy or not.[8]

Eysenck found little differences in results (in the subjects he examined) between those treated and those not treated. Since his study failed to prove any advantage of psychotherapy over no formal treatment, he remarked:

> From the point of view of the neurotic, these figures are encouraging; from the point of view of the psychotherapist, they can hardly be called very favorable to his claims.[9]

Eysenck's statement is overwhelming. But what is really shocking is the vast amount of referral to psychological counseling when research does not seem to support it.

Bergin has disagreed with Eysenck's conclusions and does not believe that the research supports Eysenck's position. However, this is not a simple matter. The controversy has been raging ever since 1952 over whether there is any difference between counseled and not-counseled persons. In 1979 the symposium "The Outcome of Psychotherapy: Benefit, Harm, or No Change?" Eysenck reported the results of reviewing the history of cures for mental patients in the hospital in which he works. He discovered that as far back as the late seventeenth century (1683-1703) about two-thirds of the patients were discharged as cured. In spite of the fact that psychotherapy did not exist at that time, the improvement rate was about the same as it is today. The so-called treatment consisted of the use of fetters, cold baths, solitary confinement, and even extraction of teeth for extreme punishment.

During his presentation Eysenck gave additional evidence for his earlier discovery that indicated that about the same number of individuals will improve over a two-year period of time whether or not they receive therapy. He confirmed, "What I said over 25 years ago still stands."[10] Then in 1980 Eysenck wrote a letter to the *American Psychologist* supporting his original position.[11] In recent years Eysenck has even more strongly supported his original position.[12]

Nevertheless, Collins says that "there is now a consensus that psychotherapy is more effective than no therapy."[13] The word *consensus* usually means general agreement or unanimity. We will let the evidence speak for itself. Let us begin by quoting Bergin, the same person quoted by Collins. Bergin says:

> . . . it is disheartening to find that there is still **considerable controversy** over the rate of improvement in neurotic disorders in the absence of formal treatment.[14] (Emphasis ours.)

In reviewing a large number of research studies, Smith and Glass came to some conclusions that encouraged psychotherapists, because at first glance their conclusions seemed to indicate that psychotherapy was more effective than no treatment at all. Because of the vast amount of research reviewed and the sophisticated statistical methods used by Smith and Glass, many who read the conclusions thought that finally, once and for all, the proof for psychotherapy had been established. However, at the annual meeting of the American Psychopathological Association, psychiatrist Dr. Sol Garfield criticized that conclusion which is based upon the approach used by Smith and Glass called meta-analysis. Garfield says that "instead of resolving forever the perennial controversy on the efficacy of psychotherapy, meta-analysis seemingly has led to an increased crescendo in the argument."[15]

Researcher Dr. Morris Parloff summarizes all of the conclusions of Smith et al and others in an article in *Psychiatry*. Parloff admits that one overall "disconcerting finding" is that "all forms of psychotherapy are effective and that all forms of psychotherapy appear to be equally effective."[16] However, this result raises the question about whether this conclusion is a testimony for or against psychotherapy as opposed to any other form of help. One must also ask whether or not it is the therapeutic techniques and therapists' training that help. Perhaps change comes from other factors, such as the belief that help is forthcoming or the sense that someone else cares or even the decision to begin working on the problem.

If top researchers are unable to assert with great confidence that psychological counseling works, why do Christians exhibit such great faith in psychology? If it is so difficult to perform studies and prove things in psychological counseling, why do Christians believe that psychological counseling is necessary for people suffering from problems of living? If both the American Psychiatric Association and the American Psychopathological Association give mixed reports about efficacy, why do Christian leaders promote the promises of the psychological way? And if there is little sound research, why are Christians so eager to substitute theories and therapists for the Word of God and the work of the Holy Spirit? Why has the church permitted the cure of souls ministry to be replaced by the cure of minds?

Researchers have determined that positive results from therapy have more to do with the counselee's desire to change[17] and on the warmth of relationship[18] than on the therapeutic theory or technique or experience of the therapist.[19] The factors which seem to be the basis for improvement exist both in and out of counseling. Therefore the idea that all seem to work equally well does not really support the incorporation of psychology into the church, especially since other studies indicate that untrained helpers do as well as trained and experienced therapists.[20] Furthermore, placebo studies indicate that almost any interesting activity (such as listening to music, being in a current affairs discussion group, reading plays) can be substituted for therapy with equal results.[21]

The all-work-equally-well idea applies to the transpersonal, religious therapies which have discarded the usual theories and techniques. Some of these incorporate astrology, meditation, and shamanic techniques. One example is Dr. Leslie Gray who at the end of her clinical fellowship in psychology at Harvard, found her own help through a Cherokee shaman rather than through her own psychotherapeutic training. She admitted that she did not get into shamanism for religious reasons, but rather because she was looking for a therapy that works. She says:

> I use what I call "core shamanism"—techniques that are not culture-bound. For example, sonic driving—drumming, rattling, chanting—enables people to reach an altered state of consciousness wherein they can have access to information that ordinarily wouldn't be available to them. . . . Unlike psychotherapists, I do not depend on interpretation and analysis. . . . I don't interpret his or her experience, or delve into the past, or look for determinants in childhood. My work is educational and spiritual; I teach shamanic techniques. . . . Neither do I give

> advice; I set things up so that clients get advice directly from their guardian spirits.[22]

According to the general conclusions of the Smith et al study, Leslie Gray's therapy would evidently work "equally well."

Dr. Gray's repudiation of psychotherapeutic theories and techniques and her commitment to shamanic techniques should speak volumes to Christians who embrace psychology rather than put their whole trust in the Lord Jesus Christ. Whereas Gray relies solely on shamanic beliefs and techniques, many Christians are not relying upon the Word of God, the work of the Holy Spirit and the cross of Christ. Why can't Christians trust counseling from the Word of God as much as Gray trusts in shamanism? Even Collins quotes Everett Worthington, Jr., who says, "The only good studies show secular and religious counseling to be equally effective with religious clients,"[23] and those studies are done from a psychological perspective.

The controversy over whether or not psychological counseling really helps people continues to rage in spite of the increase in research.[24] Garfield concludes a review of the research activities in psychotherapy by stating:

> Admittedly, we have a long way to go before we can speak more authoritatively about the efficacy, generality, and specificity of psychotherapy . . . . The present results on outcome, while modestly positive, are not strong enough for us to state categorically that psychotherapy is effective, or even that it is not effective . . . .Until we are able to secure more definitive research data, the efficacy of psychotherapy will remain a controversial issue.[25]

Dr. S. J. Rachman, Professor of Abnormal Psychology, and Dr. G. T. Wilson, Professor of Psychology, in their book *The Effects of Psychological Therapy*, point out the many serious errors and violations of sound statistical procedure in the Smith and Glass report. They say:

> Smith and Glass are naive in prematurely applying
> a novel statistical method to dubious evidence that
> is too complex and certainly too uneven and
> underdeveloped for anything useful to emerge. The
> result is statistical mayhem.[26]

After evaluating the Smith and Glass review as well as other disagreements with and criticisms of Eysenck, Rachman and Wilson support Eysenck's original position that there is no advantage of treatment over no treatment. Eysenck cited a study done by McLean and Hakstian which used a variety of treatment methods for depressed patients. One conclusion of their study was that, of the treatment methods used, psychotherapy was the least effective.[27]

For any form of psychotherapy to meet the criteria for efficacy, that therapy must show that its results are equal to or better than results from other forms of therapy and also better than no treatment at all. It must meet this criteria through standards set by independent observers who have no bias towards or against the therapy being examined. The study must also be repeatable and thereby confirmed to indicate whether a therapy can be said to be helpful.[28]

Professor of psychiatry Dr. Donald Klein, in his testimony before the Subcommittee on Health of the U. S. Senate Subcommittee on Finance, said, "I believe that, at present, the scientific evidence for psychotherapy efficacy cannot justify public support."[29] As a result of the hearings, a letter from Jay Constantine, Chief, Health Professional Staff, reports:

> Based upon evaluations of the literature and
> testimony, it appears clear to us that there are vir-
> tually no controlled clinical studies, conducted and
> evaluated in accordance with generally accepted
> scientific principles, which confirm the efficacy,
> safety and appropriateness of psychotherapy as it is
> conducted today.
>
> Against that background, there is strong pressure

from the psychological and psychiatric professions
and related organizations to extend and expand
Medicare and Medicaid payment for their services.
Our concern is that, without validation of psychotherapy and its manifest forms and methods, and in
view of the almost infinite demand (self-induced
and practitioner-induced) which might result, we
could be confronted with tremendous costs, confusion and inappropriate care.[30]

After summarizing a variety of research studies, Nathan
Epstein and Louis Vlok say:

We are thus left to conclude with the sad and
paradoxical fact that for the diagnostic category in
which most psychotherapy is applied—that of
neurosis—the volume of satisfactory outcome
research reported is among the lowest and the
proven effectiveness of psychotherapy is minimal.[31]

The following statement from Rachman and Wilson, after
extensive review of the research on the effects of
psychotherapy is both revealing and shocking:

It has to be admitted that the scarcity of convincing
findings remains a continuing embarrassment, and
the profession can regard itself as fortunate that
the more strident advocates of accountability have
not yet scrutinized the evidence. If challenged by
external critics, which pieces of evidence can we
bring forward? . . . The few clear successes to which
we can point, are out-numbered by the failures, and
both are drowned by the unsatisfactory reports and
studies from which no safe conclusions can be
salvaged.[32]

These authors conclude their book by saying:

. . . it is our view that modest evidence now supports

the claim that psychotherapy is capable of producing some beneficial changes—but the negative results still outnumber the positive findings, and both of these are exceeded by reports that are beyond interpretation.[33]

Can Psychological Counseling Be Harmful?

In addition to the concern about the effectiveness of psychological counseling, there is the concern about the harm rate. Michael Shepherd from the Institute of Psychiatry in London summarizes the outcome studies in psychotherapy:

A host of studies have now been conducted which, with all their imperfections, have made it clear that (1) any advantage accruing from psychotherapy is small at best; (2) the difference between the effects of different forms of therapy are negligible; and (3) psychotherapeutic intervention is capable of doing harm.[34]

Collins claims, "There is evidence that the people who are harmed by therapy most often are the severely disturbed or those with counselors who themselves are maladjusted."[35] It is also true that psychological therapy is the most helpful to those people who need it least.[36]

People often hear and read about the possible help given by psychotherapy, but they rarely hear or read about its potential harm. Richard B. Stuart's book *Trick or Treatment, How and When Psychotherapy Fails* is filled with research that shows "how current psychotherapeutic practices often harm the patients they are supposed to help."[37] After surveying the "best minds in the field of psychotherapy," one group of researchers concludes:

It is clear that negative effects of psychotherapy are overwhelmingly regarded by experts in the field as a significant problem requiring the attention and concern of practitioners and researchers alike.[38]

There is a growing concern among the researchers about
potential negative effects in therapy. Many researchers are
noting this danger zone in therapy. Bergin and Lambert say
that "ample evidence exists that psychotherapy can and does
cause harm to a portion of those it is intended to help."[39] Dr.
Morris Parloff, chief of the Psychosocial Treatments Research
Branch of the National Institute of Mental Health, declares:

> In my view, it seems fair to conclude that although
> the empirical evidence is not firm, there is now a
> clinical consensus that psychotherapy, if improperly
> or inappropriately conducted, can produce psy-
> chonoxious effects. Most studies do not contemplate
> the possibility of negative effects.[40]

Dr. Carol Tavris warns:

> Psychotherapy can be helpful, especially if the
> therapist is warm and empathic, but sometimes it
> slows down a person's natural rate of improvement.
> In a small but significant number of cases,
> psychotherapy can be harmful and downright
> dangerous to a client. Most of the time it doesn't
> accomplish much of anything.[41]

The average harm rate is about ten percent.[42] This calls
for a *caveat emptor* (buyer beware) warning to prospective
patients. Dr. Michael Scriven, when he was a member of the
American Psychological Association Board of Social and
Ethical Responsibility, questioned "the moral justification for
dispensing psychotherapy, given the state of outcome studies
which would lead the FDA to ban its sale if it were a drug."[43]

Even after considering the most recent research on the
subject, Scriven still refers to psychotherapy as a "weak
possibility."[44] If psychotherapy can be harmful to one's
mental health, some written warning (equivalent to the one
on cigarette packages) ought to be given to potential buyers.

When one considers the research which reveals detrimental effects of psychological counseling, one wonders if the overall potential for improvement is worth the risk.[45]

Many therapists are reluctant to publicize and advertise anything but the positive results of psychological counseling. We agree with Dr. Dorothy Tennov, who says in her book *Psychotherapy: The Hazardous Cure*:

> . . . if the purpose of the research is to prop up a profession sagging under the weight of its own ineffectiveness in a desperate last-ditch effort to find a rationale for its survival, we might prefer to put our research dollars elsewhere.[46]

Bergin once accused two well-known writers in the field of being too concerned about harming the image of psychotherapy in the eyes of government, insurance companies, and consumers. He said:

> The implication is that "harmful effects" will impinge upon our pocketbooks if we are not more careful about publishing evidence on therapy-induced deterioration.[47]

We wonder to what extent money, academic rank, and vested interests in training programs influence the outlook and reaction of therapists to research detrimental to the psychological way.

Professionals vs. Nonprofessionals.

In discussing professional versus lay counseling, Collins says, "Professionals know the ease with which counselors—especially inexperienced and untrained counselors—can misinterpret symptoms, give insensitive guidance or advice, be manipulated by counselees, or fail to understand the complexities of abnormal behavior." Though he admits that professionals can also make such errors, he says that "the trained counselor is more alert to spotting and avoiding such dangers."[48] No research is provided for the foregoing statement and no footnote used to enable one to find the research upon which his statement is founded.

We mentioned earlier that the research has not confirmed the efficacy of psychotherapy, but has confirmed its ability to harm. In addition, research supports the results produced by amateurs over professionals! In comparing amateurs and professionals with respect to therapeutic effectiveness, Dr. Joseph Durlak found in 40 out of 42 studies that the results produced by the amateurs were equal to or better than by the professionals![49] In a four-volume series called *The Regulation of Psychotherapists,*[50] Dr. Daniel Hogan, a social psychologist at Harvard, analyzed the traits and qualities that characterize psychotherapists. In half of the studies amateurs did better than professionals.[51] Research psychiatrist Dr. Jerome Frank reveals the shocking fact that research has not proven that professionals produce better results than amateurs.[52]

Eysenck declares:

> It is unfortunate for the well-being of psychology as a science that . . . the great majority of psychologists, who after all are practicing clinicians, will pay no attention whatsoever to the negative outcome of all the studies carried on over the past thirty years but will continue to use methods which have by now not only failed to find evidence in support of their effectiveness, but for which there is now ample evidence that they are no better than placebo treatments.

He continues:

> Do we really have the right to impose a lengthy training on medical doctors and psychologists in order to enable them to practice a skill which has no practical relevance to the curing of neurotic disorders? Do we have the right to charge patients

fees, or get the State to pay us for a treatment which is no better than a placebo?[53]

According to Dr. Donald Klein, New York State Psychiatric Institute, and Dr. Judith Rabkin of Columbia University, one must determine whether the helping factors are specific or general. They say that "specificity usually implies that the specific technique is necessary so that the particular outcome simply cannot be accomplished without it."[54] They say:

> A core, covert issue in the specificity debate is the uncomfortable realization that if all psychotherapies work about the same then all of our elaborate psychogenic etiological hypotheses are called into question.[55]

And, if all hypotheses are called into question, then there is no reason why the body of Christ cannot minister to one another as effectively as those who are trained in psychological theories and techniques.

Dr. Joseph Wortis, State University of New York, plainly declares, "The proposition of whether psychotherapy can be beneficial can be reduced to its simplest terms of whether talk is very helpful." He goes on to say, "And that doesn't need to be researched. It is self evident that talk can be helpful."[56] What a simple yet profound statement! Why can't ordinary Christians share their faith with one another through love and truth rather than looking for professional psychological help?

Researcher Dr. James Pennebaker, an associate professor at Southern Methodist University, indicated a relationship between confiding in others and health. He demonstrated that lack of confiding is related to health problems. One could conclude from his research that, to paraphrase an old adage, the conversation of confession is good for the soul— and apparently for the body too.[57]

The research comparing the results produced by amateurs versus professionals seriously challenges the fees charged by the professionals. After examining the specificity issue, Dr. Robert Spitzer, Columbia University and New York State Psychiatric Institute, gives a hypothetical example by supposing that a "mental health aide" can perform an equally effective service for $6 per hour rather than $30 or $50 or $120 normally paid to a psychological therapist. He concludes by challenging his colleagues on how they would feel about a mental health aide providing the service for $6 per hour rather than the higher paid psychotherapist.[58]

In discussing lay counselors and professionals, Collins says, "Well-trained nonmedical counselors who understand psychopathology are aware of physical issues and more inclined to encourage counselees to get competent medical examinations and treatment."[59] Collins provides no research for his statement. However, it does raise a question about diagnosis of mental-emotional-behavioral problems.

Our book *The Psychological Way/The Spiritual Way* includes research that shows that psychological diagnosis is a disaster. Not only do professionals make massive errors, but nonprofessionals are as good or better at diagnosis than professionals.[60] Psychiatrist Dr. Hugh Drummond admits, "Volumes of research have been done to demonstrate the absolute unreliability of psychiatric diagnosis."[61] Additional studies have shown that the psychological system cannot be relied upon to distinguish the sane from the insane in either civil or criminal matters.[62]

Dr. George Albee tells how therapists from different countries will disagree when presented with the same individuals. He discusses the usual psychiatric disagreements on the mental fitness of identical defendants in court cases. The psychiatrists for the defense predictably have different opinions from those for the prosecution. Furthermore, people who are considered affluent are generally given more favorable diagnoses than those who are poor. Albee says, "Appendicitis, a brain tumor and chicken pox are the same everywhere, regardless of culture or class; mental conditions, it seems, are not."[63]

Collins says, "It has often been suggested that there would be no need for professional counselors if church members were consistently bearing one another's burdens. In theory this is true."[64] He goes on to say that in practice "many churches are not caring or therapeutic."[65] After speaking at various churches and to numerous pastors, it seems to us that the reason the church is not a caring community is mainly because of what we refer to elsewhere as "the psychologizing of Christianity."[66] The myth that psychology has something to offer Christians with problems of living better than what the church has always had has disabled and disarmed first the clergy and then the congregation. Christians have been convinced that the best thing they can do for a suffering friend is to encourage him to get counseling, and by that they mean professional psychological counseling.

The faith in professional counselors over lay counselors is uncorroborated in reality and unsubstantiated in research. The church needs to return to caring for human problems as it did from its inception. God's Word declares:

> According as his divine power hath given unto us all things that pertain unto life and godliness, through the knowledge of him that hath called us to glory and virtue: whereby are given unto us exceeding great and precious promises: that by these ye might be partakers of the divine nature, having escaped the corruption that is in the world through lust. (2 Peter 1:3, 4.)

Rather than looking to psychologically trained "experts," we need to grow in our knowledge of the Lord, learn to walk in His love and His Word, and bear one another's burdens.

The question for the Christian to ask is not simply, "Does it work?" The question for the Christian is: which way honors and glorifies the Lord? Which way will cause us to draw closer to Him and learn to walk after the Spirit rather than according to the flesh?

6

THE SELF-CENTERED GOSPEL

Jesus' challenge to His disciples to be in the world but not of the world is only faintly heard today. The continual temptation for merging the visible church with the culture has reached astronomical proportions, so much so that the church has been nearly swallowed up by popularized versions of existentialism, humanism, and various psychologisms. Rather than Christ being the center of communion, self and self's so-called **needs** have become the focus.

That we have reached this peak of self-centeredness is not surprising when we look back at the influences of the nineteenth century. Under the influence of the German theologian Friedrich Schleiermacher, man's personal experience and perception became the source of theology rather than the Word of God.

> Faith in Scripture as an authoritative revelation of God was discredited, and human insight based on man's own emotional or rational apprehension became the standard of religious thought.[1]

Thus man's mind became the ultimate evaluator of all truth. His choice of personal experience over written revelation became the foundation for today's liberal theology. Moreover,

this emphasis on man more than on God Himself influenced
the shift from God-centered theology to man-centered theology, which has infiltrated even the most evangelical,
fundamental elements of the twentieth-century church.

The shift was subtle and gradual. Just as the starting
point for Schleiermacher's theology was anthropological
rather than theological, the doctrines of man began to precede
the doctrines of God in theology texts. The philosophy of
existentialism developed by Soren Kierkegarrd further
influenced theological thought. Dr. Paul Brownback, author
of *The Danger of Self-Love*, says,

> . . . the bottom line of existentialism is philosophical
> selfishness. People have always been selfish, but
> existentialism provided a philosophical justification
> for it.[2]

At the same time, psychology was emerging from
philosophy as a separate discipline. It's association with
medicine in the treatment of insanity and so-called neuroses
soon gave it a prestigious "scientific" status. While conservative elements of the church recognized its anti-biblical
philosophical roots, the liberal church embraced much of the
new psychological "discoveries." After all, the liberal church
was already moving in the direction of existentialism and
humanism over divine revelation.

More and more Christians, in their faith in psychology as
science, incorporated teachings of Sigmund Freud, Carl Jung,
Alfred Adler, Abraham Maslow, Carl Rogers, and others. The
shift from God to self ran parallel to psychology in its
emphasis on man's needs above its emphasis on God's will.
The change in emphasis from knowing and obeying God to
understanding and meeting the needs of self has captured the
pulpits, the altars, and the hearts of men. Rather than man
being created for God, God is reduced to being a need
supplier. Rather than being accountable to God as the
Sovereign creator and ruler of the universe, modern
Christians look to God as a big psychiatrist who will see to it
that all of their so-called needs to feel good about themselves

are met. Indeed, He is the source of all physical necessities as well as of love, joy, peace, faith, hope, and life itself. However, Jesus clarified the direction of intent when he said: "But seek ye first the kingdom of God, and his righteousness; and all these things shall be added unto you." (Matthew 6:33.)

In every instance of the shift from a Christ-centered Gospel to a man-centered gospel there is a change in priorities. There is also a shift in the order of things. God must be preeminent in all things. He is both the beginning and the end. His Word must take precedence over human experience. This does not mean that there are not any needs to be met or that Christianity is not personal. But the switch in emphasis from God to self, from God's purposes to self's needs, from our serving Him to Him serving us permeates every fiber of church life.

These distinctions may seem small, but it is a matter of direction. Two sets of train tracks that run parallel to each other in a train station may appear alike. However they may go in opposite directions. And that is exactly what happens when the emphasis moves from Christ to self in preaching, teaching, counseling, thinking, and acting. Historically, evangelical thinking has been God-centered, while humanistic psychology has been centered on self. However, as the church has embraced theological, philosophical, and psychological thought which does not put God at the center, it has had the audacity to put God at man's right hand.

Psychological Understanding of Scripture.

Because of the great emphasis on understanding man and meeting his needs, Christians are becoming more psychological in their thinking than biblical. Unfortunately, psychology has become the twentieth-century tool for understanding the Word of God. This makes logical sense, because if man's mind is the evaluator of experience above the Word of God, then man's mind becomes the evaluator of the Bible. Therefore, if the mind of man is the ultimate authority in the understanding of Scripture, then those psychological "experts" of understanding people become the new authorities in biblical exegesis.

Rather than understanding the people of the Bible through the context of Scripture, psychologists see them through the lenses of their own favorite psychological theories. For instance, in his book *The Magnificent Mind*, Collins gives new psychological "insight" into the suffering of Job. In his discussion of Andrew Weil's theory that "all illness is psychosomatic" and that "causes always lie within the realm of the mind," he proposes that perhaps Job's boils were from great duress and that they went away "only when his mind was pointed heavenward and he was able to 'see' God with his eyes."[3] He uses this in support of the use of mental imagery, which is both a psychological and occultic technique. By explaining Scripture with psychology, he gives greater credence to psychology than to the Bible.

Examples abound. A well-known Southern California Christian college president used Carl Jung's analysis of the Apostle Paul's zeal as a major point in his sermon. Peter, Isaiah, Jeremiah, Joseph, and the rest have been psychologically analyzed as well. Not only are Bible saints analyzed; biblical doctrines are trivialized and verses are yanked out of context to support whatever theory or technique is to be justified.

There is also a great confusion of terms. The word used by a psychological theorist may have an entirely different meaning from its ordinary usage. The word may carry an entire theoretical framework. For instance, when Gordon Allport uses the term *becoming*, he has an entire theory of selfhood invested in the word. His theory of becoming is from the secular humanistic perspective. The becoming self is moving in directions similar to what Maslow termed "self-actualization." There is absolutely no way that Gordon Allport would use that word in reference to becoming like Jesus. Nevertheless, in his attempt to integrate psychology and the Bible, Collins says:

In spiritual growth and psychological maturity each

believer should be in the process of what psychologist Gordon Allport has called "becoming."[4]

With the confusion of terms and meanings, psychological and spiritual maturity suddenly become equivalent. This is the concern of Don Matzat, who says of Collins' arguments in *Can You Trust Psychology*:

> Collins falls into the same trap that ensnares many who look to psychology as a means for changing lives and developing character. Accepting the form of Scripture as being the correct description of the quality of the Christian life, they ignore the substance or supernatural material of Christianity which is the life of Christ himself. Viewing Christian growth as being the positive development of the human personality into "Christlikeness," they feel justified to borrow from the techniques of psychology to accomplish that end. So they boast, "we can help produce Christlike people!!" While they acknowledge the "what" of Christian living, they ignore the "how." They therefore end up with what St. Paul calls "the form of godliness," and for all practical purpose, deny the power that produces it.[5]

Through the influence of psychology, the Christian walk is reduced to a form of human accomplishment rather than divine enablement. The source for growth and change becomes understanding the self rather than knowing God.

Because of the influence of psychology, self-esteem is a primary concern throughout the church world. Not only is it touted as the answer to the ills of mankind; it is justified through interpreting the Bible with psychological theories. The roots of self-esteem are not found in the Bible, but rather in psychology. The great emphasis on self-esteem was mainly introduced into the twentieth century through psychologist William James. His study of the self centered on self-feelings, self-love, and self-estimation. He used the word *self-esteem* to indicate positive self-feelings as contrasted with negative self-feelings. Self-esteem and self-love theories were further developed by humanistic psychologists, such as Erich Fromm, Alfred Adler, and Abraham Maslow.

Self-Esteem.

Self-esteem theories are based on faith in the autonomous human being. According to the humanistic scheme, everyone is born perfect and the final authority and measure of all things is the self. Self is therefore the god of humanistic psychology. And as self relates with itself, the therapists are the priests. The shift in emphasis from God to self has come into the church through the incorporation of such humanistic ideas as self-esteem, especially by those who embrace the teachings of humanistic psychologists.

Society's move from self-denial to self-fulfillment revealed a new inner attitude and a different view of life. Self-actualization is its major focus and self-fulfillment its clarion call. And, self-fulfillment, with all its accompanying self-hyphenated and self-fixated variations such as self-love, self-acceptance, self-esteem, and self-worth, has become the new promised land. Then as the church became psychologized, the emphasis shifted from God to self.

In his chapter, "Is an Emphasis on the Self Really Harmful?" Collins supports his position on self-esteem by quoting the secular humanist Nathaniel Branden:

> Currently being attacked as "a religion of self-worship," the movement's exponents are charged with being self-centered, self-indulgent, infantile. And . . . critics imply that a concern with self-realization entails indifference to human relationships and the problems of the world . . . .
>
> Admittedly, there is a lot about the movement that is foolish, irresponsible, even obnoxious—some people's notion of self-assertiveness, for instance. . . But individualism, self-esteem, autonomy and inter-

est in personal growth are not narcissism—the latter being a condition of unhealthy and excessive self-absorption arising from a deep-rooted sense of inner deficiency and deprivation. . . .

I do not know of a single reputable leader in the human potential movement who teaches that self-actualization is to be pursued without involvement in and commitment to personal relationships. There is overwhelming evidence, including scientific research findings, that the higher the level of an individual's self-esteem, the more likely that he or she will treat others with respect, kindness and generosity.[6]

Collins says, "This is a perspective that critics of selfism rarely report." The reason why we, the critics of selfism, do not report this statement is because it is not true. For example, Branden says, "I do not know of a single reputable leader in the human potential movement who teaches that self-actualization is to be pursued without involvement in and commitment to personal relationships." Who is Branden speaking of? Himself? He was involved in an adulterous relationship with Ayn Rand. Is he referring to Carl Rogers? Or Abraham Maslow?

Carl Rogers has said:

The man of the future . . . will be living his transient life mostly in temporary relationships . . . he must be able to establish closeness quickly. He must be able to leave these close relationships behind without excessive conflict or mourning.[7]

Dr. William Kirk Kilpatrick says of Rogers' statement, "A statement like this raises the question of how close a relationship can be that is gotten in and out of with so little cost."[8]

Adrianne Aron critiques Abraham Maslow's theory of self-actualization as it was lived in the hippie movement. She says:

> In the hippie pattern Maslow's dream of a compas-
> sionate, reciprocal, empathic, high-synergy scheme
> of interpersonal relations gets lost behind a reality
> of human exploitation. Where the theorist pre-
> scribed self-actualization the hippies produced
> mainly self-indulgence. Yet, I shall argue, the hip-
> pie result is not alien to the Maslovian theory. . . .[9]

It really is dangerous to give recognition and status to these
psychologists because it leads many Christians into false
teachings and false theologies.

Daniel Yankelovich, a pollster and analyst of social
trends, wrote a book entitled *New Rules: Searching for Self-
Fulfillment in a World Turned Upside Down*. In it he documents changes that have occurred in our society. He describes "the struggle for self-fulfillment" as "the leading edge
of a genuine cultural revolution." He claims, "It is moving our
industrial civilization toward a new phase of human
experience."[10] In describing the new rules, Yankelovich says:

> In their extreme form, the new rules simply turn
> the old ones on their head, and in place of the old
> self-denial ethic we find people who refuse to deny
> *anything* to themselves.[11] (Emphasis his.)

The cover of the book states:

> *New Rules* is about that 80 percent of Americans
> now committed to one degree or another to the
> search for self-fulfillment, at the expense of the
> older, self-denying ethic of earlier years.[12]

The new formula for society has become faith in a cause
and effect relationship between a high amount of self-love,
self-esteem, etc., leading to health, wealth, and happiness
and a low amount to just the opposite. One can see in *New
Rules* that humanistic psychology is the narcissism of our
culture. Even well-known humanistic psychologist Rollo May
says of Yankelovich's conclusions, "I can see he is right."[13]

A research study supported by the National Institute of Mental Health attempted to find a relationship between self-esteem and delinquent children. The researchers found that "the effect of self-esteem on delinquent behavior is negligible."[14] The researchers confess, "Given the extensive speculation and debate about self-esteem and delinquency, we find these results something of an embarrassment."[15]

In his book *The Inflated Self*, Dr. David Myers points out how research has revealed people's self-serving bias. While church leaders now claim that people need ego boosting and self-esteem raising, Myers' research led him to conclude:

> Preachers who deliver ego-boosting pep talks to audiences who are supposedly plagued with miserable self images are preaching to a problem that seldom exists.[16]

A research project at Purdue University compared two groups of individuals, one with low self-esteem and the other with high self-esteem, in regard to problem solving. The results of the study once more explode the myth that high self-esteem is a must for mankind. One of the researchers says, "Self-esteem is generally considered an across-the-board important attitude, but this study showed self-esteem to correlate negatively with performance." He concludes by stating that in that particular study, "The higher the self-esteem, the poorer the performance."[17]

A study designed to determine underlying causes for coronary heart disease showed that frequent self-references on the part of the subjects were implicated in coronary heart disease. Self-references were measured by the use of "I," "me," "my," and "mine." In contrast, the researchers mention that "it is interesting to note that the Japanese, with the lowest rate of coronary heart disease of any industrial nation, do not have prominent self-references in their language."[18] The researchers conclude:

> Our central thesis, stated in a sentence, is that self-involvement, which arises from one's self-identity

and one's attachment to that identity and its extensions, forms the substrate for all the recognized psychosocial risk factors of coronary heart disease.[19]

Collins readily uses the vocabulary of humanistic psychology. He both adopts it and adapts it with biblical explanations. He attempts to explain how the "Bible does not condemn **human potential**," how God "molds us into new creatures with reason for **positive self-esteem**," and how "the Supreme God of the universe enables us, through Christ, to find **real self-fulfillment**."[20] (Emphasis added.) Self-fulfillment is not the same as fulfillment through serving God. The first is the autonomous self and self-will being fulfilled. The second is a person fulfilling God's will and purpose through dying to self and living unto God. Temporary pleasure may come from fulfilling the self, but true joy comes from fulfilling His call on our lives by His grace.

Why would anyone want to borrow vocabulary from humanistic psychology, which is based upon a secular humanistic view of humanity and which does not even recognize the Supreme God of the universe? Many psychologists would say it's because these terms can be explained biblically. However, human potential, positive self-esteem and self-fulfillment all evaporate when one reads the following verses:

> And he said unto them all, If any man will come after me, let him deny himself, and take up his cross daily, and follow me. (Luke 9:23.)

> This know also, that in the last days perilous times shall come. For men shall be lovers of their own selves, covetous, boasters, proud, blasphemers, disobedient to parents, unthankful, unholy, without natural affection, trucebreakers, false accusers, incontinent, fierce, despisers of those that are good, traitors, heady, highminded, lovers of pleasures more than lovers of God. (2 Timothy 3:1-4.)

> And he said unto me, My grace is sufficient for thee:
> for my strength is made perfect in weakness. Most
> gladly therefore will I rather glory in my infirmities,
> that the power of Christ may rest upon me.
> Therefore I take pleasure in infirmities, in reproach-
> es, in necessities, in persecutions, in distresses for
> Christ's sake: for when I am weak, then am I strong.
> (2 Corinthians 12:9-10.)

Do these sound like human potential, positive self-esteem and
self-fulfillment?

Collins says, "We have dignity, value and purpose."[21]
However, the Bible says:

> The heart is deceitful above all things, and desper-
> ately wicked: who can know it? (Jeremiah 17:9)

> But we are all as an unclean thing, and all our righ-
> teousnesses are as filthy rags; and we all do fade as
> a leaf; and our iniquities, like the wind, have taken
> us away. (Isaiah 64:6.)

Collins says, "We have dignity, value and purpose . . . because
the God of the universe created us and declared that his creation was good."[22] Dignity has more to do with how one behaves than intrinsic worth. However, because Jesus said that
we are to love our neighbors as ourselves, we are to treat one
another with dignity. Although the image of God has dignity,
value and worth, humanity has frightfully tarnished that
image. For us to attempt to bolster ourselves up with self-
worth and intrinsic self-value is pointless when our old self is
counted crucified, dead, and buried (Romans 6) and our new
self is "not I, but Christ." (Galatians 2:20.) Dignity, value, and
purpose for the Christian are **in Christ**, rather than in self.
In other words, He is our dignity, value, and purpose, just as
He is our righteousness.

Humanistic psychology clouds the issues so drastically
that the new life in Christ becomes blurred with self-enhanc-

ing terms, when it is to be no longer I, but Christ. Rather than majoring in humanistic psychology and selfism, Christian counselors must major in walking in the Spirit in an eternal love relationship with Christ (Romans 8). When Christian psychologists define psychological vocabulary in biblical terms it is confusing at least and heretical at worst.

7

WHERE DO WE GO FROM HERE?

Where do we go from here? The church has lost its moorings in the Gospel of Christ, the Word of God, and the work of the Holy Spirit. Unless Christians sink their anchor into the Solid Rock they will continue to drift into the sea of psychological theories and slip right into New Age mythologies. The bigger and better always seem to be on the horizon and the very thought of going back to the basics seems narrow minded and shortsighted.

General revelation (what can be discovered in nature through scientific endeavor) has risen to the same level as the special revelation of the Word of God. General revelation is God's grace to let us learn about our physical world through scientific endeavor. It is also strong enough to let us know that God exists (Romans 1:20). However, general revelation has become the primary excuse for the proliferation of unscientific opinions masquerading as science. Thus, the cry of "All truth is God's truth" is used to bring opinions, distortions, and deceptions into the church of God. Indeed, all truth does come from God. Furthermore, truth is more than simply a selection of individual facts or truths. It is a whole entity with no contradiction or error. God's truth as revealed in Scripture is based upon His own character and personhood. Who He is is fundamental in the entire truth of His Word. As well as being true in every aspect, His Word is true in its unified whole. Psychology can never reach that point of truth. It is filled with distortions of whatever truth might be perceived, and when it is all put together it is merely an elaborate fabrication of men's minds.

On the one hand, Collins recognizes the superior position of the Word of God when he says, "The Bible is the inspired, valid, true Word of God," and when he declares, "All truths discovered by human beings must be tested against and proved consistent with the revealed Word of God."[1] However, what he has adopted and adapted from psychology has not been consistent with his intention to remain faithful to the Word of God. Collins is not alone in this regard. Christians who practice psychology do not intend to distort or diminish Scripture. They have found what they believe to be true and helpful in psychology and adopt and adapt Scripture. In the process the Bible, in both specific verses and as a whole, becomes adapted to the psychological perspective. What generally happens is that the psychologies influence the interpretation so that they **seem** to pass the test of Scripture.

The specific revelation of Scripture has to do with what God desires mankind to know about Himself, about humanity, and about relationship. Those who rely on the Word of God as being the only sure guide for walking in faith are often accused of putting the Word of God in a higher position than God Himself. However, those who love the Word do so because they love the Lord whose Word it is. Those who follow the Word do so because of the life of Christ within them. The Word of God is the external revelation for knowing God in the intimacy of relationship. It is the only external, sure guide and measure of godly living. The Word of God works in harmony with the indwelling Holy Spirit. The Holy Spirit is called "the Spirit of truth" and the Word of God is the Word of truth.

In his concern over psychology, Don Matzat says, "What is being potentially undermined via the integration of psychology and theology is not the sufficiency of Scripture, *but the sufficiency of Christ!!*"[2] (Emphasis his.) We would say that both are being undermined. The Lord Jesus Christ cannot be separated from His Word. In fact, the identification of Christ with the Word comes across very clearly in the first chapter of the Gospel of John, where Jesus Himself is called the Logos. However, Matzat is making a strong point. Psychology greatly undermines the very nature of Christianity, which is "Christ in you, the hope of glory."

Christianity depends on Jesus' life within the believer; it is not fleshly conformation to the written Word of God. Faith functions through a life, but if a person is looking to the ways of men to conform to certain principles of the Bible, that will only be a counterfeit. The fruit of the Spirit cannot come through psychological inquiry or understanding. It is a supernatural work of the Holy Spirit living in the believer.

Although many Christians who practice psychology believe that there is more depth of understanding in psychology, the exact opposite is true. Psychology can only touch the flesh or what is left of that which must be crucified. Psychological theories and therapies will not be able to perform the work of the Spirit in a person's life. Therefore, if believers are to walk even as Jesus walked, they must return to His ways, which are engraved upon the hearts of believers and expressed in His written Word. Rather than majoring in the psychological opinions of men, Christians need to major in Christ and His Word.

Nevertheless, Collins encourages students to pursue psychological studies if they want to counsel. His rhetorical question boldly asks, "Who is better equipped than a Christian psychologist to teach students how to keep the faith in the midst of psychological challenges?"[3] Just the opposite occurs. They are taught how to juggle the two and how to try to fit them together either by changing the theory to make it biblical (which is less often the case and which would annul the need for psychotherapy in the first place) or by interpreting the Bible through psychological theories.

Furthermore, Collins gives scant warning about what happens to professional therapists as a result of their counseling. Those who focus on the self through psychological theories rather than on God through His Word and Jesus Christ dwelling within them are bound to suffer. There are negative consequences to practicing psychotherapy. One survey of psychiatrists indicated:

> 73% reported experiencing significant problems with anxiety, and 58% reported problems with moderate to severe depression. These emotional difficulties were partially attributed to their work as psychotherapists.[4]

Another study revealed:

> . . . more than 90% of the psychiatrists surveyed felt they were experiencing a wide variety of special emotional problems as a result of conducting psychotherapy.[5]

This matches with other research that has reported alarming rates of suicide, alcohol abuse, sexual dysfunctions, poor personal relationships, marital problems, divorce, family problems, and so on.[6] Although the research indicates that interpersonal skills are of utmost importance in counseling, researchers found that therapists' own personal relationships suffered. They proposed:

> A lack of genuine relatedness, resulting from prolonged participation in "as if" relationships, may very well carry over into the therapist's relationships outside of therapy. The patient's idealization of the psychotherapist may cause the therapist to feel superior and consider himself or herself an "expert." These feelings of superiority may create a sense of distance from others.[7]

Another survey indicated that "50 percent of clinical psychologists no longer believed in what they were doing and wished they had chosen another profession."[8] Indeed young Christians who enter the field of psychotherapy and psychological counseling will be learning the ways of the world rather than the way of the Lord.

In his criticisms of those who are untrained in psychology and yet would dare minister to people with problems, Collins has failed to footnote statements that would seem to require it. For example, he says, "Satan is blamed for everything that goes wrong, including most illnesses. New, threatening or unfamiliar ideas (including psychological ideas) are labeled 'demonic' and quickly rejected."[9]

In spite of the fact that Collins encourages training in psychological principles and even provides that training through his own teaching and writing, he does admit: "Professional mental health education, training, and experience do not appear to be necessary prerequisites for an effective helping person."[10] While he confesses that "there is no solid evidence to guarantee that this training will make [a person who wants to counsel others] a better counselor," he nonetheless recommends that people become psychologically trained.[11]

Misuse or Abuse?

Collins says, "We do not throw out all psychology simply because some misuse it, any more than we would discard all science or education because some abuse these fields or see them as the only hope for mankind."[12] First, there is an attempt by no one we know to throw out "all psychology." Collins constantly stretches objections critics have to a *part* of psychology to include *all* of psychology. By paralleling "all psychology" and "all science" in the same sentence he leaves the impression that this type of psychology is science when in fact it is not.

Collins gives the impression that the objections to psychology are based solely upon "misuse" or "abuse." However, the objections to psychology are directed at the use of it as well as the misuse and abuse. If there were no misuse or abuse, it would not change the critics' basic position at all. It is clear in our writing that we are not objecting solely to the misuse or abuse of psychotherapy, but to its use altogether. In addition, one Christian's use of psychotherapy is another Christian's misuse or abuse. For example, Dr. Joseph Palotta is a Christian psychiatrist and hypnotherapist. He combines hypnosis and the Freudian psychosexual stages of development into a system he calls "hypnoanalysis." He says, "The universal conclusion that little boys and little girls make is that somehow the little girls have lost their penises and have nothing." He goes on to describe how "little girls feel that they have been castrated, that their penises have some-how been cut off" and that little boys "fear that they will lose their penises." He says, "The little girls develop what is termed penis envy."[13] Is that use, misuse, or abuse? Obviously it depends on whom you ask.

Collins warns that one must "study psychology with a constant awareness that the *science* of human behavior could be both **powerfully effective** and **subtly dangerous**."[14] (Emphasis ours.) Part of what he says is not true of psychotherapy, psychological counseling, or the psychologies which attempt to explain why people are the way they are and how they change. These are **not** science and **not** powerfully effective. However, Collins is absolutely right when he says that they are "subtly dangerous." Indeed, they are **dangerous**, not only to a person's mental health, but to his spiritual life as well.

The Psychological Way or the Spiritual Way?

Collins correctly quotes us as saying, "For almost two-thousand years the church did without the pseudoscience of psychotherapy and still was able to minister successfully to those burdened by the problems of living." In the next para-graph he correctly quotes us as saying, "We are not opposed to, nor are we criticizing, the entire field of psychology." He then erroneously includes us with a group of authors by stat-ing, "These authors instead are distressed with those parts of psychology that propose to help people using ideologies that appear to contradict Scripture."[15] This statement contrasts with what Collins says earlier in the book about our position. He says earlier that our "book argues that psychotherapy— the psychological way—is an ineffective, false, antibiblical, destructive, deceptive, pseudoscientific new religion filled with 'unproven ideas and abstract solutions.'"[16] This earlier statement on the part of Collins contradicts his conclusion about where we stand and requires some explanation on his part.

When we wrote our first book, *The Psychological Way/The Spiritual Way*, we were warned that we would be regarded as reactionaries and that the current demand was for books that amalgamized psychology and Christianity. Therefore, our book would not be in great demand. That warning was true.

When we completed our fourth book, *PsychoHeresy*, we were told by publishers to whom we submitted the manuscript that the names would have to be removed because of the popularity of the authors mentioned. We found out later that the more popular one becomes in the Christian world, the more protection one receives from Christian publishers. After all, if a publisher publishes a book that criticizes a famous (which always means bestselling) author, that author may not want to publish with that publisher in the future. As one of our friends wryly put it, "It's easier to criticize the apostle Paul than to criticize one of these bestselling psychological authors."

Psychiatrist Thomas Szasz has said of the psychotherapies that "all such interventions and proposals should . . . be regarded as evil until they are proven otherwise."[17] Szasz said when he endorsed our book *The Psychological Way/the Spiritual Way*, "Although I do not share the Bobgans' particular religious views, I do share their conviction that the human relations we now call 'psychotherapy,' are, in fact, matters of religion—and that we mislabel them as 'therapeutic' at great risk to our spiritual well-being."[18] Szasz, though not a Christian, recommends that mental health care be taken away from the professionals, such as the psychiatrists and psychologists, and given back to the church.

Psychologist Bernie Zilbergeld, in his book *The Shrinking of America*,[19] discusses much of the research related to the practice of psychotherapy. He has said:

If I personally had a relationship problem and I
couldn't work it out with my partner, I wouldn't go
and see a shrink. I would look around me for the
kind of relationship I admire. I wouldn't care if he
was a carpenter or a teacher or a journalist . . . or a
shrink. That's who I would go to. I want somebody
who's showing by [his] life that [he] can do it.[20]

Psychiatrist E. Fuller Torrey recommends spiritual counseling. He says, "For people with problems of living who share
the Bobgans' spiritual world view, their approach would be
the most effective."[21]

When Jesus was entering Jerusalem on a colt, people
cried out saying, "Blessed be the King who cometh in the
name of the Lord; peace in heaven, and glory in the highest."
(Luke 19:38.)   And some of the Pharisees said to Jesus,
"Master, rebuke thy disciples." (Luke 19:39.) Jesus said to
them, "If these should hold their peace, the stones would immediately cry out." (Luke 19:40.) When non-Christians and
atheists have joined the Christian critics of psychology, it
does raise many questions.

Two researchers, Orlinsky and Howard, who support the
use of psychotherapy and yet realize the problems associated
with that decision liken themselves to the optimistic little boy
who was found happily digging his way into a pile of horse
manure. When asked why he was so gleefully doing the task,
he replied that with all that horse manure "there must be a
pony in there somewhere."[22] We disagree. What you see is
what you get.

Psychology is a leaven that has come to full loaf in the
church, so much so that Dr. J. Vernon McGee said,

If the present trend continues, Bible teaching will
be totally eliminated from Christian radio stations
as well as from TV and the pulpit. This is not a wild
statement made in an emotional moment of concern.
Bible teaching is being moved to the back burner of
broadcasting, while so-called Christian psychology
is put up front as Bible solutions to life's problems.

He also refers to "so-called Christian psychology" in magazines and books and says, "So-called Christian psychology is secular psychology clothed in pious platitudes and religious rhetoric."[23] Elsewhere he says, "I see that this matter of psychologizing Christianity will absolutely destroy Bible teaching and Bible churches."[24]

We agree with Collins' statement at the end of his book. He says, "How we handle psychology and how we relate it to the Christian faith are issues" of great importance. [25] Joshua said:

> And if it seem evil unto you to serve the Lord, choose you this day whom ye will serve; whether the gods which your fathers served that were on the other side of the flood, or the gods of the Amorites, in whose land ye dwell: but as for me and my house, we will serve the Lord. (Joshua 24:15.)

Christians need to decide whether they will serve the false gods of psychology or the true and living God of the Bible.

PART TWO

COMMENTS

by Jay E. Adams

Richard Palizay and the Bobgans have writen a lucid and trenchant analysis of Larry Crabb's counseling system. In it, they explode the claim that the system is biblical, demonstrating Crabb's fundamental dependence on Adler, Maslow, Ellis, and—especially—Freud. Their insightful treatment of the corpus of Crabb's writings clearly reveals how Crabb uses the Scriptures out of context and for purposes for which they were not given.

Contrary to what some think, from Crabb's own words, Palizay and the Bobgans show that there has been no basic change in his views. Differences in later books stem only from the use of varied biblical images with which the system is painted and repainted.

In Crabb's works pagan theorists are praised, while the efforts of truly biblical counselors are debunked as "nothing buttery." Crabb also decries the teachings of integrationists as "tossed salad." But Palizay and the Bobgans demonstrate that Crabb himself is as fully an integrationist as those from whom he attempts (unsuccessfully) to divorce himself. Crabb's well-known allusion to "spoiling the Egyptians" is singularly inept. The Egyptians were spoiled of clothes, silver and gold—not values, ideas, beliefs and methodologies having to do with the problems in living addressed by counselors. The Israelites were forbidden to turn to the Egyptians for the latter (Leviticus 18:3) and God rebuked them when they did so (Jeremiah 2:18; 42:13-19). It is one thing to buy automobiles manufactured by unregenerate Shintoists; it is another to turn to the unsaved for counseling beliefs and practices.

Palizay and the Bobgans uncover Crabb's basic problem—the reason why he has adopted the integrationist position: contrary to 2 Timothy 3:17, he does not believe the Scriptures are sufficient to enable Christian counselors to counsel adequately. This fundamental flaw lies beneath all the other errors apparent in the system. Palizay and the Bobgans wonder why so many Christians, including pastors and teachers, fail to discern these all-to-obvious weaknesses, and hope these chapters will enlighten many.

In my opinion, I believe Crabb sincerely **wants** to be biblical and **thinks** that his system is. But so long as he continues to build his basic system out of pagan materials, according to the erroneous speculations of unsaved men, he will never achieve his goal. Painting such views in biblical hues does not transform them. To be biblical, the system itself, from the ground up, must be built of biblical materials according to God's plan. This Crabb has not yet done.

PART TWO

INSIDE-OUT THEOLOGY

Dr. Lawrence Crabb, Jr., has written a number of books on counseling and Christian growth. From his background in psychology he comes to Scripture with a viewpoint that sounds both appealing and workable. He sees Christians struggling with difficult problems of living and wants to help. He also addresses serious problems having to do with superficiality and ineffective Christian living. He encourages people to develop a close relationship with God and to recognize their dependence on Him. Crabb's goals for a deeper walk with God, loving relationships, and effective Christian living have inspired many to follow his ideas and methods. However, the way he hopes to solve the problems and lead people into a closer walk with the Lord depends more on psychological theories and techniques than on the Word of God and the Work of the Holy Spirit.

8

INTEGRATION

Crabb's rationale for integrating psychology with the Bible is based on his observation of superficial, ineffective Christians, his confidence in psychology, and his contention that the Bible does not give direct answers to people with problems of living. Crabb touches the common sense of the church when he points out the fact that there are Christians who are struggling with difficult problems of living. And, he touches the nerve of the church when he admonishes Christians for being materialistic and superficial. Christians can agree with him on a number of points. Yes, some Christians have serious problems of living. Yes, materialism and superficiality have greatly weakened individual Christians and the church as well. And Christians do need to grow in love for one another in the Body of Christ. They need to learn to walk in full dependence upon the Lord who is conforming each one to the image of Jesus Christ.

The Problem of Superficial Living.

We agree that there are serious problems in the church. Ineffective, superficial living does not honor Christ. Superficiality is not a new problem. Jesus faced that problem and said:

> Well hath Esaias prophesied of you hypocrites, as it
> is written, This people honoureth me with their lips,
> but their heart is far from me. Howbeit in vain do
> they worship me, teaching for doctrines the com-
> mandments of men. (Mark 7:6-7.)

Jesus did not mince words when he criticized religious
leaders for masking their sinful hearts with an outward show
of obedience. He saw the relationship between superficiality
and replacing God's Word with man's wisdom.

> Woe unto you, scribes and Pharisees, hypocrites! for
> ye are like unto whited sepulchres, which indeed
> appear beautiful outward, but are within full of
> dead men's bones, and of all uncleanness. Even so
> ye also outwardly appear righteous unto men, but
> within ye are full of hypocrisy and iniquity.
> (Matthew 23:27-28.)

Jesus cried, "Woe," to the scribes and Pharisees, not only
because of the deceitfulness of hypocrisy, but because of the
eternal consequences of a disobedient heart.

Early in His ministry Jesus stressed the importance of
the inner life of attitudes and motives. They were His central
concern in His Sermon on the Mount. Notice how His opening
words refer to the inner person.

> Blessed are the poor in spirit: for theirs is the
>   kingdom of heaven.
> Blessed are they that mourn: for they shall be
>   comforted.
> Blessed are the meek: for they shall inherit the earth.
> Blessed are they which do hunger and thirst after
>   righteousness: for they shall be filled.
> Blessed are the merciful: for they shall obtain mercy.
> Blessed are the pure in heart: for they shall see God.
> Blessed are the peacemakers: for they shall be called
>   the children of God. (Matthew 5:3-9.)

Such inner attitudes are not only receptive to the will of God, but bring forth fruitful actions. Therefore, we agree with Crabb when he declares that Christianity is more than outward actions.

We strongly agree with Crabb that superficiality is a serious problem. We say a hearty "Amen" to his plea for genuine love for one another in the Body of Christ. We also believe that Christians should be in the process of learning to walk in full dependence upon the Lord who saved us and who is conforming each one of us into the image of Jesus Christ. But, the inner man is not transformed into the likeness of Christ through psychological systems or techniques devised by men. The spiritual transformation of the inner man is outside of the domain of secularly based systems.

Crabb's Confidence in Psychology.

We agree with Crabb on the crucial importance of Christian sanctification being an inner work with outward consequences. However, we disagree with his psychological explanations and methods by which he hopes to achieve that inner change. While Crabb contends that his understanding about the nature and behavior of man is thoroughly biblical, his books reveal a heavy reliance on his background in clinical psychology. Though he claims to be a biblical counselor, his explanations and ways of change have been borrowed from psychology. On the one hand, he says that "the Scriptures provide the only authoritative information on counseling."[1] But, on the other hand he declares that "psychology and its specialized discipline of psychotherapy offer some valid insights about human behavior which," according to his own opinion, "in no way contradict Scripture."[2]

Like other integrationists, Crabb seeks to combine psychological theories and therapies with the Bible.[3] In his book *Effective Biblical Counseling*, he describes his method of integration as "Spoiling the Egyptians."[4] The label "Egyptians" represents psychological and psychiatric theorists. He argues that if a counselor will "carefully screen" concepts from psychology he will be able to determine their "compatibility with Christian presuppositions."[5] He contends that his method of screening will enable the church to glean "useful insights" from psychology without compromising commitment to Scripture. Crabb identifies his position as striking the balance between what he calls "Tossed Salad" (integrationists who are careless in their integration) and "Nothing Buttery" (those who have a "simplistic model of counseling" since it is based exclusively on the Word of God). [6] He claims that a Christian who spoils according to his guidelines "will be better equipped to counsel," than either the "Tossed Salad" or "Nothing Buttery" counselors.[7]

Problems with Integration.

While an integrationist may truly admire the Bible, his unwavering reliance on psychology shows an equal, if not greater, confidence in secular theories and therapies. In fact, adding unverified psychological theories and techniques to biblical data actually reveals a halting confidence in the Scriptures. It sends out a constant signal that the Scriptures in and of themselves are not enough for life and godliness. **Integration implies that God gave commands without providing all the necessary means of obedience until the advent of psychology.** It indirectly faults God for leaving Israel and the church ill equipped for thousands of years until psychoanalytic and humanistic psychologists came along with the necessary insight. It seems to discount the possibility of living the Christian life solely through spiritual means provided by God in His Word and through His Holy Spirit.

Integrationists face the constant dilemma of defending their dual faith in Scripture and psychology. The Bible's claim to be sufficient in all matters of life and conduct is a troublesome burr in the saddle of integrationists as they ride out to plunder the Egyptians. Numerous passages extol the sufficiency, power, and excellency of God's Word. For instance 2 Peter 1:2-4 says:

> Grace and peace be multiplied unto you through the knowledge of God, and of Jesus our Lord, according as his divine power hath given unto us all things that pertain unto life and godliness, through the knowledge of him that hath called us to glory and virtue: Whereby are given unto us exceeding great and precious promises: that by these ye might be partakers of the divine nature, having escaped the corruption that is in the world through lust.

The Bible is not meant to work independently from God Himself. The Bible is sufficient because the Lord Himself works through His Word. If a person tries to use the Bible apart from Christ ruling in His heart, he may claim that the Bible lacks practical answers for life's difficulties. However, it is through the Bible that God reveals Himself and works His divine power in Christians' lives. The Bible is more than words on a page. Every word is backed by His mighty power, His perfect righteousness, His love, His grace, and His wisdom. Thus God not only gives precious promises and instructions for living; He enables a believer to obey His Word. That is why the Bible is sufficient for life and conduct.

Paul declared that he would not depend upon the wisdom of men, but on the power and wisdom of God. Not only is human wisdom foolishness in comparison with God's wisdom; human words lack the divine power necessary to transform a person into the likeness of Christ and to enable him to live the Christian life according to God's will. God uses the wisdom and power of the Scriptures to enable believers to please Him and bear fruit:

> All scripture is given by inspiration of God, and is profitable for doctrine, for reproof, for correction, for instruction in righteousness, that the man of God may be perfect, thoroughly furnished unto all good works. (2 Timothy 3:16-17.)

No psychological doctrine can even come close to that claim, nor can it add power for change.

While sincere integrationists believe that there are psychological theories about the nature of man and therapies for change that do not contradict Scripture, the root remains the same. Jesus was always concerned about ungodly roots and about following the traditions of men instead of the Word of God. Paul also warned:

> Beware lest any man spoil you through philosophy and vain deceit, after the tradition of men, after the rudiments of the world, and not after Christ. (Colossians 2:8.)

Thus the problem always haunting an integrationist is the source from which he has borrowed: psychological counseling systems which were devised by agnostics and atheists to answer questions about the human condition without regard for the Creator and His Word.

A Sufficient Bible Without Direct Answers?

Crabb attempts to alleviate the problem of integration in the opening chapters of *Understanding People* by arguing that the sufficiency of Scripture means that it is sufficient as a framework. Then he proceeds to supplement that framework with psychological insights.[8] He says:

> Yes, the Bible is sufficient to answer every question about life, but not because it **directly** responds to every **legitimate question**.[9] (Emphasis added.)

Then he argues that psychology can be used to fill in the direct information to unanswered questions that he regards as legitimate. Repeatedly using the terms *directly* and *legitimate*, he attempts to build a case for seeking definitive answers outside the Scriptures.

Crabb agrees that the Bible answers some important questions, but contends that it lacks the so-called direct information necessary to address the legitimate questions that real people ask about the harsh reality of their real world.[10] He says that "no passage literally exegeted directly responds" to a host of legitimate questions.[11] Therefore one must supplement Scripture with creative thoughts gleaned from psychology to answer such questions.[12]

By such reasoning, Crabb seems to be saying that the Scriptures are both sufficient and insufficient. While claiming to believe in the sufficiency of Scripture, he goes outside of the Scriptures and turns to psychological opinions for answers to questions such as these:

> What am I supposed to do with my deep desire to be a woman because I'm so scared of being a man?
>
> How do I handle my terrible fear that if I ever expressed how I really feel, no one would really want me?
>
> Why do I feel so threatened when someone successfully proves that I've been wrong about something?
>
> Why do I not want to admit my internal struggles?[13]

In Crabb's opinion, the Bible does not clearly deal with questions being asked by desperate people.[14] He reasons that if one sticks only with the exegesis of Scripture he will not answer vital questions or else he will give only shallow and simplistic answers.[15]

Crabb uses the term *legitimate* to argue that people have a fundamental right both to ask and to seek answers to such questions.[16] Nevertheless there are examples in Scriptures in which people did not insist on that right. After extolling the Word of God, David asks, "Who can understand his errors? Cleanse thou me from secret faults." He did not despair because God did not give a full explanation of why he sinned. Instead, he trusted God and asked Him to cleanse him. He believed in the cleansing power of the Word of God.

But, according to Crabb, any counselor who does not address those questions has a "shallow understanding of problems and solutions that sounds biblical but helps very few."[17] In fact, he declares that a counselee could be "significantly harmed" if counseled by shallow thinkers who have not yet addressed those legitimate questions.[18] Crabb implies that counselees are entitled to answers to those legitimate questions, because if no one addresses their legitimate questions they will be forced to accept "superficial solutions."[19]

If such questions do not come from Scripture, on what basis does Crabb identify them as "legitimate"? The answer points to a major problem in his methodology, which is heavy reliance on his own preference and opinion. He picks the questions and chooses to classify them as "legitimate" according to his own subjective opinion. He then concludes that since the Bible does not directly address those questions, counselors have both the right and obligation to dip into the psychological opinions of men to bring help to problem-laden, spiritually ailing Christians.

In *Understanding People* Crabb gives three illustrations which produce questions which he says that the literal exegesis of Scripture will not answer.[20] The three cases concern a man with desires to dress as a woman; a woman with sexual hang-ups; and an anorexic. The unanswered question is the same in each case, namely, why do they display such bizarre behavior? In Crabb's opinion the Bible does not directly answer this crucial, legitimate "why?"

With each of his three illustrations Crabb cites Scriptures prescribing the correct course of action which will please God.[21] The Scriptures directly tell each person **what** God desires them to do. But according to Crabb the Scriptures do not tell them what he considers to be the more crucial and fundamental matter: **Why** do people desire bizarre and sinful action? While the Bible does not provide simplistic psychological answers, it does answer the big "why?" Sinful behavior is the result of man's sinful nature.

It may be interesting to look at the great variety of psychological opinions when dealing with what Crabb identifies as "legitimate questions." But, the danger in looking for answers to such questions outside of the Bible is that psychological systems tend to place answers outside of the person himself. Because of the underlying philosophy that people are innately good and are corrupted by society, mainly parents, psychological theories look for reasons for unacceptable attitudes and behavior in circumstances outside of the person. **That is why those kinds of answers are not found in the Bible**. Even when Satan or other people may tempt one to sin, God says through his word that even then they are drawn into sin by their own lust (James 1:14). God holds people responsible for their own sin. Thus, according to the Bible itself, it is neither necessary nor profitable to go outside Scripture for answers. The Bible answers the truly crucial questions about the nature of man and why he behaves the way he does.

Crabb complains about counselors who do not know or use answers found in psychology. Such counselors have before them God's clear word on the nature of man and right conduct, but they do not have what Crabb would consider a **direct** answer to the crucial question "Why?" They use God's clear Word. They believe in pursuing obedience to God's will when He has spoken clearly on the pleasing course of conduct. But, what does Crabb say of such counsel? He condemns it as promoting mere "external conformity."[22] In fact, he contends that such counsel would leave such people "utterly unhelped, and worse, significantly harmed."[23]

Evidently Crabb equates simple obedience to the Word of God with superficiality and external conformity. Surely he does not think that the Bible is limited to only external concerns! Obedience to the law of the Spirit in Christ Jesus (Romans 8:2) includes both inner and outer obedience. In fact Paul's explanation of walking according to the Spirit in Romans 8 deals with the inner life and motivation, not with anything superficial. How can one indict counsel from the Bible alone as anything superficial or merely external?

One wonders about Crabb's severe criticism of all Christian counselors who have not yet dealt with his legitimate questions. What about those who have ministered through the centuries without being privy to insights derived from psychology which supposedly deal directly with Crabb's legitimate questions? And what about Jesus?

Jesus would not have answered the questions according to any psychological theories even if they had been around.

He does not excuse, justify, or fix up the old self. He enables His disciples to obey His commands by His own presence in their lives. He says:

> Abide in me, and I in you. As the branch cannot bear fruit of itself, except it abide in the vine; no more can ye, except ye abide in me. I am the vine, ye are the branches: he that abideth in me, and I in him, the same bringeth forth much fruit: for without me ye can do nothing. (John 15:4-5.)

But, Crabb proposes to transform the self through psychological insight, using the wisdom of the world for spiritual matters.

The Bible answers questions about human behavior in terms of God's holiness and man's depravity. Details of the old self-life may not be fully understood, but Jesus gives the way out of self and into Him. What Crabb identifies as legitimate questions may indeed be part of the load that Jesus wants His children to leave at the foot of the cross. The answer to all of the impediments and confusions of the old self-life is to come to Christ, to take His yoke of relationship and guidance, and to really know Him in a personal, vital way. Jesus says:

> Come unto me, all ye that labour and are heavy laden, and I will give you rest. Take my yoke upon you, and learn of me; for I am meek and lowly in heart: and ye shall find rest unto your souls. For my yoke is easy, and my burden is light. (Matthew 11:28-30.)

The Bible continually stresses that it is personal knowledge of the Father and the Son that leads to life and godliness, rather than details about the self that the Bible does not provide. And it is the Spirit who enables us to crucify self, that Christ may be glorified in and through us.

There is therefore now no condemnation to them

which are in Christ Jesus, who walk not after the flesh, but after the Spirit. For the law of the Spirit of life in Christ Jesus hath made me free from the law of sin and death. (Romans 8:1-2.)

The life of Jesus, mediated to us by the Holy Spirit, is the very source of the solution to each one of the above problems. On the other hand, psychological answers are not only speculative, irrelevant and inconsequential; they are also misleading and can be ultimately destructive. The conflicting variety of answers from various psychologies illustrates how uncertain their answers really are. One psychological counselor's answer may disagree sharply with another's even if both of them are Christians. In contrast to the wide diversity of opinions among the various psychological systems, the Word of God is true, reliable, and life changing.

Such questions and their diverse psychological answers can actually become a smoke screen for not hearing and obeying God's will. They can easily prevent or delay a person from putting off the sinful self-life and putting on the righteousness of God through surrender to Him. Psychological explanations for behavior may actually serve to keep one from the radical change that God desires to bring through His Spirit. On the other hand, when a person comes to the point of desiring God's complete sovereignty in his life in every detail, the Lord will enable him to know and understand all that is essential for a life of holiness, godliness, and righteousness. God can do a far deeper work than any fanciful combination of psychological opinions about questions supposedly left out of Scripture.

Millions of Christians will never seek answers beyond the Bible to understand why they do what they do. Yet, they will obey God when the Spirit speaks through His Word. Surely the Spirit of God and the Word of God are not leading them to mere external conformity! Millions of Christians will never read Crabb's psychological answers as to the "why?" They will only be able to rely on their own relationship with God and the study of His Word. Surely the Spirit of God and the Word of God will not leave them with a shallow and deficient view of man! Millions of lay Christians will never enter into any more than study, memorization, and obedience to the direct statements of Scripture. Surely this does not mean that the Spirit of God and the Word of God can only lead them into a shallow, simplistic, and superficial method of counseling others.

An Unwarranted Censure of Scripture.

Crabb's contention that counsel limited to questions directly answered by the Bible results in "a shallow understanding of problems and solutions that sounds biblical but helps very few"[24] is in direct opposition to the orthodox view of the sufficiency of Scripture. Such a claim weakens one's entire approach to Scripture and can lead to creative twisting of the plain meaning of the Word. Results of implementing such an approach to Scripture are disastrous. Even direct statements from the Bible can be adjusted to make room for the importation of psychological answers to questions supposedly unanswered through exegetical study.

Crabb's line of argument seems to demand a whole host of detailed and specific information which is not in the Bible. This is the wholesale excuse of all integrationists to shift from the Bible to the world. Rather than using biblical language, they use psychological jargon. But, just because God does not employ the labels and techniques of modern psychology, we should not be fooled into thinking that problems of living have not been sufficiently addressed by Scripture. There is no need to go beyond the direct statements of God in order to address such matters. God deals directly with essential matters of life and godliness. Therefore the Scriptures can and should be the sole and sufficient guide for living and counseling.

A Biblical Approach to Problems of Living.

A Christian's answer to problems of living depends on his relationship with God and obedience to His Word. If one starts with the premise of the **absolute** sufficiency of Scripture, then he will work **out from** the Bible **into** the world and its problems. It is a process of moving from Scripture into the world as led by the Holy Spirit. Thus, a true biblical counselor will interpret people and their problems through the lens of the Bible, not through the lenses of psychology. Those integrationists who use the double lenses of psychology and the Bible will only produce double vision. And how can counselors with double vision point out the right way to struggling Christians?

God does not interpret man according to such psychological terminology or doctrine. Therefore the church should not use it. Certainly God was not ignorant of these matters when He guided His servants to record His Word. Surely God does not regret that Freud, Jung, Maslow, and others did not live in the first century so that his apostles might have incorporated their notions into the gospels and epistles. Nor is Paul's presentation of sanctification shallow and deficient because it lacks the so-called insights of psychological theory.

God never intended for His people to doubt the power and sufficiency of His Word. The Spirit says boldly that the Word of God can pierce to the core of man's being. Hebrews 4:12 declares:

> For the word of God is quick, and powerful, and sharper than any two-edged sword, piercing even to the dividing asunder of soul and spirit, and of the joints and marrow, and is a discerner of the thoughts and intents of the heart.

The Lord through His Word can perform surgery on the heart of man in a way that no psychologist could ever hope.

Indeed the heart of man is deceitful and desperately wicked. It is beyond human ability to discern its wicked ways, as God says so forcefully in Jeremiah 17:9-10. However human depravity and treachery do not prevent the Word of God from doing what it says it will do. The Word and the Holy Spirit cut through to the inner man. The Heart-Knower who searches the heart and examines the mind, who discerns a person's thoughts from afar and knows our words before they are on our tongue, has spoken in the Bible.

The apostle Paul recognized that change on the inside is brought about through the Holy Spirit in conjunction with the Word of God. He prayed:

> That [the Father of our Lord Jesus Christ] would grant you, according to the riches of His glory, to be strengthened with might by His Spirit in the inner man; that Christ may dwell in your hearts by faith; that ye, being rooted and grounded in love, may be able to comprehend with all saints what is the breadth, and length, and depth, and height; and to know the love of Christ, which passeth knowledge, that ye might be filled with all the fulness of God. Now unto him that is able to do exceeding abundantly above all that we ask or think, according to the power that worketh in us, unto him be glory in the church by Christ Jesus throughout all ages, world without end. Amen. (Ephesians 3:16-20.)

Only Jesus' love and life bring about the kind of heart change that bears eternal fruit and that honors God instead of men. Jesus gave His own life to change people on the inside. He did not give a technique, but rather His very own life to will and do His own good pleasure in and through each believer. No psychotherapist or psychological technique can perform wonders akin to what Christ does through His Word and His Spirit!

9

THE USE AND PRAISE OF PSYCHOLOGY

Crabb's confidence in psychology permeates his earlier books. But some of his followers believe that his later books indicate that he has moved away from his dependence upon psychological presuppositions, understandings, and techniques. Yet, his extensive indebtedness to psychology is as thorough in his most recent books as in earlier ones. In *Understanding People*, Crabb says, "Readers familiar with my earlier books will recognize movement in my concepts **but not, I think, fundamental change**."[1] (Emphasis added.) Furthermore, his subsequent book, *Inside Out*, reveals a strong affiliation with psychological opinion and practice.

In *Effective Biblical Counseling*, after his defense of "Spoiling the Egyptians," Crabb recommends over twenty secular psychologists to help Christians become "better equipped to counsel."[2] Men such as Freud, Adler, Maslow, Rogers, *et al* are extolled as potentially beneficial.[3] Crabb's belief that psychologists offer a substantive body of truth for the church can be seen in his own statements.[4]

> Again let me insist that psychology does offer real help to the Christian endeavoring to understand and solve personal problems.[5]

Crabb not only praises the movement as a whole but also exalts certain "bright lights" from within the camp. For example, Crabb sharply censures those who reject the psychological opinions of Carl Rogers,[6] even though it is difficult to follow Rogers' teachings without being influenced by the presuppositions which underlie them.

Special Praise for Freud and His Psychology.

The Freudian concept of the unconscious serves as the cornerstone of Crabb's model of man and methodology of change. The Freudian *unconscious* is not simply an adjective to describe that part of the brain that stores bits of information which are not presently in awareness. In Freud's psychoanalytic theory, the unconscious is a reservoir of drives and impulses which govern an individual beyond his conscious awareness. Freud changed an adjective into a noun and thus gave it form and substance. The Freudian unconscious not only holds memories and information; it also motivates present thinking and acting. Furthermore, it is out of reach through ordinary mental activity.

Freud's use of the word *unconscious* is technical and specific. According to the *Dictionary of Psychology*, when *unconscious* is used as a noun it is "the region of the mind which is the seat of the id and of repressions." And when the word *unconscious* is used as an adjective in the technical sense, it is defined as "characterizing an activity for which the individual does not know the reason or motive for the act." It is a hidden, elusive part of man which supposedly "cannot be brought to awareness by ordinary means." It is supposedly the residence and source of a person's drives, motivations, actions, and even essence of life. "Thinking which goes on without awareness," "memories which have been forced out of the conscious level of mind into the unconscious," and "motivation of which the individual is unaware" are all part of Freud's creation of the unconscious.[7]

Crabb's use of the word *unconscious* is very similar to the above psychological description. His commitment to the

Freudian theory of the unconscious is evident from the following quotations from *Understanding People*.

> Freud is rightly credited with introducing the whole idea of *psychodynamics* to the modern mind. The term refers to psychological forces within the personality (**usually unconscious**) that have the power to cause behavioral and emotional disturbance. He taught us to regard problems as *symptoms* of **underlying *dynamic processes* in the psyche**.[8] (Italics his; bold emphasis added.)

He continues, "I think Freud was correct. . . when he told us to look beneath surface problems to **hidden internal causes**." (Emphasis added.) Crabb does not agree with all that Freud taught and even sees errors in his theories, but he insists that "the error of Freud and other dynamic theorists is *not* an insistence that we pay close attention to **unconscious forces** within personality."[9] (Italics his; bold emphasis added.) In spite of Freud's rejection of Christianity, Crabb says, "I believe that [Freud's] psychodynamic theory is both provocative and valuable in recognizing elements in the human personality that many theologians have failed to see."[10]

In his earlier books Crabb uses the word *unconscious* directly and explains its hidden nature and power for motivation. In his book *Inside Out* he relies on metaphors and descriptive phrases such as "heart," "core," "beneath the surface," "hidden inner regions of our soul," "dark regions of our soul," "beneath the waterline," "underlying motivation," "hidden purpose," and "reservoir of their self-protective energy."[11] In fact the very title *Inside Out* points to the Freudian notion of the unconscious.[12] Crabb clearly portrays the unconscious as a real and powerful part of every person. He further suggests that doctrines of the unconscious are indispensable to the church.

Because of the influence of Freudian thought in our twentieth century culture, most people believe in some kind of unconscious. However, their interpretation of what the unconscious is or does will vary from one person to another. One person may do something out of habit and say he does it unconsciously. Or another may say that there must be an unconscious because he does not have to think about every single thing he does while driving a car. On the other hand, Freud stated that the unconscious is a place where all kinds of powerful drives and mysterious motivations cause people to do what they do, whether they want to or not. The implications of such a powerful seat of urges driving people to do all kinds of things against their will flies in the face of God holding people responsible for their actions. If people look for unconscious reasons for their behavior, they can excuse all sorts of behavior. **But, the idea of the unconscious as a hidden region of the mind with powerful needs and motivational energy is not supported by the Bible or science**.

We are tremendously complex beings, but psychological explanations about the inner workings of the soul are merely speculation. The only accurate source of information about the heart, soul, mind, will, and emotions is the Bible. Not only is the Bible accurate; the Lord Himself knows and understands exactly what lies hidden beneath the surface of every person. He knows and He brings cleansing to those inner parts that we may never understand. David prayed:

> Search me, O God, and know my heart: try me, and know my thoughts: and see if there be any wicked way in me, and lead me in the way everlasting. (Psalms 139:23-24.)

Teaching a Freudian concept of the unconscious is a disservice to Christians. Rather than relying on the Word of God and the indwelling Holy Spirit to search their hearts, they will learn to rummage around in some kind of Freudian unconscious and remain focused on the self.

Crabb does not merely praise the unverified notions of Freud. He actually incorporates a Freudian type of unconscious into the very heart of his teachings on sanctification. In a discussion entitled "The Beginnings of Change" he presents the unconscious as the key element of change.[13] He teaches that Christian growth comes from gaining **insight into the unconscious**. Crabb declares that failure to face the so-called reality of an unconscious reservoir of "beliefs, images, and pain" will result in "disastrous externalism."[14] He contends that failure to deal fully with the "unconscious" will result in "pressure, judgmentalism, legalism, and pride rather than deep love for God and for others."[15]

Thus without Scriptural warrant, Crabb teaches that the unconscious is a crucial factor in sanctification. Without providing a **biblical** definition of *the unconscious* (aside from a misinterpretation of the biblical use of the word *heart*), Crabb makes it a central element of his counseling system. Even though he does not provide biblical verification for his view, Crabb criticizes pastors and other Christian leaders for failure to emphasize the unconscious.[16] According to Crabb, leaders who ignore this Freudian notion produce unconscious "robots or rebels" who ignorantly conform to external expectations while continuing in their unconscious rebellion.[17] Indeed, without the law of the Spirit of life in Christ Jesus (Romans 8:2) leaders can produce rebels and robots, whether or not they use psychological ideas of the unconscious.

Crabb suggests that ignorance of the crucial role of the unconscious allows error to spread throughout the entire evangelical church.[18] He says, "Perhaps the major error of evangelical churches today involves a shallow and deficient understanding of sin."[19] But his analysis of the problem is that the church has failed to grasp the absolute centrality of the unconscious. Crabb levels the blame for the spread of this "error" on church leaders who have ignored this Freudian notion. He explains,

> Many pastors preach an "iceberg view" of sin. All they worry about is what is visible above the waterline.[20]

There is a real problem when preachers concentrate on external things and ignore sinful motives, resentment, unforgiveness, self-will, self pity, and self-centeredness. However, Crabb is talking about ignoring the Freudian unconscious.

The iceberg is Freud's classic model of the unconscious. The entire iceberg represents the mind, and only the tip is accessible to the person. It includes all information and memories which are accessible through recall as well as present thoughts and mental activity. The huge mass beneath the waterline does not simply represent all that is presently outside conscious awareness. It supposedly contains all that drives, motivates, and determines behavior outside conscious volition. Psychologists Hilgard, Atkinson, and Atkinson point this out in their standard work on psychology.

> Freud compared the human mind to an iceberg: the small part that shows above the surface of the water represents conscious experience, while the much larger mass below water level represents the **unconscious—a storehouse of impulses, passions, and inaccessible memories that affect our thoughts and behavior**. It was this unconscious part of the mind that Freud sought to explore by the method of free association . . . . By analyzing free associations, including the recall of dreams and early childhood memories, Freud sought to help his patients become aware of much that had been unconscious and thereby to puzzle out the basic determinants of personality.[21]

This explanation of personhood is based on conjecture, not scientific investigation. Not only does this concept of the unconscious make it "a storehouse of impulses, passions, and inaccessible memories;" it also assigns power to "affect our thoughts and behavior." The bizarre interpretations that Freud placed on his patients' free associations, dreams, and memories illustrate the distortion that results from trying to rummage about in a so-called unconscious.[22]

Crabb confidently uses Freud's iceberg illustration to explain the mind and its contents.[23] Although he denies that his concept of the unconscious is "a derivative of secular Freudian thinking smuggled into Christian theology," his use of the iceberg image and metaphor reveals a Freudian view of the unconscious.[24] Crabb follows Freud when he teaches that the content above the water line represents the conscious mind, while the content below the water line represents the unconscious.[25] Crabb, like Freud, also assigns motivating power to the unconscious.

Crabb likens pastors who focus only on conscious activity to the ill-informed sea captain who steers his vessel around the tip of an iceberg while remaining ignorant of the existence of "a mountain of ice beneath the surface."[26] Those pastors fail to take into account the great mass of crucial material motivating the person from the unconscious. He also claims that evangelical Christianity's ignorance of that "great mass of sinful beliefs" and motives has produced a masquerading of spiritual health.[27]

Crabb warns that if the church continues to spurn this enlightenment about the unconscious her counselors will actually be in a worse condition than the unregenerate psychotherapists and their clientele. After quoting Richard Lovelace at length because Lovelace supports Crabb's argument so well, Crabb declares:

> Unless we understand sin as rooted in unconscious beliefs and motives and figure out how to expose and deal with these deep forces within the personality, the church will continue to promote superficial adjustment while psychotherapists, with or without biblical foundations, will do a better job than the church of restoring troubled people to more effective functioning. And that is a pitiful tragedy.[28]

While the first part of that statement is drawn from Lovelace, the part about psychotherapists doing a better job is Crabb's addition. Crabb's belief in the indispensable value of Freud and psychotherapy is abundantly clear. No one would be more surprised than Freud himself at this change of events. He could never have imagined that the very religion he intensely hated would one day so heartily embrace and promote his doctrines.[29]

The Influence of Anna Freud, Alfred Adler and Others.

Freud's theory of the unconscious has had a profound influence on counseling psychology. His followers either elaborated or modified his doctrine of the unconscious. Freud's daughter Anna wrote extensively on ego-defense mechanisms of the unconscious, which include unconscious denial and repression. Crabb commends Anna Freud for her "classic work on ego-defense mechanisms," which play a significant role in his own system. He declares that her writings are "appropriate and helpful reading for a Christian."[30] The heavy emphasis on the defense mechanism of denial continues throughout all of Crabb's work. It is essential to *Understanding People* and for changing from the *Inside Out*.

Freudian theory has met with growing criticism both in and out of the field of psychology. Furthermore, acceptance of Freud conflicts with the biblical view of conscious choice and responsibility. Therefore, Crabb is careful to say that he does not believe in unconscious *determinism* or its complement of early determinants of behavior. At first this seems like a contradiction. However, it is simply a modification of Freud's theory, similar to that found in Alfred Adler.

We are not accusing Crabb of being totally Freudian, because he does not incorporate the Oedipus Complex or the early psycho-sexual stages of development. However, one can see the Freudian influence in Crabb's theory that people are motivated by the contents of the unconscious. In the sense of the iceberg metaphor, the centrality of the unconscious is the same even though Crabb's content would be somewhat different from Freud's. **Just as with Freud's therapeutic system, eliminating the theory of the unconscious would be tantamount to eliminating Crabb's entire system as well.**

Crabb's adaptation of the Freudian unconscious is much

the same as Alfred Adler's (a follower of Freud). Like Adler, Crabb teaches that while people are responsible and make choices, their unconscious motives direct a substantial amount of behavior. In like manner Crabb also teaches that unconscious motives often result in self-defeating behaviors. Like Adler, Crabb promotes a combination of unconscious motivation and personal responsibility and insists that a person be held responsible for wrong attitudes and actions which originate from wrong assumptions in the unconscious.

The following is an overall description of Adler's theory:

> Adler's theory shared some of psychoanalysis's [Freud's] tenets: psychic determinism, the purposeful nature of behavior, the existence of many motives outside conscious awareness, and the notions that dreams could be understood as a mental product, and that insight into one's own unconscious motives and assumptions had curative power. Adler, however, rejected the energy model of libido and replaced it with a future-oriented model of striving toward a subjectively determined position of significance. . . . Adler's human was an active striver trying to cope with the tasks of life but hampered by mistaken apperceptions and faulty values.[31]

Keep this in mind when we look at the details of Crabb's system.

Adler's influence on Crabb's integration model of counseling is seen in his emphasis on the need to promote insight in order to move a counselee beyond hidden motives underlying behavior. Adler says, "Fundamental changes are produced only by means of an exceedingly high degree of introspection."[32] Adler further declares:

> . . . individual-psychology can intervene to some purpose, and by means of an intensified introspection and an extension of consciousness, secure the domination of the intellect over divergent and

hitherto unconscious stirrings.[33]

Similarly Crabb contends that we need the help of another person to accomplish deep change through intensified introspection. Just as Adler used both individual and group therapy, so does Crabb. The emphasis on exposing contents of another's unconscious for the purpose of insight and therefore growth is very similar to Adler.[34]

Adler's influence on Crabb concerning what neither would like to refer to as early determinants of behavior can be seen in Crabb's adaptation of Adler's "Early [childhood] Recollection Technique"[35] In this technique the counselor asks the counselee to recall and describe early painful memories in order to find a key to present feelings and behavior. This projective technique supposedly provides insight into the direction and meaning of life.[36] However, as with all projective techniques, it is simply creative guess work, a kind of creative feeling around in the dark caverns of the Freudian unconscious in search of light.

Crabb has also seemingly adopted and adapted Adler's theories concerning the direction of movement, self-defeating behaviors, unrealistic assumptions, denial, and safe-guarding tendencies. Adler emphasized that all behavior is directed to the goal of overcoming inferiority and thereby gaining a sense of worthwhileness in both relationship and tasks of life. Similarly, Crabb teaches that all behavior is motivated by needs for worthwhileness (deep longings) through security (relationship) and significance (impact).

Crabb also follows Adler in the emphasis on emotion. Adler believed that emotions are aroused when a person gains real insight into his own hidden motives, wrong assumptions, use of denial and other safe-guarding techniques.[37] Later when we consider Crabb's methods of change we will see the strong emphasis on feeling pain from the past. Crabb's stories about people resisting insight therapy into the hidden regions of the unconscious also follow Adler's explanations concerning counselees resisting treatment through self-protecting strategies.[38]

Freud greatly influenced Adler, especially in terms of the

importance of unconscious motivations. Then Adler influenced a number of other psychological theorists, including Karen Horney, Carl Rogers, and Albert Ellis.[39] Basic assumptions of these psychologists as well as those of Abraham Maslow hold predominant places in Crabb's system.

Albert Ellis's Rational Emotive Therapy appears to have played a significant role in the development of Crabb's Rational Circle. He teaches that thoughts about oneself greatly affect behavior. And, since Ellis is an avowed humanist, his teachings are centered in self. He not only leaves God out of the picture, but says that "unbelief, humanism, skepticism, and even thoroughgoing atheism not only abet but are practically synonymous with mental health" and that "devout belief, dogmatism, and religiosity distinctly contribute to, and in some ways are equal to, mental or emotional disturbance."[40] For Ellis, self-interest is better than self-sacrifice, and unconditional self-acceptance is a prime feature of mental health. He says:

> Nonreligious philosophies, like RET, teach that you can always choose to accept yourself *because* you decide to do so, and that you require no conditions or redundant beliefs in God or religion to help you do this choosing.[41] (Emphasis his.)

Then Ellis puts down those Christians who try to combine Christianity with teachings on self-acceptance by saying:

> Ironically, when you do decide to adopt a religious view and choose to accept yourself conditionally (because you believe in a grace-giving god or son-of-god), *you* choose to believe in this religion and you consequently create the grace-giver who "makes" you self-acceptable.[42] (Emphasis his.)

It is amazing that Christians choose to drink from such antichristian psychological belief systems.

In *Effective Biblical Counseling*, Crabb lists a number of psychologists and recommends their books. The following summary statement from the end of his chapter "Christianity and Psychology" illustrates Crabb's confidence in psychology. All names in the parentheses are in his original statement.

> Man is responsible (Glasser) to believe truth which will result in responsible behavior (Ellis) that will provide him with meaning, hope (Frankl), and love (Fromm) and will serve as a guide (Adler) to effective living with others as a self- and other-accepting person (Harris), who understands himself (Freud), who appropriately expresses himself (Perls), and who knows how to control himself (Skinner).[43]

But Glasser's responsibility has nothing to do with God or His measure of right and wrong; Ellis equates godlessness with mental health; the hope that Frankl gives is not a sure hope because it is man-centered; the love of Fromm is a far cry from the love that Jesus teaches and gives; Adler's guide is self rather than God; Harris's acceptance disregards God's law; Freud hardly understood himself and he repudiated God; Perls' expression focuses on feelings and self; and Skinner's methods of self-control work better with animals than humans. Why not give credit where credit is due? To the Lord and His Word! **Why not look to God's Word concerning responsibility, truth, meaning, hope, love, guidance for effective living, understanding oneself, expression, and self-control instead of rummaging around in the broken cisterns of the opinions of unredeemed men?**

10

NEED THEOLOGY

Crabb's model of counseling centers on his belief that unconscious needs direct and motivate behavior. He declares, "In order to understand biblical counseling, we must identify clearly the deepest personal needs of people."[1] When he speaks of "deepest personal needs" he is referring to a need for worthwhileness which he divides into needs for security and significance.[2] In his later books he refers to those needs as deep longings for relationship and impact.

Crabb presents the unconscious as a powerful reality submerged beneath the conscious mind. He places great importance on the contents of the unconscious in terms of the way they affect all of behavior. They include personal needs of security and significance,[3] basic assumptions on how to meet those needs,[4] "relational pain" and "relational strategies."[5]

In *Inside Out* Crabb uses the terms *deep longings*, *thirst* and *wrong strategies* to describe the unconscious—its contents, power, and influence.[6]

Summary of Crabb's Foundational Proposition.

A foundational proposition in Crabb's system is that **every person has two substantive needs (longings) in the unconscious (core of his being) which motivate**

behavior. That this concept is central to Crabb's model is obvious just by skimming the contents of his books. Thus in order to grasp Crabb's system, one must understand that basic proposition. It functions as the fundamental, regulative, and distinctive principle in Crabb's model of man. The following is a summary of the model he builds on that proposition. Footnotes will not be used in this summary but documentation will be provided later.

In seeking to define man's innermost nature, Crabb proposes that at the core of man's innermost being are two real, profound, substantive realities known as personal needs or longings that provide the motivational energy behind overt behavior. Crabb earlier identifies them as the need for security and significance but later as deep longings for relationship and impact. According to Crabb, both exert their power from the deepest level of man, namely, the unconscious.

From their place in the unconscious, those needs/longings motivate individuals into action at the conscious level. They are presented as ruthless drives, persistent demands, and powerful murmurings deep within the unconscious. People are supposedly driven in a consuming way to satisfy two powerful needs. And according to Crabb, anyone who fails to satisfy those needs will be empty and discontent, whether he realizes it or not.

In Crabb's system all sin is directly related to inadequate attempts to satisfy the two needs apart from God. However, failure to satisfy the two needs/longings is not readily obvious to the person because of the strategic role of the unconscious. Because the two needs and the beliefs about satisfying their demands exist in the unconscious, people do not know the cause of their problems. In fact, they may not even realize they have problems.

According to Crabb, unmet needs produce loneliness, sorrow, and intense pain. Therefore, counseling people into an awareness of their unconscious needs and strategies is difficult. Because of the "intense pain" of unmet needs and because of the "excruciating hurt" from the failure of their unconscious strategies, people build "self-protective" layers to insulate themselves against further injury.

According to Crabb, those self-protective layers cause people to deny the reality of their true goals and motives. Through the process of denial, people supposedly develop layers to insulate themselves from painful unconscious realities and to obstruct attempts to expose their true motives. Although strategies of self-protection manifest themselves at the conscious level, people supposedly do not consciously know that what they are doing is for the purpose of self-protection. Crabb uses the distinction between the two levels of the mind to infer that while people may appear happy on the surface, there is a huge possibility that they are really miserable and lonely inside.

Crabb gives an example of a man he calls Frank, who is highly motivated and successful. Frank's conscious overt activities include business success, a lovely wife and home, three intelligent children, and positive church experiences. In fact, Frank "feels really good about life and shares with passion the joys of living for Jesus."[7] But Crabb contends that what is seen on the surface does not reveal the true source of Frank's motives. According to Crabb, Frank's "upbeat, assertive, knowledgeable" manner which leads to outward success and an outward life "above reproach and worthy of respect" is actually his way to protect himself "from ever having to admit he can't resolve a problem." Crabb contends that beneath Frank's outward joy and life of accomplishment there is a desperately fearful man "longing for a level of respectful involvement he's never enjoyed" and a sense of painful inadequacy.[8] Therefore this man, like all others, is supposedly unaware of his pain and seeks to protect himself through Freudian ego-defense mechanisms of unconscious repression and denial. In other words, the man in his unconscious life is the opposite of the man in his conscious life.

Counseling according to Crabb's theory then must be a process of exposing unconscious pain and self-protective strategies. The counselor must strip away defensive layers to expose the confused world of the unconscious. Once the layers have been peeled away, pains and hurts of the unconscious can be exposed. Crabb considers approaches which do not peel the layers to be superficial and simplistic.

According to Crabb's system, unmet needs, wrong strategies about satisfying them, pain and hurt of failure, and so forth must be unearthed and faced honestly even though the process can be excruciating. He contends that real change is only possible if a person is willing to start from the inside, meaning the unconscious.

After unconscious causes of the problems have been exposed, the counselor can set about the process of reprogramming both the conscious mind and the unconscious. This is accomplished through a focused effort to program into the mind a new strategy about how to satisfy the two needs. Again this is not an easy task. The person must jump from the cliff of safety and trust God to meet his two needs in the unconscious. Only then, according to Crabb, can he learn to depend both consciously and unconsciously on God.

Crabb's Model of Four Circles.

Crabb has devised a "four-circle model of personality," in which the unconscious plays the dominant role.[9] His four circles are: Personal, Rational, Volitional, and Emotional. Each circle represents different aspects of the individual as he relates to life through conscious and unconscious activity.

The Personal Circle. Crabb identifies the Personal Circle as a person's "Capacity for Relationship and Impact."[10] Crabb identifies this capacity as a God-created need. He says,

> The basic personal need of each personal being is to regard himself as a *worthwhile human being*.[11] (Emphasis his.)

According to Crabb, the need to be worthwhile has two components: the need for security and the need for significance, or deep longings for relationship and impact. He theorizes that the deep longings are related to a relentless fear of rejection, of not being acceptable, of not being of value or significance. In fact, Crabb teaches that the primary motivating force in every person is fear of not being accepted, of not being secure and significant. And the goal of behavior is to be accepted as worthwhile, with security and significance.[12]

In Crabb's model the Personal Circle of powerful needs is the core of every person, and it is primarily unconscious. Thus, even though a person may be superficially aware of having those needs, their power and thrust come from the unconscious. From this hidden, nearly inaccessible realm, the two needs motivate everything a person does. Crabb compares the needs for significance and security with Freud's drives for power and pleasure.[13] We also see the influence of Adler, Maslow, and Rogers in Crabb's Personal Circle.

The Rational Circle. The key feature of the Rational Circle is its unconscious beliefs and strategies about how to meet the needs for security and significance (deep longings for relationship and impact). While the Rational Circle includes all mental processes, such as thoughts, concepts, beliefs, and images,[14] the emphasis is on so-called unconscious beliefs and motives.[15] Thus the Rational Circle largely works from the unconscious to satisfy the so-called needs of the Personal Circle. Crabb contends that unconscious denial, erroneous thinking, wrong conclusions, and wrong beliefs in the Rational Circle need to be replaced with accurate thinking so that needs for security/relationship and significance/impact can be met more effectively.[16] The influence of Freud, Adler, Maslow and Ellis can be seen in Crabb's Rational Circle.

The Volitional Circle. Crabb's Volitional Circle represents a person's choosing capacity.[17] He says that people choose their behavior and are therefore responsible. Yet, according to his system, a great deal of choice in terms of strategies and goals is based upon the unconscious assumptions, beliefs, and strategies of the Rational Circle about how to meet the demands of the two needs/longings in the Personal Circle. Although the Volitional Circle largely represents conscious activity, it operates according to the needs and dictates of the unconscious.[18] Crabb's Volitional Circle shows the influence of Freud, Adler, Ellis, and Glasser.

The Emotional Circle. The Emotional Circle is where

counselees experience feeling. They are encouraged to get in touch with their feelings, since the really deep emotions exert their power from the unconscious. According to Crabb's system, emotional experiences, whether pleasant or unpleasant, relate directly to success in satisfying the demands of the two needs/longings. Certain emotions are triggered by the vast array of unconscious beliefs and thoughts about how to satisfy the two needs. Thus emotions play a key role in exposing the unconscious. The idea is that if a person can experience those emotions in his conscious awareness, he may be able to penetrate the contents of his unconscious. Then by bringing more and more material into the conscious realm, he will be able to think more accurately, choose with greater awareness, and develop more effective strategies for meeting his unconscious needs.[19] The influence of Freud, Adler, Rogers, and Perls is evident in Crabb's Emotional Circle.

Crabb's four circles will serve as the framework for our critique. Special attention will be given to Crabb's psychological theory of the unconscious since the whole thrust of his methodology centers around its contents.

Need Psychology/ Theology.

Crabb's model may sound good on the surface. After all, who has not felt the stirrings of the soul longing for satisfaction? His emphasis on personal needs and longings finds eager reception in the church. His plea for meaningful intimate relationships with God and with fellow believers causes people to be hopeful about his methods. And the implied promises for love, purpose, and meaning saturate the pages of his books. However, Crabb's doctrine of man with two unconscious needs motivating all behavior is psychologically based. And his doctrine of change, with unconscious beliefs and strategies for meeting the needs, is also grounded in psychological ideas.

Because Crabb's model borrows significantly from humanistic psychology, it is necessary to consider its basic tenets. Humanistic psychology is based on the belief that people are born good and that society (especially parents) corrupts them. Humanistic psychologists further believe that certain needs motivate everything a person does, that a person's life plan is to fulfill those inborn, unmet needs, and that when those needs are met the person will be able to realize his full potential and be socially responsible. They identify those psychological needs with such words as: *self-esteem, worthwhileness, emotional security*, and *significance*.

Their hope for mankind is this: when individual psychological needs are met then people will be personally fulfilled and socially responsible. They will be loving, peaceful, creative, industrious, and unselfish. They will no longer try to fill their emptiness (unfulfilled needs) with alcohol, drugs, or any other kind of overindulgence. In short, according to their theories, if everyone were to reach self-actualization (all needs being met) we would have a utopian society.

Many Christians have bought into the humanistic lie that when people's needs are met, they will be good, loving people. Through the influence of humanistic psychology, they believe that people sin because their needs are not met. Some say that teenagers rebel because their needs have not been met. They contend that failure to live the Christian life is because Christians do not have enough self-esteem or they do not understand that all of those so-called psychological needs are met in Christ. They reduce the Gospel to the good news of self-worth, self-esteem, emotional security, and significance. And they believe that if only Christians would see that God meets all of those needs they will be able to live the Christian life effectively.

Scripture, however, does not bear this out. Adam and Eve had it all. There was no need in their lives that was not being met to its very fullest, and yet they chose to sin, have their own way, disbelieve God, believe a lie, and love self more than to love and obey God. They followed both the words and example of Satan, who as Lucifer had had it all: beauty, power, authority, love, and all that an archangel could have and be. But Lucifer wanted to be God. And what about Israel? The more their needs were met, the less they relied on God. The more their needs were met, the more sinful they became.

Even the fulfilling of legitimate needs will not make a person a saint or promote sanctification.

And here we must delineate between true human need, according to the Bible, and what humanistic psychologists place at the center of human need. The Bible places God's will and purpose at the center rather than so-called psychological need. In His gracious will Jesus gives of Himself, not according to what psychologists identify as essential personal needs, but according to His perfect love and intimate knowledge of each person.

Throughout the Bible the panorama of God's plan for humanity unfolds according to His own will and purpose, which includes, but goes far beyond, human need. But since those psychological theories were devised by people who were seeking to understand themselves and humanity apart from God and who were looking for solutions separated from the sovereignty and will of God, their central interest was what they believed to be human need and human fulfillment without God.

Because humanistic psychology is based on humanism rather than theism, it ignores longings for worship, godly righteousness, discipline, faith in God, spiritual truth, pleasing God, loving God, obeying God, and other intricacies that God knows about each person. Instead, all is centered in the self. And when Christians try to amalgamate humanistic psychology with the Bible, they tend to ignore, distort, or subsume all spiritual blessings under what they call psychological needs.

The idea that humans are motivated by powerful needs in the unconscious is an unproven assumption that many Christians have come to believe. In fact, people do not think twice when someone says that people are motivated by inner needs. Tony Walter in his book *Need: The New Religion*, says:

> It is fashionable to follow the view of some psychologists that the self is a bundle of needs and that personal growth is the business of progressively meeting these needs. Many Christians go along with such beliefs.[20]

Walter further contends that needs now constitute a new morality and says:

> One mark of the almost total success of this new morality is that the Christian Church, traditionally keen on mortifying the desires of the flesh, on crucifying the needs of the self in pursuit of the religious life, has eagerly adopted the language of needs for itself. . . we now hear that "Jesus will meet your every need," as though he were some kind of divine psychiatrist or divine detergent, as though God were simply to service us.[21]

But Walter further declares that "human need was never central to Christian theology. What was central was God's grace not human need. Christianity is at root God-centered, not man-centered."[22]

Psychological systems, however, are man-centered and were proposed as alternative means of understanding the human condition and wrestling with problems of living. God's law was replaced by humanistic values which turned into needs, which gave them a moral force. Abraham Maslow built his hierarchy of needs on his own beliefs and values. And since he placed a high value on self-worth, self-esteem, and self-actualization, he justified those values by making them into needs. And while humanistic psychologists have removed the *ought*'s and *should*'s of external moral codes (such as the Bible), they have presented their own morality of needs. Walter notes:

> . . . the human project as the progressive meeting of human need has been unmasked; it is a secular religion, or at least a secular morality. I suggest that atheists and agnostics who pride themselves on having dispensed with morality and religion should ponder whether they have not let both in again through the back door.[23]

Indeed, need psychology has the force of morality and the

power of religion. And Walter identifies this new morality and new religion as **not** compatible with Christianity. He says:

> There is one feature of some of the major writings on need that points towards need as a form of morality. Marx, Fromm, Maslow and others have noted the incompatibility between human beings orienting their lives to meeting their needs, and a traditional Christianity that would deny the needs of the self and would give charity to others not because their needs entitled them to it but out of sheer disinterested love. . . . Life as a project of meeting needs becomes almost a substitute, disguised religion.[24]

Nevertheless, Crabb attempts to combine need psychology with the Bible. He makes the needs of men appear synonymous with God's will and purpose.[25] He equates those needs with God-given capacities.[26] Thus in his system it follows that the underlying need to be worthwhile is a God-given capacity. He relates the need for significance (also called "impact") with the capacity to fulfill God's purposes and the need for security (also called "relationship") with the god-given capacity for relationship with God. In his attempts to join together man-centered psychological theories with the Bible, Crabb has created a "Need Theology."

Need theology turns everything around. Not only does the human take center stage, but his so-called psychological needs are of prime importance. In Crabb's system the unconscious needs for security and significance direct, motivate, and energize every aspect of a person's life. Those needs are not regarded as something negative, but rather as positive capacities to be filled. **This is an unknown view of the innermost nature of man in the long annals of church history**.

Because of the centrality and the legitimacy of the needs in Crabb's theology, they play an essential role in his doctrine of sin. In his system sin is defined as the attempt to fulfill the demands of those unconscious needs apart from God. However, according to the Bible the sin problem is much deeper than strategies for meeting those unconscious needs apart from God. Thus in Crabb's model, the basic inner nature (the self) is not the problem. Yet the Bible reveals something quite different about the human heart and its sinfulness. Paul likened the condition of the unredeemed sinner as "dead in trespasses and sins" and "children of disobedience: among whom also we all had our conversation in times past in the lusts of our flesh, fulfilling the desires of the flesh and of the mind, and were by nature the children of wrath" (Ephesians 2:1,3). Nowhere in Scripture is the doctrine of sin interpreted in light of supposed strategies about satisfying two unconscious needs.

In Crabb's doctrine of salvation, the way of the cross turns into a message of escape from the tyranny of unmet needs. Both regeneration and sanctification are reinterpreted in light of unconscious needs. Thus real change according to Need Theology is learning how to meet the demands of the two with God's help rather than independently. However, Jesus did not die on the cross to satisfy a supposed need for self-worth, but to redeem human beings from the clutches of sin and Satan. He changes their lives, not by teaching them new strategies for seeking and finding security and significance, but by actually giving them new life. He does not merely alter wrong thinking about unconscious need fulfillment; he changes the very desires of the heart. Christ changes believers' motivation to love for God and others. Paul tells about this wonderful, life-transforming change: "Therefore if any man be in Christ he is a new creature: old things are passed away; behold all things are become new" (2 Corinthians 5:17).

The way of sanctification through Need Theology is to explore the caverns of the unconscious where the needs reside, to uncover the pain of unmet needs, and thereby to become dependent on God. Although a Christian is to examine himself in the light of God's Word to see that he is walking in the Spirit, biblical sanctification is quite different from concentrating on unmet needs, feeling the pain of the past, and then learning about God meeting those needs. According to the Bible, the focus of the vision of the believer is drawn from self to Christ through the Holy Spirit and the Word of God. Believers become more like Him as they look at Him and to Him:

> But we all, with open face beholding as in a glass the glory of the Lord, are changed into the same image from glory to glory, even as by the Spirit of the Lord. (2 Corinthians 3:18.)

It is by looking at Jesus, not at themselves, that believers take on His character through the gracious work of the Holy Spirit. Furthermore sanctification calls for taking up one's cross, not taking up new strategies for need fulfillment.

Although Crabb objects to criticism about his teachings having "a man-centered focus on fulfillment rather than a God-centered emphasis on obedience to Him and preoccupation with His Glory,"[27] what he teaches does indeed lead to a humanistic rather than a godly emphasis. The reason why this happens is because Crabb's integration includes the doctrines of men whose psychologies center on man and his innate goodness, his worthwhileness, his psychological reasons for behavior, and his goal of fulfillment.

No matter how much Crabb desires his system to free people to love and serve God and to relate warmly with people, the focus on human need will counteract his goal. The Bible calls believers to walk by faith rather than by any needs or desires of the self-life. Crabb encourages people to focus on themselves so that they can become better Christians, but A. W. Tozer says:

> Faith is the least self-regarding of the virtues. It is by its very nature scarcely conscious of its own existence. Like the eye which sees everything in front of it and never sees itself, faith is occupied with the Object upon which it rests and pays no attention to itself at all. While we are looking at God we do not see ourselves—blessed riddance. . . .

Sin has twisted our vision inward and made it self-regarding. Unbelief has put self where God should be, and is perilously close to the sin of Lucifer who said, "I will set my throne above the throne of God." Faith looks *out* instead of *in* and the whole of life falls into line.[28]

Jesus set the tone of the Christian way both by His life and His doctrine. Paul urges us to follow after His excellent example of self-denial in Philippians 2:2-8. Indeed the Lord Himself set the denial of self as a fundamental requirement of Christian discipleship:

If any man will come after me, let him deny himself, and take up his cross, and follow me. For whosoever will save his life shall lose it: and whosoever will lose his life for my sake shall find it. (Matthew 16:24-25.)

Denying self is quite the opposite from seeking to satisfy self. Maslow's system and all of the humanistic, psychoanalytic, behavioristic, and transpersonal psychologies have set out to oppose and destroy the way of the Cross. How can Christians hope to successfully incorporate such psychological viewpoints into the biblical way of life?

11

THE UNCONSCIOUS:
A KEY TO UNDERSTANDING
PEOPLE?

For Freudians, the unconscious mind provides the magic key that unlocks the true knowledge of the person. The notion of a magic key grows out of their opinion that the unconscious directs and motivates behavior. Hence, if you desire to understand people, you must deal first and foremost with the unconscious. Only in this way can one unravel the "tangled web" of bizarre and troubling behavior.

In Crabb's opinion Christian counselors cannot hope to properly analyze and counsel people unless they also understand and analyze the unconscious.[1] He clearly states that each of us has been programmed in the unconscious mind.[2] He teaches that thoughts and evaluations made at the conscious level are powerfully influenced by the unconscious:

> The sentences we consciously tell ourselves strongly influence how we feel and what we do. We now can see where these sentences originate. The content of the sentences we tell ourselves in our conscious minds draws upon the wrong assumptions held by our unconscious minds.[3]

While Crabb believes this to be true, there is no evidence to support his assumption that people's wrong assumptions or sentences said to themselves originate in a Freudian-based unconscious.

Nevertheless, Crabb contends that conscious activity is constantly motivated by the content of the unconscious in a powerful and pervasive manner. He says:

> Though we may not be consciously aware of what we are telling ourselves at every given moment, the words that fill our minds control much of what we do and feel. Much of our behavior is a direct product of what we are **thinking unconsciously**.[4]

> Not only the motives but also the unique theme or style of our interactions remains unidentified. . . .[5]

> Therefore the sinfully wrong strategies by which we manipulate people with our well-being in mind are intentionally hidden from view. They take their place in the **unconscious**.[6] (Emphasis added.)

Belief that unconscious thinking controls and determines behavior not only saturates his books; each case history that Crabb interprets inevitably reveals unconscious assumptions and beliefs **controlling** conscious activity. For example, he says:

> Consider what happens as a girl watches her mother cry because her daddy doesn't come home at night. This unfortunate girl may learn the belief that men hurt women. She may then (unconsciously) set for herself the goal of never becoming emotionally vulnerable to a man. When she marries, her goal will motivate her to keep her distance, never to relax in her husband's love, never to give herself freely to him.[7]

Psychologists cannot predict behavior. But when a person has problems later in life, a psychologist may try to find out what happened earlier and then apply his theories to explain what happened and why. If behavior cannot be predicted, as Freud readily admitted, such understanding is only guess-work.

Crabb believes that this woman's conduct as a wife and mother is controlled by past events and unconscious beliefs motivating her from her unconscious. According to this system it is impossible for a person to change without discovering and confronting those so-called unconscious thought-patterns. He contends that *"if no work is done beneath the water line, then work above the water line results in a disastrous externalism."*[8] (Emphasis his.) Remember that "below the water line" represents the unconscious. Crabb goes on to say that the unconscious contents truly determine the way in which people live. He says:

> We must learn to deal with problems below the water line that typically remain unidentified but still have serious effects on how we live. . . . There are, I believe, processes going on within our personalities that **determine** the directions we move. . . .[9] (Emphasis added.)

The Unconscious: Scientific Fact or Fiction?

Crabb speaks of his Freudian-based theory of the unconscious as though it were a scientifically established fact. But it is mere opinion. No one has ever proven that the Freudian unconscious exists. Nor has anyone scientifically verified the contents of the unconscious.

Just because psychological systems and personality theories **seem** to explain the person and his behavior, that does not mean that the explanations are accurate. When we consider that there are numerous competing systems, each of which pretends to explain personhood, something must be amiss. World-renowned scholar and philosopher of science Sir Karl Popper examined these psychological theories. He says:

> These theories appeared to be able to explain

practically everything that happened within the
fields to which they referred. The study of any of
them seemed to have the effect of an intellectual
conversion or revelation, opening your eyes to a new
truth hidden from those not yet initiated. Once your
eyes were thus opened you saw confirming instances
everywhere: the world was full of *verifications* of the
theory. Whatever happened always confirmed it.[10]
(Emphasis his.)

At first glance this looks like promising evidence. However,
Popper insists that constant confirmations and seeming
ability to explain everything do not indicate scientific
validity. What looks like a strength is actually a weakness.
He says, "It is easy to obtain confirmations or verifications,
for nearly every theory—if we look for confirmations. . . .
Confirming evidence should not count *except when it is the
result of a genuine test of the theory*."[11] (Emphasis his.) And
he indicates that psychological theories such as Freud's and
others' do not meet scientific requirements: "A theory which
is not refutable by any conceivable event is nonscientific.
Irrefutability is not a virtue of a theory (as people often think)
but a vice."[12] He concludes that "though posing as sciences,"
such theories "had in fact more in common with primitive
myths than with science; that they resembled astrology
rather than astronomy."[13]

One can interpret the same feeling or behavior in a great
variety of ways. But that is all it is, speculation and interpretation. One can even impose psychological interpretations on
the Bible, but the interpretations distort the true meaning of
Scripture. And then, with a particular psychological interpretation, the Bible can appear to verify that same psychological
system. This can be done by nearly every psychological
system and theory, including the theory of the unconscious.

The Freudian unconscious as the key element in
understanding and solving problems is based upon pure
conjecture. Popper is not the only one who has compared such
theories with astrology. Researcher Carol Tavris says:

> Now the irony is that many people who are not
> fooled by astrology for one minute subject them-
> selves to therapy for years, where the same error of
> logic and interpretation often occur.[14]

Another researcher also refers to such psychological theories
as myths because "they are not subject to disproof."[15]
**Anyone can devise a system of explaining human
nature and behavior and then interpret all behavior in
light of his explanation**. This is true not only of theories of
the unconscious; it is true for graphology, astrology, phrenolo-
gy, palm reading, and a host of other questionable practices.

Crabb's readers could conclude that his integration
material on the unconscious is beyond dispute. Yet Crabb
never gives scientific support for the concept. The existence
and contents of the Freudian unconscious and Crabb's
adoption and adaptation of the Freudian unconscious have
never been proven. Nevertheless the idea of the unconscious
so pervades our society and the church that nearly everyone
takes it for granted. Examples of academic negativism about
Freudian notions are given later in the Meier and Minirth
section.

Crabb's Commitment to the Unconscious.

Although there is no biblical or scientific proof for the
existence of the Freudian unconscious, Crabb structures his
entire system on the rudiments of this Freudian fabrication.
He declares, "There is an unconscious."[16] Then instead of
supporting his statement with evidence to prove that there is
an unconscious that powerfully directs and motivates all
behavior, he makes this general statement about awareness:
"We are simply not aware of all that we are doing in our
deceitful hearts."[17] However, this general observation does
not support Crabb's elaborate psychological theory of the unconscious. Then as a further attempt to assert the existence of
the unconscious, he declares, "And *we don't want* to be aware
of what we really believe and the direction we in fact are
moving."[18] (Emphasis his.) This statement implies an across-

the-board application to all Christians. But, there are many who are aware of what they believe and are desiring to be:

> . . . filled with the knowledge of his will in all wisdom and spiritual understanding; that [they] might walk worthy of the Lord unto all pleasing, being fruitful in every good work, and increasing in the knowledge of God; strengthened with all might, according to his glorious power, unto all patience and longsuffering with joyfulness; giving thanks unto the Father, which hath made [them] meet to be partakers of the inheritance of the saints in light. (Colossians 1:9-11.)

Crabb not only insists on the existence of the unconscious, but on the necessity of a counselor or other initiate to expose the contents of the unconscious. He says, *"It is therefore true that no one sees himself clearly until he is exposed by another."*[19] (Emphasis his.) This denies the sovereign work of God in a person's life. The Word of God places itself as the mirror to expose sin and the Holy Spirit enables a person to see his error and correct it. While there are times when the Lord uses another believer, that is not the usual manner. And one must be careful about exposing another. One can confront another's external sin, but only God can see inside a person, read his thoughts and motives, and expose internal sin.

The unconscious is the cornerstone of Crabb's counseling model. He reveals firm commitment to psychological theories of the unconscious throughout his writing. In *Inside Out*, he uses such terms as *inside, underground* , and *beneath the surface*, rather than the word *unconscious*.[20] The oft-stated notion that real change requires an inside look[21] or looking "beneath the surface"[22] is none other than a veiled reference to the unconscious. His "inside" theme points to the same personality theory contained in *Understanding People*, in which he emphasizes the centrality of the unconscious as the key to understanding and change.[23] When he proclaims the necessity of looking at the "deepest parts of the soul," or of a deep "inward look," he is clearly referring to a psychoanalytic theory of the unconscious.

Are Theories of the Unconscious in the Bible?

Although a Freudian-based theory of the unconscious serves as the foundation of Crabb's system, his books do not give adequate biblical support for such a centralized and dominant emphasis. There are lengthy discussions on such things as unconscious motivational factors, the contents of the unconscious, and how to change unconscious beliefs, but little attempt to verify those discussions from the Scriptures.

In *Effective Biblical Counseling* Crabb offers his definition of the unconscious to be *"the reservoir of basic assumptions which people firmly and emotionally hold about how to meet their needs of significance and security."*[24] (Emphasis his.) The same general definition can be found in psychology textbooks. The supposed scriptural warrant for Crabb's definition and for his entire presentation on the unconscious is a study he did on the New Testament Greek term *phronema*, which is translated *mind.* He says:

> I recently listed every verse in which this word (or a derivative) is used. From my study of these passages, it appears that the central concept expressed by the word is a part of personality which develops and holds on to deep, reflective assumptions. . . . Let me tentatively suggest that this concept corresponds closely to what psychologists call the "unconscious mind."[25]

It looks like Crabb was looking for biblical confirmation for the existence of "what psychologists call the 'unconscious mind.'"

Crabb himself is so uncertain of the results of his study, that he can only "tentatively suggest" that it confirms his detailed discussion of the unconscious. We must have more certainty than that, especially when presenting a view of personality that is supposed to be consistent with Scripture.[26]

Indeed, Crabb's seeming hesitation about the results of his word study is well founded. The New Testament Greek term *phronema* does not refer to the notions presented in Crabb's discussion of the unconscious. His description of the unconscious as the reservoir of basic assumptions about how to satisfy our two deepest needs is not implied by the term *phronema.*

Phronema and the verb form *phroneo* refer strictly to conscious thought processes. According to Vine's dictionary, *phronema* refers to what a person has in mind, the thought, or the object of thought. *Phroneo* means "to think, to be minded in a certain way. . . to think of, to be mindful of."

Phroneo has to do with "moral interest or reflection, not mere unreasoning opinion."[27] There is no hint in the immediate context or in the biblical use of the Greek word that it corresponds to the psychological version of the unconscious or unconscious thought. Every usage in the New Testament refers to conscious thought processes, that is, to rationally controlled thought at the conscious level. One could search both ancient and modern lexicons and Bible dictionaries and not find anyone define *phronema* as the reservoir of unconscious assumptions about how to meet two particular needs.

Continuing his search for biblical support for his theories on the unconscious, Crabb quotes Romans 12:1-2.

> I beseech you therefore, brethren, by the mercies of God, that ye present your bodies a living sacrifice, holy, acceptable unto God, which is your reasonable service. And be not conformed to this world: but be ye transformed by the renewing of your mind, that ye may prove what is that good, and acceptable, and perfect, will of God.

Crabb uses this as biblical proof for unconscious beliefs and motives.[28] He uses the phrase "renewing the mind" as a direct parallel to his theory of dealing with the unconscious throughout his books.[29] Nevertheless Romans 12:2 will not support Crabb's notions of the unconscious. The renewing of the mind has to do with the rest of Romans 12. Paul is speaking of conscious thinking, such as:

> For I say, through the grace given unto me, to every man that is among you, not to think of himself more highly than he ought to think; but to think soberly, according as God hath dealt to every man the measure of faith. (Romans 12:3.)

Paul then goes on to explain the operation of each member in the body of Christ. He continues with admonitions to "love without dissimulation," to "abhor that which is evil," to "cleave to that which is good," to be "kindly affectioned one to another with brotherly love," not to be "slothful in business," to be "fervent in spirit," to serve the Lord, to rejoice in hope, to be patient in tribulation, to distribute to the needy, to exercise hospitality, and so forth (Romans 12:4-21.) Paul is talking about consciously thinking about things differently from the way the world thinks. He is talking about conscious attitudes, conscious choices, and conscious thoughts behind conscious actions being changed, because of the new life in Jesus. Finding the unconscious with deep needs, strategies, and pain in Romans 12:2 requires a very imaginative and poor handling of the text.

If insight into the unconscious is central to understanding people, God would have made it central to His doctrine of man. However, such a doctrine had not been discovered throughout the centuries. It seems a bit odd that such a crucial doctrine would have been hidden all these years and now only be discovered through the help of minds that are darkened to the Word of God. Even now, with the invention of the so-called unconscious, one must distort Scripture to make it fit.

In addition to superimposing his notions of the unconscious upon the biblical term translated *mind*, Crabb seeks to equate the word *heart* with the unconscious:

> My understanding of unconscious elements within the personality is rooted in the biblical teaching

> that, above all else, our hearts are deceitful and
> desperately wicked.[30]

According to God's revelation the heart is deceitful. However,
the deceitfulness of a person's inner being does not prove or
even imply that a person's heart or inner being is the
unconscious described by Crabb. The word *heart* as employed
in Scripture will not support his psychological agenda concerning the unconscious, its crucial role, or its contents.

Psychological notions of the nature and function of the
unconscious find no support in the Bible. Nowhere does God
state that an entity known as the unconscious provides the
key to understanding conscious activity. Nowhere does God
teach that there is an unconscious reservoir of images,
motives, and beliefs which drive and direct behavior. No
scriptural evidence shows the Spirit leading a sacred author
to define repentance and change in the light of a
psychological theory of the unconscious. Nowhere does God
teach that pleasure, joy, or serenity on the conscious level
may be self-protective measures that function to deny the
reality of terrors, fears, and pain in the unconscious. In
attempting to promote such a theory Crabb operates
according to the dictates of psychology rather than the Word
of God.

The doctrine of the unconscious is an entire ideology
existing independent from and contradictory to what
Scripture teaches about the human condition. It subverts
clear biblical teaching on the nature of man. It alters the
focus of sanctification from the way of the cross to the
psychological notion of exposing the unconscious. It reduces
the spiritual work of the Holy Spirit in the inner man to a
psychological work in the unconscious. And, the supernatural
transformation of the inner man is replaced by a human
method of changing oneself through an altered perception of
how so-called needs are met.

The Bible stresses the glorious presence and power of the
Holy Spirit in the inner man. Thus, we would pray with Paul:

> Of whom the whole family in heaven and earth is

named, that he would grant you, according to the riches of his glory, to be strengthened with might by his Spirit in the inner man; that Christ may dwell in your hearts by faith; that ye, being rooted and grounded in love, may be able to comprehend with all saints what is the breadth, and length, and depth, and height; And to know the love of Christ, which passeth knowledge, that ye might be filled with all the fulness of God. Now unto him that is able to do exceeding abundantly above all that we ask or think, according to the power that worketh in us, unto him be glory in the church by Christ Jesus throughout all ages, world without end. Amen. (Ephesians 3:15-21.)

Belief in the Freudian unconscious harmonizes with Hinduism rather than with Christianity. In his book *The Religions of Man*, Houston Smith says, "The Hindu concept of man rests on the basic thesis that he is a layered being."[31] He says:

Hinduism agrees with psychoanalysis [Freud] that if only we could dredge up a portion of our lost individual totality—the third part of our being [the unconscious]—we would experience a remarkable expansion of our powers, a vivid refreshening of life.[32]

Just as in psychoanalysis, Hindus believe that the unconscious contains both yearnings (drives) and suppressions (ego-defense mechanisms). We say this to illustrate the fact that any attempt to understand the thoughts and intents of the heart and the why's and wherefore's of human behavior is a religious exercise. The religion may be psychoanalytic, humanistic, transpersonal, Moslem, Hindu, or Christian. However if a Christian dips into the cisterns of psychological opinions, he cannot be offering the pure water of the truth of God.

12

PERSONAL CIRCLE: UNCONSCIOUS MOTIVATORS OF BEHAVIOR

Central to Crabb's model of man are two dominant unconscious needs which motivate behavior from within the Personal Circle. His controlling concept of two powerful unconscious needs is central to understanding what he says at any given point. According to Crabb, behavior can only be properly understood in relation to those two unconscious needs.

Examining the concept of personal needs can be somewhat confusing because of the chameleon-like nature of the very term itself. The term *needs* can take on a variety of meanings according to the purpose of the person employing it. For example someone will say, "What do you need (want)?" A Christian will speak of the need for a Savior. Ministers speak of meeting the needs of their people in terms of shepherding them and nourishing them in the Word. Thus it is necessary to examine Crabb's concept of needs.

Crabb's theory of needs represents his essential understanding of human nature. Crabb includes much more doctrinal baggage under the term *needs* than the average person. For him the word *needs* functions as a technical term to describe man's innermost nature. The words *personal needs* and *personal longings* function as an umbrella under which he gathers his entire understanding of a person's innermost nature.

The Nature and Location of Everyone's Two Needs.

In his earlier books Crabb calls the two unconscious needs "security" and "significance." Later he changes his terminology to "longings" for "relationship and impact." However, as Crabb himself indicates, his change in words does not involve any change in the doctrine. He says:

> Readers familiar with my earlier books will recognize movement in my concepts but not, I think, fundamental change. For example, my preference now is to speak of *deep longings in the human heart for relationship and impact* rather than *personal needs for security and significance.*[1] (Emphasis his)

Because Crabb affirms that both personal needs and deep longings identify the same doctrine of man in his system, we use the phrases interchangeably throughout this critique.

The following is Crabb's description of the needs and their location:

> **Deep inside** each of these people rumbled a **persistent demand**, one which they **couldn't clearly hear** themselves saying, yet one which was **driving them ruthlessly in disastrous directions**. If we could listen to the **faint but powerful murmurings** of their **unconscious minds** we would hear something like this: I **need** to respect myself as a worthwhile person. . . . Sorting through this "stream of unconsciousness" a simple organization emerges: people have one basic personal **need which requires** two kinds of input for its satisfaction. The most basic **need** is a sense of **personal worth**, an acceptance of oneself as a whole, real person. The

two required inputs are *significance* . . . **and**
security.[2] (Italics his; bold emphasis added.)

Thus the needs for security and significance are ruthless
drives in the unconscious. As he says in *Inside Out*, "The
consequence of living with no satisfaction of our crucial
longings is the beginning of hell."[3]

Crabb even assigns an independent existence to the two
needs. He says:

> The intangible identity that I know as "Me" has **two
> real and profound needs**, which are **substantive
> personal realities** not reducible to biological or
> chemical analysis. They have a **personal exist-
> ence, independent of the physical body**, that
> constitutes the core of what it means to be a spirit.[4]
> (Emphasis added.)

Not only are they "substantive personal realities"; they
constitute "the core of what it means to be a spirit." Thus in
Crabb's system the two needs constitute the essence of
personhood. He says:

> **The need to regard oneself as worthwhile by
> experiencing significance and security is
> unalterably a part of the human personality.**[5]
> (Emphasis added.)

However, the Bible points to a different picture of mankind. Rather than being driven by the need for worthwhileness experienced as needs for security and significance, the
Bible teaches that humans are driven by the sinful self. The
problem is self at the center as an insatiable, rebellious
tyrant. Since the Fall, man has required a Savior from sin,
not a satisfier of psychological needs. Instead of two so-called
unconscious needs being met, the power of sin must be broken. The domination of sin is so great that a person must be
born of the Spirit, regenerated by the very life of God. This
work of God is never described as the satisfaction of uncon-

scious needs crying out for security and significance. The separation of man from God through sin is so vast that a person cannot repair the breach by engaging in Crabb's techniques of realizing inner pain and discovering that God can make one secure and significant. In fact, it is only by God's grace that a person even realizes that he is undone by sin. Only by God's grace does a person exercise the kind of faith that enables him to walk in the Spirit, with an obedient heart that desires to please God rather than self.

The Bible says that a sinner's inclination is rebellion against rather than yearning for God. Therefore, the needs that Crabb identifies with all people cannot be equated with yearning for God in the biblical sense. The very nature of sin is to be one's own little god rather than submitting to Christ. Before a person is made new through Christ, the essence of his personhood is the sinful self. After regeneration, it is the Holy Spirit enabling him to know, love, and serve God. The Bible, not psychology, is God's revelation concerning the essence of man before and after salvation.

The error of Crabb's counseling system lies not merely in the choice of the term *needs*, but in the doctrine of man he fabricates under that label. It does not matter if he exchanges the term *needs* for terms like *longings* or *felt lacks* or *sense of emptiness*. The biblical distortion in this material is not a matter of labels. Rather, the problem lies in Crabb's interpretation of the fundamental nature of man. The labels can constantly be shifted, but the doctrine remains the same.

The Motivational Omnipotence of Man's Two Needs.

In Crabb's model the two unconscious needs function as omnipotent motivators of conscious activity. Crabb's clearest presentation of unconscious motivation is in his propositions on motivation in *Effective Biblical Counseling*.[6] Although in later books he shifts from his five propositions on motivation to a four-fold explanation of the image of God, the doctrine remains the same.[7] Crabb's secularly-derived explanation of motivation almost sounds biblical when he discusses it in terms of the image of God. But, the shift in terminology does not reflect a shift in doctrinal content. Crabb sees man's innermost nature filled with hidden, unconscious causes of behavior.

Crabb teaches that behavior is **directly** related to two substantive needs in the unconscious.[8] His five propositions on motivation relate to the power of the unconscious on both the conscious mind and on behavior. In his first proposition Crabb says:

> Motivation typically depends upon a need state, or in simpler language, we are motivated to meet our needs.[9]

His "need state" and "needs" refer to security and significance in the unconscious. He presents the same idea in his description of the image of God with its longings for relationship and impact.[10]

Crabb's second proposition refers to unconscious beliefs about how to satisfy the two deep and profound needs. He says:

> Motivation is a word referring to the energy or force which results in specific behavior. . . . I am motivated to meet a need by doing certain things which *I believe in my mind* will meet that need.[11] (Emphasis his.)

The words *in my mind* refer to the entire Freudian notion of the iceberg. In other words, motivation comes largely from those beliefs in the unconscious having to do with meeting the two needs.

According to Crabb, behavior is not only motivated by unconscious beliefs, but directed by them. In his third proposition, he says:

> Motivated behavior always is directed toward a goal. I believe that *something* will meet my need.

That something becomes my goal.[12] (Emphasis his.)

Conscious choices are therefore goal-oriented and motivated by unconscious beliefs about how to satisfy the two needs. This proposition agrees with Adler's emphasis on all behavior being goal-directed by needs in the unconscious.

In his fourth proposition on motivation, Crabb says:

> When the goal cannot be reached . . . a state of disequilibrium exists (subjectively felt as anxiety). The need which is denied satisfaction becomes a source of negative emotions. . . . I then am motivated to protect my need to feel worthwhile from further injury by minimizing my feelings of insignificance or insecurity.[13]

Crabb emphasizes denial of feelings and self-protection strategies throughout all of his books. In *Inside Out* Crabb refers to "retreat into denial," running from pain through denial, and "a powerless lifestyle of denial."[14]

In his final summary proposition on motivation Crabb declares:

> All behavior is motivated. . . . In order to understand any unit of behavior, **you must know what need is motivating the behavior**. . . .[15] (Emphasis added.)

This final proposition brings us full circle, back to **motivating needs in the unconscious**, to which, in his closed system, every action is ultimately connected. Crabb analyzes all behavior and problems of living in light of his Need Theology. Again, Crabb identifies motivation with those two substantive, unconscious needs. All behavior is thus interpreted in light of a psychologically-based need structure.

Crabb illustrates how his theory of motivation works in a person. This person describes his problem in terms of what he has learned about his wrong assumptions about how to meet his unconscious needs:

I listen to the preacher tell me that the love of money is the root of all evil. . . . I fully agree with what the preacher is telling me, but I still feel an inner drive compulsively spurring me on to make money. I try to shake it but I can't. Prayer, repentance, dedication all make me feel better for a while, but the lust for money remains strong. My real problem is not a love of money but rather a wrong belief, a learned assumption that personal significance depends on having money. *Until that idea is deliberately and consciously rejected, I will always want money*, no matter how many times I confess to God my sin of wanting money. . . . But again, as long as **I unconsciously believe that money equals significance, I will never stop lusting after money because I always will be motivated to meet my needs.**[16] (Italic emphasis his; bold emphasis added.)

The man has obviously learned Crabb's system and terminology. He identifies his problem as "a wrong belief, a learned assumption that personal significance depends on having money," and he thinks that his unconscious belief causes him to lust for money. He has thus concluded that his lust for money is motivated by unconscious needs rather than by the law of sin in his life. But, the heart of his problem is not simply an unconscious assumption about gaining significance; it is sin reigning in his life. He is still self-serving in wanting to be important, to be seen as successful, to be regarded highly, and to control his own life. The Bible does not interpret such self-service in light of psychological needs in the unconscious.

Unconscious Needs, the Law of Sin, or the Law of the Spirit?

There is no debate over the significance of the issue of motivation. Crabb is attempting to address a very vital area of counseling. However, in attempting to wed the issue of motivation to his psychological system of unconscious needs, he has moved away from the doctrine of the Scriptures. In Romans 6-8, Galatians 5 and elsewhere, the Bible speaks of only two "laws" of motivation: the law of sin and the law of the Spirit. The law of sin speaks of a person under the power or rule of sin, and the law of the Spirit speaks of the rulership of the indwelling Holy Spirit. The Bible does not even hint at any third law such as Crabb's proposal of unconscious psychological needs that motivate behavior. Yet Crabb is attempting to make this third law the primary source of information. He interprets every problem in light of it.

The historic position of the Christian church has viewed sin as inherent rebellion, as a corrupt nature, and as the internal tyrant of the heart. Its corrupting power makes the heart deceitful and unknowable apart from God. Unbelievers are under the power of sin. But believers, who have been redeemed and given new life, are enabled to resist the power of sin through the power of the indwelling Holy Spirit. The Bible always assigns the inner motivating powers in light of these two realities. And the Bible never defines indwelling sin as unconscious beliefs related to two unconscious needs. It never explains either the role of the Spirit or the power of sin in light of two substantive entities in the unconscious known as needs or longings.

The Holy Spirit motivates and enables believers to love and obey God. The apostle John declared, "God is love" (John 4:8). And then he said, "Herein is love, not that we loved God, but that He loved us, and sent us His son to be the propitiation for our sins. Beloved, if God so loved us, we ought also to love one another" (John 4:10-11). Here is the motivation of the person who is walking according to the Spirit rather than according to his old sinful, self-serving ways. The only way a person can follow the Great Commandment to love God with all of his heart, soul, mind and strength is by Jesus' life mediated to the sinner by the Holy Spirit. The Holy Spirit illumines the Word, assures the believer of sonship with the Father, guides the believer, and enables him to love and obey.

> For as many as are led by the Spirit of God, they are the sons of God. For ye have not received the spirit of bondage again to fear; but ye have received the Spirit of adoption, whereby we cry, Abba, Father. The Spirit itself beareth witness with our spirit, that we are the children of God: And if children, then heirs; heirs of God, and joint-heirs with Christ; if so be that we suffer with him, that we may be also glorified together. (Romans 8:14-17.)

The focus of the Bible in relationship to sanctification is not on so-called psychological needs, but on knowing and obeying the will of God (Romans 6:11-13). It is on conscious obedience, on conscious warfare against known temptations and transgressions, and on conscious submission to the power of the Spirit (Galatians 5:16-25 and Romans 8:13). Through God's enabling, it is possible to change attitudes, thoughts, and behavior without fully knowing motives. God does not promise to expose and reveal all of the tangled motives of anyone's heart.

The motivation for Christian living is not inherent within believers in the form of two supposedly unsatisfied needs. Rather it lies in the person of Christ (Galatians 2:20). It is outside of people and only becomes a part of them through the gracious intervention of God into their inner man. Christ motivates them to obey God by mediating grace to them in the person of the Holy Spirit. Thus God never speaks of motivation in terms of a simplistic theory of two all-powerful unconscious needs. Crabb's attempt to introduce a third and more powerful "law" in the inner man moves away from the biblical description of man. His borrowed psychological "law" of two substantive needs/ longings represents a severe breach from biblical teaching.

Psychological Sources.

Crabb's language and theory of motivation come right out of psychology.[17] For instance, the following words and ideas of Abraham Maslow closely parallel some of

Crabb's words and ideas concerning the relationship of personal needs to motivation.

> All people in our society . . . have a need or desire for a stable, firmly based, usually high evaluation of themselves, for self-respect, or self-esteem, and for the esteem of others. These needs may therefore be classified into two subsidiary sets. These are, first, the desire for strength, for achievement, for adequacy, for mastery and competence, for confidence in the face of the world, and for independence and freedom. Second, we have what we may call the desire for reputation or prestige (defining it as respect or esteem from other people), status, dominance, recognition, attention, importance, or appreciation.[18]

Notice the similarity to Crabb's idea that people need to have a sense of personal worthwhileness, with the subcategories being significance and security. Maslow's writings also teach that needs profoundly affect conscious behavior. He says:

> But thwarting of these needs produces feelings of inferiority, or weakness, and of helplessness.[19]

> . . . a healthy man is primarily **motivated by his needs** to develop and actualize his fullest potentialities and capacities.[20] (Emphasis added.)

Does the Bible teach that an unredeemed person will reach his full potential through the satisfaction of two all-powerful needs?

Without God's gracious intervention, no one is spiritually healthy. Rather than reaching some great potential of self-actualization, one's own lusts will drive him into sin and rebellion and ultimately to death and hell. But, someone may argue that what Maslow says does apply to Christians because God enables them to develop their full potentialities. Yet, we will only become what God has designed us to become by the motivation that comes from His life in us and from our great love for Him in response to His love for us. How can a new man in Christ continue to be motivated by self or self's needs? It is a contradiction to Jesus' call to deny self, take up one's cross, and follow Him.

The Nature of Man.

In defining man's innermost nature, Crabb gives no clear distinction between a believer and an unbeliever. All are basically the same in their spirit. Crabb says:

> The intangible identity that I know as "Me" has two real and profound needs, which are substantive personal realities not reducible to biological or chemical analysis. They have a personal existence, independent of the physical body, that constitutes the core of what it means to be a spirit.[21]

That is his definition of the biblical term *spirit*. He then says,

> The image of God is reflected in these two needs. God is a personal being who in His essential nature is *love* and who, as a God of design and purpose, is the author of *meaning*.[22] (Emphasis his.)

Crabb teaches that since human nature is limited because of the fall, the attributes of man created in the image of God become human needs. For him the corruption of the fall is that capacities for love and meaning (identical of the needs for security and significance in Crabb's system) are filled in the wrong ways.

While it is true that fallen man does try to fulfill his needs and desires in wrong ways, the essence of the fall is more than simply how a person fulfills his needs. At the Fall, love and meaning became self-centered and self-directed. Love for God was replaced with love for self. God's purposes and will were replaced by self-will. Love was distorted and misdirected and self became its own little god. The essence of natural man is sin, not unmet needs for security and significance.

But Crabb's view of the human heart makes no distinction before or after conversion in the essence of its longings. In *Understanding People* Crabb says:

> The longings of the human heart, I submit, cannot be changed. And even if they could, to do so would make mankind less than God designed us to be. Our longings are legitimate. . . . The problem is not centrally with our longings.[23]

And yet, the entire New Testament argues that the longings do change. The desire to please self is replaced by a desire to love and please God.

Jesus made a clear distinction between the nature of a believer saved by grace through faith and the nature of an unredeemed sinner. (John 15.) He made a distinction between the children of God and the children of the devil. (John 8:44 and 10:27-29.) Paul made these same distinctions throughout his letter to the Ephesians. John said that the world does not even know (understand) the sons of God. (John 3:1.)

Some of the unredeemed may very well identify with much of what psychology says, because self (with all of its self-seeking, self-regard, self-will, self-excusing, self-blaming, self-love, self-worth, self-hate, self-fulfillment, and self-pity) is at the center. And Christians can become confused when they see that they, who have been liberated from the domination of sin, still struggle against its power (Romans 6-8). However, they are nevertheless new creations in Christ. John describes it this way:

> But as many as received him, to them gave he power to become the sons of God, even to them that believe on his name: Which were born, not of blood, nor of the will of the flesh, nor of the will of man, but of God. (John 1:12-13.)

The believer has God's life in him. And it is the very Spirit of

God who enables him to love God and others. And while he struggles between the tension of the law of sin and the law of the Spirit, he is nevertheless essentially and radically different from the unbeliever in his inner man (Galatians 5 and Romans 6-8).

The description of love for God and others is the opposite of self-seeking love:

> Charity suffereth long, and is kind; charity envieth not; charity vaunteth not itself, is not puffed up, doth not behave itself unseemly, seeketh not her own, is not easily provoked, thinketh no evil; rejoiceth not in iniquity, but rejoiceth in the truth; beareth all things, believeth all things, hopeth all things, endureth all things. (1 Corinthians 13:4-7.)

As Paul tells us in Galatians 5:15-25, this kind of love only exists through the power of the indwelling Holy Spirit, not through some psychological exercise. A believer does not exercise *agape* love by focusing on his own needs and longings or by looking at himself. He does so through the life of God and by looking at His character:

> But we all, with open face beholding as in a glass the glory of the Lord, are changed into the same image from glory to glory, even as by the Spirit of the Lord. (2 Corinthians 3:18.)

There is a vast difference between a believer and an unbeliever. The believer can please God because God's life is in him to motivate and enable him to do so. The unbeliever cannot please God because of his self-seeking, sinful nature. Unfortunately, however, many who profess faith in the Lord Jesus are still following self rather than God. They are acting as if they are dominated by sin. While believers do sin and revert to the ways of the old self, God's life is in them to motivate them to confession, repentance, and walking again in the Spirit unto love and obedience.

The Thirst of the Two Needs/Longings

Crabb reiterates his psychological theory of unconscious need motivation in biblical garb. He uses the metaphors in John 7:37-38 to present his psychological understanding of the capacities of personhood:

> If any man is thirsty, let him come to Me and drink. He who believes in Me, as the Scripture said, "From his innermost being shall flow rivers of living water." (New American Standard Bible.)

From these few words Crabb develops an elaborate system of Thirsty Souls to verify his theory of motivational needs/longings and Hollow Cores to verify his theory of the unconscious. Crabb says that Jesus came to quench thirst, but that the Scriptures "seem quiet on the subject." In fact he declares, "Thirst is never defined."[24] Crabb tells us that even the apostle Paul failed to clear up the meaning of this crucial theme. He contends that until now the real issue of thirst has been largely neglected.[25] It seems a little odd to call something a biblical theme, and then to say that Scriptures are strangely silent on the exact meaning of the theme.

However, the word *thirst* as used in the Bible has not been neglected. In the above passage, *thirst* is a metaphor referring to intense spiritual desire for knowing God and experiencing His presence. In the above instance, the context tells us that the thirst Jesus quenches leads to an abundant, overflowing life resulting from the indwelling Holy Spirit. It is thus a thirst for God, His presence, His revelation, and His righteousness. Jesus said, "Blessed are they that do hunger and thirst after righteousness, for they shall be filled" (Matthew 5:6). Words carry their own meanings, but when used as metaphors, their meaning is revealed through the context in which they are used. Thus the meaning of *thirst* has not been a mystery through the ages. One can turn to lexicons, Bible dictionaries, commentaries, sermons, and devotional literature and come across the word *thirst* in the context of where and how it is used in the Bible.

Since Crabb erroneously contends that thirst is "never defined," he says:

> If we permit ourselves to ask only those questions that the Bible *explicitly* answers, we must put aside our questions about thirst and move on to other matters.[26] (Emphasis his.)

Crabb then gives his own **psychological definition** of *thirst*: deep longing for relationship and impact. The words *thirst* and *longings* function as technical terms for Crabb. They refer to much more than the average person would imply when using them. Crabb defines personhood in terms of unrelenting thirst for the satisfaction of the two needs/longings that are vital, powerful, profound realities of the Hollow Core. They cannot be ignored; they cry out for satisfaction. He says, "As image-bearers designed to enjoy God and everything He has made, we are thirsty people who long for what was lost in the Fall."[27] At first this may sound orthodox, but from the evidence throughout his books, what he contends was lost is the satisfaction of the needs for security and significance, also referred to as relationship and impact.[28]

The word *thirsty* in the context of Crabb's books signifies the unrelenting drive for satisfaction of the *"deep longings in the human heart for relationship and impact,"* which are really the *"personal needs for security and significance."*[29] Therefore he is talking about a Freudian-like unconscious with needs that motivate behavior. Thus, any longing for relationship with God in this context is to meet the needs of the self. Remember that the central need behind the needs for security and significance is the need for regarding oneself as worthwhile.[30]

Besides John 7:36-37, Crabb cites Psalms 42:2 and 63:1, Isaiah 55:1, and John 6:35 in defense of his theory of unconscious needs/longings. Each passage uses the word *thirst*. However, to cite passages which speak of "longing (thirsting) for God" as support for his doctrine of Need

Theology is invalid. The Psalms describe the **believer** as longing for God, not for the satisfaction of two unconscious needs that constantly press for gratification. None of the passages teach Crabb's concept of two substantive, all-powerful needs/longings at the core of man's being.

Because Crabb comes to the Bible with his theory of two needs/longings firmly fixed in his model of man, he sees hidden implications in biblical passages. Thus it appears that he does not seek answers to man's innermost nature from the clearly intended meaning of the biblical text. Rather, he seeks confirmation. A determination to understand the Bible's clearly intended meaning should prevent one from being satisfied with hidden implications for documentation.

The Personal Circle as a Hollow Core.

Crabb amplifies his theme of thirst with what he calls a "Hollow Core." And he uses the same verse for a biblical reference:

> If any man is thirsty, let him come to Me and drink. He who believes in Me, as the Scripture said, "From his innermost being shall flow rivers of living water." (John 7: 37-38)[31]

Crabb does not explain the purpose and content of the Lord's invitation. Nor does he explain its relationship to regeneration and the workings of the Holy Spirit. Crabb's interest centers on the Greek term *koilia*, which is translated "innermost being." Here is his line of reasoning: (1) *Koilia* refers to a deep part within the core of our being. (2) *Koilia* literally means an open, empty space. Metaphorically it refers to an empty space that "desperately longs to be filled."[32] (3) Therefore, everyone has a Hollow Core that is empty, but yearns to be filled. The awful emptiness is caused by everyone's two unfilled needs/longings. Crabb leaps from the mere definition of *koilia* to an elaborate theory of a so-called Hollow Core with its identifiable content and incredible powers. Not only has one word become an entire theory; it becomes the drama of an empty core with "monstrous power" which controls the direction of every person's life.[33]

On the basis of **implication**, which he draws from the word *koilia*, Crabb presents a "dimension of personality" that he calls the "Hollow Core." Then he takes a principle from the natural world and uses it to explain the dynamics of that Hollow Core by saying:

> Nature, whether physical or personal, abhors a vacuum. Internal emptiness becomes an absolutely compelling force that drives people to sacrifice anything, eventually even their own identities, in an effort to find themselves.[34]

Crabb jumps from the biblical term *koilia* into a strictly defined theory about an internal vacuum that controls the very direction of a person's life. He takes a quantum leap from a single verse to a definitive doctrine about an "absolutely compelling force" driving people's lives from deep within their being. Here are some of the things he says about the Hollow Core:

> But when the Hollow Core is empty . . . our **souls are torn apart** with an **unbearable ache**, a throbbing loneliness that **demands relief**, a morbid sense of pointlessness that **paralyzes** us with anger, cynicism, and frustration.[35] (Emphasis added.)

> . . . it becomes a **monstrous power** that **relentlessly controls** the core direction of our lives.[36] (Emphasis added.)

> . . . if the **horrible reality of the Hollow Core** remains unchanged, the counselee remains a **slave** to the god of his own longings for satisfaction.[37] (Emphasis added.)

An unsaved sinner will indeed remain a "slave to the god of

his own longings for satisfaction" unless he is saved. But for
Crabb the Hollow Core is the unconscious, not the old nature
dominated by sin.

The all-powerful motivational factors in the unconscious
continue to be Crabb's dominant explanation of behavior. For
example, in describing one woman, he says:

> Doubt and lust became **overpowering obsessions**
> she could not escape. **Beneath** it all was a **terribly
> frustrated longing** to have someone see all of her
> and remain deeply involved.[38] (Emphasis added.)

Crabb graphically describes the thirst in the Hollow Core
when he says: "The pain of aloneness and pointlessness is
piercing. It *demands* relief."[39] (Emphasis his.)

Along with his expanded use of the word *koilia*, Crabb
says that in John 7:37-38, "the Lord appeals directly to this
deep ache" in our Hollow Core.[40] Thus, he must believe that
the Lord had the same concept in mind and spoke directly to
this aching, empty, pain-filled Hollow Core. Yet, consider the
implications. First, recall briefly that Crabb identifies the
content and power of the Hollow Core as the two deep
needs/longings. The hollowness or emptiness of the Core is
caused directly by failure to satisfy those two deep
needs/longings.[41] If they are unsatisfied they produce an
unbearable ache, throbbing loneliness, paralyzing anger, cyn-
icism, and frustration.[42] Crabb describes the Hollow Core
with its content and power in much the same way as he
describes the unconscious.[43] Therefore, Crabb is attempting
to make the Lord's invitation function as a defense for his
psychological theories of the unconscious, of two powerful
unconscious needs/ longings, and of the unconscious
strategies to satisfy the two needs/longings.

In his argument for the Hollow Core, Crabb demonstrates how his psychological preoccupation controls his
biblical interpretation. But, he has not demonstrated that
Jesus used the term *koilia* to refer to the two needs in the unconscious and the unconscious strategies for satisfying them.
If Jesus had taught about a Hollow Core producing pain and

driving people in disastrous directions, he would have been talking about the old sinful self, fulfilling its lustful desires. But for Crabb, the Hollow Core is the residence of the two legitimate needs/longings.

The Legitimacy of Crabb's Two Substantive Needs.

Crabb stresses that man's two substantive longings are legitimate God-given capacities. He says:

> The longings for relationship and impact, though in themselves **not sinful**, would never have been felt had sin not severed fellowship with God. All Adam's descendants struggle with the grim reminder of our dependency, a core that is hollow because we are separated from God. Fallen man is thirsty.[44] (Emphasis added.)

Crabb continually declares that man is driven by two basic needs for security and significance (deep longings for relationship and impact),which he proclaims are sinless in themselves. He says, "The longing is legitimate. . . . To deny the longing is to neglect a part of me that God made."[45] Crabb is referring to those needs/longings when he boldly declares: "Christ's invitation to come to Him on the basis of perceived thirst grants legitimacy to the longings of our soul."[46] Crabb also declares that "God assumes that His people are thirsty but He never condemns them for that thirst. Thirst is not the problem."[47] Recall here that for Crabb *thirst* refers to the two powerful needs in the unconscious that motivate all behavior.

Crabb follows the logic of Maslow's hierarchy of needs. These include basic physical needs for food, clothing and shelter. Obviously these needs are not sinful in themselves. They are physical necessities of the human body. However, when other concerns, such as personal worthwhileness, positive self-regard, emotional security, and personal significance are added to the list, one cannot arbitrarily say that they are legitimate. If man is born perfect and is innately good, as Maslow and the other humanistic psychologists believe, then anything that enhances the self in a seemingly positive way is legitimate. However, from a biblical point of view, which says that all are born in sin and are corrupt at the very core, even the desire for security can be corrupt if it is to please self rather than to love and please God.

For Crabb the condition of natural man is emptiness rather than being full of self and self-interests. He illustrates sin at the action level rather than at the very heart level of loving self more than God. Here is an example:

> In order to make these changes, both parents would need to look inside themselves to see their own unsatisfied thirst and their self-protective styles of relating. . . . [The father's] longings for respect and for relationship with his son are legitimate; **his strategy of keeping his distance to protect himself from rejection is sinful.**[48] (Emphasis added.)

Even though the man's longings may appear legitimate and not sinful, only the Lord can judge the man's heart. Are the longings stimulated by wanting to feel better about himself or by self-sacrificial love for his son? If the father is driven by his own needs for security and significance or relationship and impact rather than love for God and others, then those longings can hardly be without sin.

The solution being offered here is for the parents to look inside themselves. Remember that by the phrase "look inside" Crabb calls for **insight into the unconscious**. Thus they are to look at their own unsatisfied needs and seek satisfaction from God.

Crabb judges the longings, which he says motivate all of mankind (including believers and unbelievers), to be legitimate and not sinful. He contends that sin enters in only through strategies based on   unconscious beliefs and assumptions used to meet these so-called legitimate, sinless needs for security and significance, or relationship and impact. He does not consider the nature of the person behind the longings—whether it is the old sinful self or the new man created in Christ Jesus.

A serious problem with Crabb's insistence on the legitimacy of the two needs/longings is that it does not really agree with the biblical doctrine of total depravity. He contends that the needs/longings constitute the deepest and fullest meaning for the central part of **every** person.[49] According to his system, every problem man encounters is directly tied to the existence of those two needs/longings motivating all behavior. If the two are not sinful in themselves,[50] then it follows that the most fundamental part of man's being is exonerated from total depravity. Rather than the unregenerate sinner requiring a new nature, Crabb seems to believe that what both believers and unbelievers require is **knowledge** that God created them with capacities for relationship (security) and impact (significance) that He will fill. Thus, according to Crabb's teaching, change does not require a radical renewal of man's very nature. It only demands that one learn a simple formula about God and unconscious needs.

While Crabb declares again and again that the needs/longings are not sinful in themselves, he evidently realizes that he may have a doctrinal problem on his hands. He says in a footnote at the end of *Understanding People*: "In our fallen condition, every legitimate longing shares in the corruption. Longings will never be pure until we're in heaven."[51] Nevertheless, in the very text which the footnote qualifies, he says that the problem is **not** with the two longings.[52] Instead, he contends that the sin problem pertains to unconscious beliefs about how to satisfy the longings.[53] He also says without qualification, that the two longings are "in themselves not sinful"[54] and he repeatedly calls them "legitimate."

The confusion over the legitimacy of the two needs that are not sinful in themselves and yet share in the corruption comes from Crabb's attempt to combine biblical doctrine with humanistic psychology, which centers on human goodness, need, and potential. Therefore, he is having to juggle the doctrine of total depravity with the humanistic doctrine of the innate goodness of man. Crabb is thus more concerned about sinful ways of meeting needs than about the condition of sin which permeates the entire person and directs him towards selfish goals and pleasing self.

Crabb's model does not represent a thorough understanding of such key passages as Genesis 3 and 6, Psalm 32 and 51, Romans 1-8, and Ephesians 1-4. It does not explain how the fall has impaired the natural man. It does not explain how sin affects the motives, intentions, and conduct of believers. It does not take demonic forces into consideration. **Nor does his model give proper recognition to the work of the Holy Spirit in changing man.**

13

RATIONAL CIRCLE: GUIDING FICTIONS AND WRONG STRATEGIES

According to Crabb's model of man, problems occur because the unconscious contains many faulty and damaging messages and beliefs.[1] Such messages contained in the unconscious, although faulty and damaging, still control and direct conscious activity. Thus, a person follows the dictates of the unconscious messages to the detriment of his own well-being.

While Freud developed the original theory of the unconscious, it was Adler who called the faulty beliefs and messages "guiding fictions." In the course of his writings, Crabb uses such phrases as "basic assumptions,"[2] "wrong strategies,"[3] and "relational strategies."[4] All of his labels refer to the same thing, namely, a person's wrong, damaging beliefs, assumptions, or strategies about how to satisfy the two deepest needs/longings. They are always relegated to the unconscious (beneath the surface, inside, etc.) and they are in the Rational Circle of Crabb's Four-Circle model.

Crabb's teaching on false assumptions and wrong strategies may be summarized briefly. Painful disappointments are created by the failure to satisfy the two basic needs/longings which constantly press for gratification. The drive to satisfy them is so earnest and consuming that people develop strategies for satisfying them from early childhood on. The strategies then move into the unconscious, the original location of the two needs. The strategies are wrong in that they cannot provide the lasting satisfaction that the person seeks to gain.

Even though the strategies cannot succeed, people still operate according to the dictates of those unconscious wrong assumptions. Since firmly-held beliefs in the unconscious direct an individual's conduct, a person's main problem is his unconsciously-held false assumptions.   Hence Crabb, along with Adler, teaches that in order to truly understand and help people, one must unearth and change their unconscious programs.[5] For example, in the midst of his discussion on the unconscious, he says,

> There are, I believe, processes going on within our personalities that determine the directions we move, the strategies we use to protect ourselves from personal circle pain and to pursue anticipated pleasure.[6]

"Personal circle pain" refers to the failure to satisfy the two deepest needs/longings. The "strategies" refer to the unconsciously-held assumptions about how to satisfy the two needs.

Crabb's ideas about his Rational Circle have been influenced by Albert Ellis's Rational Emotive Therapy, which is a system of changing thoughts and beliefs in order to change behavior. Ellis's own humanistic belief system focuses on self-acceptance, self-affirmation, self-effort, and self-talk to reprogram the mind. Crabb says:

> My thesis is that problems develop when the basic needs for significance and security are threatened. People pursue irresponsible ways of living as a means of defending against feelings of insignificance and insecurity. In most cases these folks have arrived at a wrong idea as to what constitutes significance and security. And these **false beliefs are at the core of their problems**.[7] (Emphasis added.)

Crabb then quotes Proverbs 23:7 as supposed biblical support: "As [a man] thinketh in his heart, so is he." However, the context of the verse does not support his statement. This is just one example of how Crabb misuses Scripture in his attempt to give biblical support to his psychology. Proverbs 23:7 is actually a warning to watch out for duplicity:

> Eat thou not the bread of him that hath an evil eye, neither desire thou his dainty meats: For as he thinketh in his heart, so is he: Eat and drink, saith he to thee; but his heart is not with thee. The morsel which thou has eaten shalt thou vomit up, and lose thy sweet words. (Proverbs 23:6-8.)

The "he" referred to in Proverbs 23:7 is a person not to be trusted. The passage cannot be used to teach that if a person changes his unconscious beliefs he will overcome problems related to feelings of insecurity and insignificance.

The following quotations demonstrate that Crabb consistently promotes this concept of unconscious wrong beliefs and strategies. In his 1975 book, *Basic Principles of Biblical Counseling*, Crabb says:

> The two critical points to understand are, first, that each of us tends to unconsciously perceive the world of people (at least the world of people close to us) in a rather stereotyped fashion which was learned in childhood, and, second, we entertain a basic belief about what pattern of behavior is appropriate in our world to meet our personal needs. To the degree that that belief is in error we will experience problems in living.[8]

Later in *Effective Biblical Counseling* (1977) Crabb describes the unconscious as *"the reservoir of basic assumptions which people firmly and emotionally hold about how to meet their needs of significance and security."*[9] (Emphasis his.) He then declares that each person has been "programmed in his or her unconscious mind."[10] He continues:

We all develop some *wrong assumptions* about how
to get our needs met. . . . We often are not aware of
our basic wrong belief about how to meet our needs.
Yet that ungodly belief determines how we evaluate
the things happening to us in our world and that
evaluation in turn controls our feeling and
behavior.[11] (Emphasis his.)

Then in *Marriage Builder* (1982), he says:

Imbedded in our make-up are certain beliefs about
how to become worthwhile or how to avoid injury to
our self-esteem, how to be happy or how to avoid
pain. . . each of us reliably develops *wrong beliefs*
about how to find the meaning and love we need.
And a belief about what I need implies a goal that I
should pursue. . . . *Beliefs determine goals.*[12]
(Emphasis his.)

In this context, beliefs are unconscious even though the goals
may be conscious. In the same book he gives several
examples, including this one:

Suppose a boy is reared by parents who neglect him
to pursue their own interests. He may develop the
belief that there is no one who will attend to his
needs. That wrong belief may lead him to strive for
absolute self-reliance as the goal he must achieve to
avoid personal pain.[13] (Emphasis his.)

Crabb's 1987 book, *Understanding People*, continues the same
theme. In his section "Contents of the Unconscious," he says:

But still the pain exists, and we are motivated to
find relief. As relational beings we devise strategies
for responding to life that will keep the pain out of
awareness and, we hope, gain at least a measure of
the satisfaction we want. The particular strategies
we develop emerge as the product of our images of

ourselves and the world and our beliefs about what can be done.[14]

And, according to Crabb's diagram in the same section, the beliefs, images, and pain are all in the unconscious.[15] He describes the unconscious strategies further:

> . . . beneath every method of relating can be found a commitment to self-interest, a determination to protect oneself from more relational pain . . . the sinfully wrong strategies by which we manipulate people with our well-being in mind are intentionally hidden from view. They take their place in the unconscious.[16]

And finally, in his 1988 book, *Inside Out*, Crabb says:

> An inside look, then, can be expected to uncover two elements imbedded deeply in our heart: (1) thirst or *deep longings* for what we do not have; and (2) stubborn independence reflected in *wrong strategies* for finding the life we desire.[17] (Emphasis his.)

In the same book Crabb relegates the two longings and wrong strategies to the unconscious.[18] According to Crabb, personal problems can be traced to unconscious wrong assumptions.[19]

Does the Bible Teach Unconscious Programming?

Crabb teaches that "real change" involves altering unconscious beliefs, strategies, and images. However, none of his books provide adequate biblical support for the so-called unconscious material. The closest attempt at biblical documentation is his reference to Paul's admonition to "renew our minds" from Romans 12:1-2.

I beseech you therefore, brethren, by the mercies of

God, that ye present your bodies a living sacrifice,
holy, acceptable unto God, which is your reasonable
service. And be not conformed to this world: but be
ye transformed by the renewing of your mind, that
ye may prove what is that good, and acceptable, and
perfect, will of God.

Crabb reads into that passage of Scripture his own
psychological theory of the unconscious. He thus uses the
verse to stress the importance of renewing what he believes to
be unconscious beliefs and strategies about how to satisfy the
two needs/longings.[20]

Crabb's interpretation of Romans 12:1-2, Ephesians 4:23,
and related passages follows this line of reasoning. (1) Crabb
contends that the church has a shallow and deficient understanding if it does not recognize sin to be rooted in those unconscious beliefs, strategies, and motives related to the two
needs/longings for security/relationship and significance/im-
pact. (2) He argues that real change requires exposing and
altering the sinful content of the unconscious. Anything less
promotes superficial adjustment and mere external conformity. (3) Therefore, Crabb concludes that the biblical concept of
renewing the mind must refer to the process of exposing and
altering the unconscious.

In his section titled "A Shallow View of Sin," Crabb says:

Unless we understand sin as rooted in unconscious
beliefs and motives and figure out how to expose
and deal with these deep forces within the
personality, the church will continue to promote
superficial adjustment.[21]

Crabb continues:

Many pastors preach an "iceberg view" of sin. All
they worry about is what is visible above the water
line. . . . A great mass of sinful beliefs and
misdirected motives is never dealt with under that
approach. The result is external conformity that

masquerades as spiritual health.[22]

Therefore he contends:

> Real change means change in the inner man, where
> a *deceitful heart*, full of motives hidden even to our-
> selves, and a *darkened mind*, holding ideas that we
> may consciously disown, must be exposed and con-
> fronted by the message of God.[23] (Emphasis his.)

On the surface this last statement sounds very true.
However Crabb is referring to the unconscious, full of wrong
beliefs which must be exposed through certain techniques.
And the message of God to which he usually refers is that
Christ has already met the needs/longings for significance/
impact and security/relationship. Thus, Crabb's interpretation of New Testament teaching on real change amounts to
psychologizing biblical theology. One can examine his books
to find further evidence concerning his psychological notion
of sanctification.[24]

Paul was not teaching any theory of the unconscious in
the context of Romans 12:1-2. Biblically "renewing the mind"
is not accomplished through reprogramming the unconscious.
"Renewing the mind" has to do with thinking according to
God's ways rather than man's. In the context of the passage,
it is related to sacrificial living with a sacrificial attitude of
service. The way of the world is just the opposite from self-
sacrifice. The transformation is from serving self to doing
God's will. Romans 12 speaks nothing about any personal
needs for security and significance, but focuses on doing the
will of God rather than the will of self.

Deep Fear, Self-Protection, and Thick Layers.

Another foundational concept in Crabb's model is a view
of self-protection based upon Freudian ego-defense
mechanisms. Self-deception is part of the entire schema of the
unconscious, with its two resident needs, power, strategies,

and motives. Its connection with the unconscious becomes evident by asking and answering three questions. (1) From what do people seek protection in Crabb's model? The answer is "pain." (2) What causes this "pain"? The answer is "two unmet needs/longings." (3) Wherein do the two unmet needs/longings and the pain exist? The answer is "the unconscious." Thus, Crabb's hypothesis about self-protection depends upon his psychological theory.

In order to accept Crabb's doctrine of self-protection, one must also believe in his doctrine of the unconscious, with its two resident motivational needs/longings. In his book *Encouragement: The Key to Caring*, Crabb paints the scenario of a businessman named Vic.[25] Vic outwardly shows signs of success. He is also pleasant, personable, and socially at ease in most public situations. However, no one, including Vic, truly knows the "real Vic." Why this ignorance of the "real Vic"? Crabb begins to tell us by saying, "Beneath the look of confidence lies deep fear: 'I have to be more successful than dad or I'll be unhappy just like him.'" After describing Vic's external success, Crabb continues:

> Because Vic is a professing Christian, part of his success package includes church attendance, prayer before mealtimes, and occasional family devotions. **But all these things serve to hide, even from himself, the deep sense of inadequacy that drives him toward the visible reminders of success. His fear is deep, his layers thick.**[26] (Emphasis added.)

According to Crabb, "no one *really* knows him." (Emphasis his.) Not only that, Vic doesn't even know how miserable he really is. Crabb says:

> His fears remain conveniently shielded from view, so well hidden that not even he is aware that his purpose in living is to prove a point and reduce a fear. . . . Because fear continues to quietly dominate his life, his layers stay firmly in place, thickened to

the point that he will let nothing puncture his false sense of security. Vic is blind to his own spiritual poverty.[27]

No one knows the "real Vic" because even though everything may be just fine on the conscious level, a man may well be seething with terror and undermined by inadequacy at the unconscious level.

Thus Crabb analyzes Vic as having deep unconscious "fear," hidden by thick "layers" built up to protect a fragile self-image. Therefore, to get at the real Vic one must "peel away" those "self-protective layers" and expose the unconscious world of pain, fear, and emptiness. This Freudian notion that a man may be consciously happy while unconsciously miserable, consciously peaceful while unconsciously terrorized, and consciously confident while unconsciously fearful permeates Crabb's books.[28] It is a duality that has no support in the Bible.

All of the confidence about what is inside makes it seem that psychologists have inside knowledge, that they can read right past the layers into the unconscious. What a psychologist says may indeed sound plausible to someone who has placed confidence in him. However, if a counselee does not agree that he is miserable and frustrated on the inside while he is happy and peaceful on the outside, he may very well be accused of denial and self-protection. Carol Tavris, in her book *Anger: The Misunderstood Emotion* describes what can happen with this kind of Freudian mind-set. She says:

> Sitting in a cafe one afternoon, I overheard the following exchange between two women:
>
> Woman A: "You'll feel better if you get your anger out."
>
> Woman B: "Anger? Why am I angry?"
>
> Woman A: "Because he left you , that's why."
>
> Woman B: "Left me? What are you talking about? He *died*. He was an *old man*."
>
> Woman A: "Yes, but to your unconscious it's no different from abandonment. Underneath, you are

blaming him for not keeping his obligation to you to
protect you forever."

Woman B: "That might have been true if I were
ten years old, Margaret, but I'm forty-two, we both
knew he was dying, and we had time to make our
peace. I don't feel angry, I feel sad. I *miss* him. He
was a darling father to me."

Woman A: "Why are you so defensive? Why are
you denying your true feelings? Why are you afraid
of therapy?"

Woman B: "Margaret, *you are driving me crazy.
I don't feel angry, dammit!*"

Woman A (*smiling*): "So why are you shout-
ing?"

It is not entirely easy to argue with a Freudian
devotee, because disagreement is usually taken as
denial or "blocking."[29] (Emphasis hers.)

Crabb would no doubt call that an amateur attempt at
getting past the layers, but he does emphasize the same
theme of defensive self protection through the denial of real
feelings.

Crabb's analysis of Vic rehearses Freudian rather than
biblical doctrine. Crabb has adopted and adapted the view
that because of pain involved in unconscious beliefs, people
repress them through denial. To avoid further injury to their
already damaged self, they protect themselves from
undesirable and painful unconscious material.

The technique of denial is well-known to Freudians as
one of the ego defense mechanisms. People supposedly build
defensive layers to avoid the excruciating pain of facing the
emptiness and disappointments existing in their unconscious.
According to the theory, they are terrified at the thought of
honestly facing their unconscious pain. Hence, people are
primarily motivated by fear. They are unconsciously terrified!

Crabb teaches that the central motivational power
known as fear drives all men to build self-protective layers.
He says that "fear consumes the core of every person."[30] In
his model, fear is the core motivation behind everything.

Crabb explains its relationship to our two needs:

> Because we are fallen beings, our capacities have become desperate longings energized by a fear that we will never find the satisfaction we desire.[31]

Thus, according to Crabb, everyone is thus energized by fear at the unconscious core of his being. At the core, all are driven by fear to protect self from the pain of unmet needs. That is an amazing description of all people! What about Paul and the apostles? Were they driven by fear to evangelize the world? What about missionaries who have given their lives for the sake of the gospel? And although some people are driven by fear because they are not trusting and obeying God, one cannot define all motivation with the single word *fear*.

Concepts of fear and denial completely dominate the counseling methodology in Crabb's later books. In fact, he contends that fear and denial constitute a fundamental problem with most Christians. Crabb especially criticizes seminary graduates, pastors, and professors as   poorly equipped to handle the problems of real people in the real world because they are unaware of the real difficulties of life.[32] He suggests that these men are ill-equipped because they too are caught in the jaws of pretense, denial, and self-protection. But, of course, they are not aware of this because it is unconscious.[33]

Crabb emphasizes denial of feelings and self-protective strategies throughout all of his books. In *Inside Out* Crabb refers to "retreat into denial,"   running from pain through denial, and "a powerless lifestyle of denial."[34] He says, "Perhaps much of what passes for spiritual maturity is maintained by a rigid denial of all that is happening beneath the surface of their lives."[35] Crabb says that self-protecting strategies build "insulating layers of friendliness and appropriate involvement [which] work to keep us from touching the terrible pain of previously felt disappointment."[36] Thus even the finest qualities (even the fruit of the Spirit) and godly activities can be condemned by Crabb as being sinful, because they may appear to prevent one from centering on the pain of disappointment.

According to Crabb, Christians must honestly face the painful material in their unconscious if they want to grow. But, in order to gain an honest look at the inside, they must discover and then discard their self-protective strategies.[37] He contends that refusal to "honestly face" all of that pain stored in the unconscious is the chief cause of shallow Christian living. In Crabb's opinion, such denial leads to shallow conformity, judgmentalism, and legalism.[38]

Again, Crabb lays some of the blame for that shallowness on the evangelical seminaries, because they have failed to prepare ministers to psychologically deal with pain, beliefs, and images in the unconscious mind.[39] Hence, ministers deal only with the conscious mind and leave the crucial contents of the unconscious unattended. The implication is that this lack is the reason why so many churches are in such a low state of spiritual vigor. Concerned about shepherds who only deal with the tip of the iceberg, while neglecting the great mass of unconscious pain, beliefs, and images,[40] Crabb says:

> We rarely consider the value of what I believe is central to real change: taking a hard look at the commitment to self-protection that displays itself most clearly in our ways of relating to people.[41]

He then illustrates his point:

> The gentle pastor has convinced others *and himself* that his patience is the fruit of the Spirit, when it may be nothing more than ugly self-protection. To change from the inside out requires that we repent of our self-protective commitment.[42] (Emphasis his.)

According to Crabb, the gentle pastor is not aware of unconscious pain, fear, and strategies which explain the motives of his behavior. Hence, he has deceived himself and others through his self-protective "style of relating."[43]

Crabb's counseling involves stripping away those self-protective layers to get to the real person hiding underneath.

Moreover, in Crabb's integration model, the very essence of Christian sanctification involves deep probing into the unconscious.

Does the Bible Support Crabb's Theory of Self-Protection?

Crabb discusses the concept of self-protection at length and regularly imposes it upon various biblical passages. However, he does not demonstrate that either the intent or the context of any Bible passage agrees with his psychological notion of self-protection. An example of his psychological view of Scripture can be seen in his interpretation of the doctrine of repentance in light of his notion on self-protection.[44] He contends that repentance must involve insight into one's own inner pain that "triggered" the outward sin. One must recognize that beneath the sinful behavior there is the greater sin for which he must repent: the sin of self-protection.

According to Crabb, one cannot truly repent without the process of insight into so-called unconscious needs that cry out for fulfillment. Without biblical support, Crabb contends that a Christian has only half-repented if he does not take self-protection into account. He gives an example of a man who loses his temper and yells at his wife. If he only confesses his sinful behavior, his repentance is not complete. He must become aware of his "relational pain and protective strategies" if he is to repent more fully.[45]

Moreover, Crabb contends that a person must realize that he himself has been a victim before he can even understand his sinful commitment to self-protection and then repent at his deepest level. Crabb says:

> I believe there's a simple reason why sin in the heart, that commitment to self-protection that manifests itself in so many defensive styles of relating, is so rarely recognized as deep and serious. We can't recognize self-protection until we see what

we're protecting. Until we face our disappointment as a victim, we cannot clearly identify the strategies we've adopted to insulate ourself from further disappointment. *Only a deep awareness of our own profound disappointment (pain in our heart) can enable us to realize our desires for satisfaction have become demands for relief (sin in our heart).*[46] (Emphasis his.)

He declares that it is necessary to get "in touch with the damage to our soul **caused by other people's sinfulness**" in order to identify and repent of the "sin in the heart, that commitment to self-protection."[47] (Emphasis added.) Thus he reverses the way of repentance, asking people first to focus on the sins of **others**. Talking about and reexperiencing the sins committed against one are Crabb's proposed activities for initiating real repentance. But, the Bible does not teach believers to focus on, talk about, and reexperience the pain of past sins committed against them. These activities are not biblical requirements preceding forgiveness of others.

Crabb offers no Scripture that verifies his theory of repentance. Nor are there any Scriptures that warrant subsuming the doctrine of repentance under psychological ideas of self-protection and rehearsing the sins of others. Rather than laying a proper biblical foundation, Crabb presents lengthy discussions that wed psychological theories of ego-defense mechanisms to the biblical doctrine of repentance and forgiveness.

One example of the way Crabb interprets the Bible through the lens of self-protection is in his treatment of Hosea 14:1-7.[48] He interprets every exhortation and promise in that passage by relating them to his notion of self-protection. One would hardly have understood Hosea in this manner prior to the advent of psychoanalysis. There is no indication in the context that suggests interpreting the passage in light of self-protection theory. Nor is there internal biblical evidence that the Holy Spirit taught such a concept anywhere in Hosea. On the basis of his own ideas, Crabb interprets the entire passage in light of his theory of self-protection.

Questioning Crabb's Theory of the Rational Circle.

Crabb's analysis of individuals and methods includes unproven psychological theories about why people are the way they are and how they change. If we are to be like the Bereans, it is necessary to question such theories and techniques to see if there is scriptural reason or justification for them. The Bible does not present an unconscious as a reality existing in clear distinction from the conscious mind. Nor does it reveal an unconscious which contains an organized world of images, beliefs, pain, and two substantive longings. It is strange that analysis of and insight into the unconscious are not addressed in Scripture if they are fundamental to sanctification, as Crabb maintains.

No one can speak with certainty about the actual contents of an unconscious mind. There is no evidence outside of personal opinion to verify such detailed explanations of the contents as Crabb proposes. The church should resist the intrusion of such theories unless clear scriptural verification is presented. The burden of biblical proof lies on Crabb, not on those who are skeptical and disbelieving. Christians have both the right and duty to doubt Crabb's opinions until the Word of God has been shown to promote them.

If Crabb is to continue to feed the church psychological opinions about the nature of man and the method of change, he must present abundant biblical evidence. His illustrative examples and redefined biblical words do not supply necessary biblical support or justification. Since the Word of God speaks very **directly** about both the nature and purpose of man and the way of change and growth, it is Crabb's obligation to provide scriptural reason for adding philosophies of men to the revealed Word of God. But, to date, he has not provided legitimate evidence from exegetical, biblical, or systematic theological sources to support the psychological theories promoted in his Rational Circle.

14

VOLITIONAL AND EMOTIONAL CIRCLES AND THE PROCESS OF CHANGE

Crabb defines the conscious mind "as that part of the person which makes conscious evaluations including moral judgments."[1] However, Crabb immediately qualifies that definition by saying that the unconscious determines the sentences which people consciously speak to themselves.[2] A person may indeed think consciously and evaluatively. However, according to Crabb, underneath the conscious thinking is a whole host of submerged, but powerful beliefs and images.

Crabb's Volitional and Emotional Circles have both conscious and unconscious material. According to Crabb, people are often unsuccessful or else make only superficial change at the choice level because of the strong influence of the unconscious. Though they may try to change their behavior and their feelings, much of their effort is wasted. Crabb contends that, to be real, change must begin on the inside, that is, the unconscious. He contends that simply changing external behavior is superficial and further exacerbates internal problems.

According to Crabb's system, the conscious mind expresses the content of the unconscious. The conscious mind serves the unconscious and supplies it with information. Crabb seems to make the conscious mind useful **only by**

making it subservient to the unconscious. Thus we are
all merely actors at the conscious level, carrying out the
programmed content of the unconscious.

Crabb presents this forced, contrived relationship
between the unconscious and the conscious mind in almost
every illustration. Here is one example out of the many:

> In order to understand why the pastor begins to
> show nervous mannerisms in the pulpit, or why he
> glumly loses interest in his work, or why he coolly
> ignores his critics, you must study. . . **what
> sentences are running through his conscious
> mind** as he considers the event of criticism. Then
> you must look for **the source of those sentences
> in an unconsciously held assumption** about
> significance.[3] (Emphasis added.)

He teaches that conscious thinking, choosing, acting, and
feeling are external responses to contents of the unconscious,
especially the pain caused by others not having met a
person's needs. Volitional and Emotional Circles only make
sense if they are interpreted in light of the Personal and
Rational Circles.

The Volitional Circle.

The Volitional Circle is where people make active
choices.[4] It represents their capacity to set a direction, choose
behavior, and pursue their goal.[5] As noted earlier, Crabb has
been influenced by Adler in his emphasis on goal-oriented
behavior. Adler gave great importance to his fundamental
proposition that "every psychic phenomenon, if it is to give us
any understanding of a person, can only be grasped and
understood if regarded as a preparation for some goal."[6]

It cannot be disputed that people do make conscious
choices about their activities and do set goals. However, what
is questionable is the dependence and subservience of Crabb's
choices and goals to unconscious needs and strategies. In his
model, choices are made on the basis of what lies beneath the

waterline, that is, in the unconscious. He gives this example of what might be going on in a person:

> With the **pain of unmet longings driving her** to find relief, and with her images and beliefs guiding her search, the stage is set for a visible direction to emerge as she looks for a way to handle her world. The first element of that direction is a goal. Beliefs about what brings satisfaction always carry with them a goal to be pursued. When someone reaches an understanding of what must be done to relieve personal circle pain, that understanding quickly translates into a goal.[7] (Emphasis added.)

Unmet needs/longings in the unconscious drive her, and the images and beliefs of the unconscious guide her. And since unmet needs and longings drive her to wrong conclusions and self protective actions, her sin is not her fault, but rather the fault of others who have not met her needs. She is further exonerated by saying that this is beyond her conscious awareness and conscious control, since everything done at the conscious volitional level is under the direction of the unconscious. What kind of choice or responsibility is that?

The Emotional Circle.

The Emotional Circle represents the capacity to experience life "with feeling."[8] Again no one will deny that emotions are a very real part of human existence. However in Crabb's system, the emotions, like the will, are predicated upon what lurks beneath the waterline. According to Crabb's perspective, emotions can be understood only as they are interpreted in light of the unconscious content of the Personal and Rational Circles. In fact, according to Crabb, the emotions of many people may be largely submerged in the unconscious so that they do not consciously feel their deep emotions. Thus, the only way to grasp the significance of human emotions is to view them through the narrow perspective of Crabb's unproven theory of the unconscious.

Conscious and unconscious emotions play a large part in the kind of psychological counseling that is based upon theories of the unconscious and hierarchy of needs. Emotions can serve to make a person vulnerable to change. Emotions can be like cracks in the layers of self-protective strategies. If an event occurs to touch the emotions, a person becomes vulnerable. He may either become defensive and add to his layers of self-protection, or he can be willing to experience the emotion. The emotional experience can serve as a wedge through the layers of self-protective strategy to expose contents of the unconscious. Furthermore, when insight occurs an emotional response is expected.

The emotions that Crabb elicits are those of disappointment and pain that the counselee feels because of the sins of others. He encourages people to enter their pain and experience their disappointment. He believes that by doing this a person will be driven to God to find satisfaction for thirst. However, such activity may inappropriately serve to relieve a person from guilt feelings. Although Crabb may not see this, the natural consequence of focusing on personal disappointments is relief from guilt. After all, if a person's sin is due to unfulfilled needs, then it's really not his fault that he is sinful. It's really the fault of others and perhaps even God for not fulfilling the needs in more obvious ways.

Appeals for Change.

Being willing to change and to go through the painful process of change must occur at the conscious level, even according to Crabb's system. People are responsible for their choices. But how? Rather than making obvious changes at the conscious level, people must choose to really change by being willing to look inside. Yet is that action unconsciously motivated? Perhaps one could say that in Crabb's system the second-worst sin of all is to refuse to look inside to discover the primary sin of self-protection.

Presumably, unless Crabb believes that people can

indeed decide to do something about exposing their unconscious material, he would not have bothered to write his
books. He uses reason to speak to a person's conscious evalu-
ative thinking in the conscious part of the Rational Circle.
Here he seeks to convince people to believe that they can
truly change from the inside out, **if** they use his method. He
appeals to the Volitional Circle by persuading them to be
willing to expose their inner needs and manipulative strategies. And through his real life stories and promises of change
and growth, he appeals to the Emotional Circle. He thus
addresses the conscious mind to bring people to a point of
exposing the so-called unconscious. And through all of the
argumentation there is both direct and implicit criticism of
those who refuse or resist this kind of processing.

Crabb's Psychological Sanctification Process.

According to Crabb, any attempt to change without cleaning
out the hidden basement (the unconscious) will result in
merely superficial external conformity.[9] Counselors thus
work to expose what they believe to be self-protective layers
which people have supposedly built up in order to avoid the
pain stored in the unconscious mind. They try to expose self-
protective techniques such as denial as well as the unconscious material itself.

The reason they must work on self-protective strategies
is because, for Crabb, these constitute the essence of sin. For
him sin is primarily all that a person does to prevent or
relieve himself of pain brought on by others. Thus, like
humanistic psychologists, Crabb teaches that wrong beliefs,
thoughts, and behavior are responses to one's environment
(primarily parents and significant persons). It is really society
that brings on the corruption by not meeting what Crabb calls
"legitimate needs." Humanistic psychologists believe that
when needs are met, people will be healthy and respond in
loving ways. When people's needs are met they will be able to
love others and be socially responsible. The primary difference between Crabb and his secular counterparts is that
Crabb offers God as the primary need meeter, while the

secularists have only human resources.

Crabb says that the exposure process is not easy. In fact
it is quite difficult and very painful, so much so that the word
pain is repeated throughout *Inside Out*. It's in the first
sentence and on the last page. One learns that although it's
not okay to deny and relate to people from defensive layers, it
is okay to hurt. It's not only okay to hurt; it's absolutely
essential. Crabb contends that pain is necessary for growth
and that most people try to avoid it. Therefore people use all
kinds of self-protective measures "to prevent painful unconscious material from becoming conscious."[10] Or, as he says in
Inside Out, "Most of us cope with life by pretending."[11]
Hence, everyone is supposedly involved in denial. There is
repeated reference to the Freudian ego-defense mechanisms
of denial and repression in the unconscious and self-
protective layers, which have been built up to prevent an
honest exposure.[12]

According to Crabb, deep change requires work from the
inside (unconscious) to the outside. It consists of stripping
away the self-protective layers. Crabb says:

> Many of the people we deal with in counseling are
> hiding behind all sorts of defensive overlays
> designed to protect a fragile sense of self-acceptance
> or to prevent further rejection or failure from reach-
> ing an already crippled self-identity. Counseling
> involves a **stripping away of the layers,
> sometimes gently, sometimes forcefully**, to
> reach the real person underneath. The context of all
> such efforts must be genuine acceptance, or as
> Rogers puts it, unconditional positive regard for the
> worth of the individual.[13] (Emphasis added.)

The exposing process can be gentle but firm nudging, through
encouraging the person to talk about his feelings. Crabb
suggests a way to do this:

> Start by asking for feedback about yourself: "I think
> I have a hard time getting really close to people. I've

wondered if I communicate that I'm too busy or too
important for real friendship. I'd appreciate hearing
how each of you experiences me in this group, even
right now as I share this. **How do I make you
feel?**"[14] (Emphasis added.)

As a person focuses on his feelings, he supposedly gains
insight into his unconscious.

Not only will a therapist encourage the admission and
expression of feelings, he may sometimes seek to evoke those
emotions. However, Crabb cautions that not just anybody
should try this. He says that *"meaningful involvement must
precede efforts to expose each other's sin."* (Emphasis his.) He
continues:

No one should appoint himself Minister of Exposure
to the entire congregation. When someone tells me I
come across as pushy, my ability to receive that
input well depends partly on how persuaded I am
that the one who's given the input genuinely cares
about me.[15]

Thus, exposure can be quite direct. But, according to Crabb,
as long as all is done with Rogers' "unconditional positive
regard" and the right motive, almost anything can be said to
expose what might be lurking beneath the surface.[16] Direct or
implied accusations of denial may also be used to expose a
person's self-protective strategies.

Crabb also recommends group involvement in exposing
layers and strategies as well as individual counseling. And
while harm is not intended, such a process can result in
personal attack in order to puncture holes in the layers so
that the person can finally see **that** he is denying and **what**
he is denying. In *The Journal of Humanistic Psychology*, John
Rowan describes what happens in the secular setting:

I have seen people bullied and intimidated in groups
because they weren't expressing feelings, or even
because they weren't expressing the *right* feelings,

such as anger. . . . I have even seen people criticized because they weren't expressing feelings *all the time*! [17] (Emphasis his.)

Notice the importance of feelings. In the kind of therapy that seeks to unearth hidden motives and beliefs in the unconscious, an emotional response is expected to accompany insight. If there is not enough strong emotion, it may indicate that the layers have not been penetrated. Thus a strong emotion is like a sign that progress is being made.

Although Crabb would no doubt deny ever intimidating or bullying anyone, the very process of exposure itself can be quite intimidating. Also, a subtle verbal and nonverbal bullying and intimidation can occur in the process of attempting to expose the so-called contents of the unconscious. And Crabb does insist that real change requires an exposure of unconscious motives and beliefs.[18] He also emphasizes feelings and believes that strong emotions accompany real insight and growth. In discussing a particular case, he says:

> The first act of changing his current relational style had to be to open himself to **feeling the pain of his past**. Only then would he be in a position to realize how deeply determined he was to never feel that pain again. . . moving on to deeper levels of involvement with others required this man to **more deeply feel his pain** and to face his self-protective sin. The more deeply we enter our disappointment, the more thoroughly we can face our sin. Unless we **feel the pain of being victimized**, we will tend to limit the definition of our problem with sin to visible acts of transgression.[19] (Emphasis added.)

Notice the emphasis on having been victimized. Rather than facing our own depravity and our own failure to love God and others, we are to concentrate on past offenses that others have committed against us. Practically speaking, the process of talking about the past and acutely feeling disappointments of the past could very well involve dishonoring parents. One wonders where the Bible encourages people to expose the sins of others publicly for one's own benefit. It is certainly the opposite of biblical forgiveness and the admonitions to do good to enemies and overcome evil with good. Furthermore by magnifying disappointments from the past a person could even be encouraged to blame God.

This return to feel the pain of the past is based on the Freudian theory of abreaction. The *Dictionary of Psychology* defines *abreaction* as "the discharge of tension by reliving in words, feelings, and actions" a painful event from the past.[20] Supposedly reliving the pain of past experience relieves a person from its unconscious grip. However, research has never proven this idea. On the other hand, there is great suspicion that quite the reverse is true. Rather than being rid of pain in the unconscious, a person may actually be creating new pain and making the proverbial mountain out of a mole-hill. And, although there may be a false relief from guilt and there may be a sense of relief after pain and crying, nothing really changes except a shift in responsibility for the sin and a stronger commitment to the technique of abreaction and the system that incorporates it. Similar forms of abreaction and ensuing commitment occur in rebirthing, primal therapy, inner healing, est, and Gestalt as well as in psychoanalysis.

However, in such settings any really helpful change is not dependent upon those theories or techniques. According to the research, actual change occurs because a person wants to change, not because of the counseling methodology.[21] Therefore, if anyone changes for the better under such a process it has more to do with personal commitment to change than the process itself. Additionally, a person's expectation for change also has more to do with whether a person changes than with the process or method used. Researcher David Shapiro says that "treatments differ in effectiveness only to the extent that they arouse in clients differing degrees of expectation of benefit."[22]

A method of counseling is always dependent upon the theory behind it. And if one believes that one needs to strip off layers and feel the pain that resides in the unconscious, then "no pain, no gain," or "pain is gain." Not only that, the insight a person gains generally has more to do with what the therapist is looking for than with what is really there. If the therapist looks for a painful past, the counselee will give it to him. If he looks for archetypes in dreams, the counselee will dredge those up. As with all psychotherapeutic systems, everything a person does can be interpreted according to the system.

Crabb not only advocates such exposure in counseling. He encourages small groups to meet together for the same purpose. Rather than Bible study, the members interact to *"give feedback lovingly* and to *receive feedback non-defensively."*[23] He gives an example of a small group encouraging a man to focus on his times of disappointment and "his refusal to enter deeply into the experience of his disappointment."[24] The man's response to the probing was to say, "Am I to focus on my pain and think about nothing other than how badly I've been victimized? I'm more interested in knowing how I can get on with my life. What's past is past. I want to learn to relate effectively to people now."[25] Crabb then criticizes the man for his "self-protective commitment to never experience the level of pain he'd felt in his childhood."[26]

Crabb misuses Scripture to support this practice of probing.[27] He quotes Hebrews 3:13:

> Take heed, brethren, lest there be in any of you an evil heart of unbelief, in departing from the living God. But exhort one another daily, while it is called To day; lest any of you be hardened through the deceitfulness of sin.

This verse has nothing to do with exhorting one another to feel the pain of being victimized or to follow the process developed by Crabb. The exhortation is to remain true to the faith lest one develop unbelief and turn away from God. The "evil heart of unbelief" is not the unconscious, but the conscious choice of unbelief and deliberate turning away from God. The hardening does not refer to building protective layers around the unconscious fear and pain. It is the stubbornness of unbelief. The same chapter refers to the

Israelites having hardened their hearts when they were tempted in the wilderness. Such a hardening is a refusal to believe and obey God.

Since Crabb contends that everyone supposedly has a center core of unconscious needs, fears, and pain, covered with layers of self-protection, his methodology is not limited to counselees with visible problems. His therapy or processing is for everybody. He believes it is essential for all of us to recognize that we have a problem with sexual identity. In fact, he considers the problem so serious that there will be no real change until we face it. He says:

> Until we sense the deep discomfort we feel in relating as men and women, we haven't touched the core of our struggle.[28]

He continues:

> At the very center of our soul, we feel shame and fear that is attached to our identity as male or female. Males lack the healthy confidence that they're intact men who can move into their world unafraid of being completely destroyed by failure or disrespect. Females lack that quietly exhilarating awareness that they're secure women who can embrace their world with no worry of having their essential identity crushed by someone's abuse or rejection.[29]

He says that these feelings of shame relate to doubts about our sexual identity and "provide powerful motivation to protect ourselves from further wounds."[30] They are so powerful that:

> *We will not face our self-protective maneuvering nor be passionately convicted about its sinfulness until we see its function is to preserve whatever is left of our identity as men and women.*[31] (Emphasis his.)

This is an interesting combination of Freud's libido (sexual energy), Jung's animus and anima (unconscious elements of masculinity and femininity), and Maslow's hierarchy of needs. Crabb attempts to support this theory with Romans 1:26, 29-32. However, the explanation of those sinful behaviors, including sexual sins and other forms of immorality, has already been given in the earlier verses. The explanation God gives is not uncertain sexual identity, but rather worshiping and serving the creature (the human self) more than the Creator.

> . . . when they knew God, they glorified him not as God, neither were thankful; but became vain in their imaginations, and their foolish heart was darkened. Professing themselves to be wise, they became fools, and changed the glory of the uncorruptible God into an image made like to corruptible man. . . . Wherefore God also gave them up to uncleanness through the lusts of their own hearts, to dishonour their own bodies between themselves: who changed the truth of God into a lie, and worshipped and served the creature more than the Creator, who is blessed for ever. Amen. (Romans 1:21-25.)

Crabb offers his psychological method to all Christians, because he believes that exposing the unconscious needs, fears, pains, and wrong strategies is a necessary means for personal Christian growth. He contends that this is the way people become truly dependent on God. He says:

> Until we admit that nothing and no one else really satisfies, we're never going to depend on Christ. And the only way to admit that there is no real satisfaction apart from Christ is to feel the disappointment in every other relationship.[32]

For Crabb, the basis for dependence on God is our need to be respected and loved, rather than our own inability to love and obey God. And while God does indeed bless His children, dependence on God begins with the Holy Spirit revealing our own depravity, not with our own disappointments and victimization by others.

In attempting to bring people to dependence on God through making miserable mountains out of past disappointments and by focusing on feelings of being victimized, dependence can easily shift from God to a more temporal source of help, that is, the process itself. And it appears to be an endless one, for one can never rid himself of sin by recalling past hurts and disappointments and feeling them to the uttermost. It's like an endless wheel with group members taking turns. It seems as though God's truth, grace, peace, and joy are replaced by confusion, works, probing and pain. Nevertheless, Crabb says that if Christians are to be genuine and inspire others to desire what they have, they must go through that kind of processing.[33]

Theological Appraisal of Crabb's Theory of Sanctification.

Crabb's doctrine of change involves exposing unconscious pain and changing unconscious strategies. As such, his doctrine of sanctification reduces to the notion that one must alter his unconscious beliefs and strategies about how to satisfy his two deepest needs/longings. Again, as with the other psychological doctrines that uphold this model of counseling, one cannot find any orthodox theologian throughout church history who interprets the biblical doctrine of sanctification in such a manner.

Crabb's view of sanctification is not based on either an orthodox understanding of Scripture or a careful study of such key sanctification passages as Romans 6-8; Ephesians 4-6; 2 Corinthians 3; and Galatians 5. Nevertheless Crabb proposes that his method should influence how one approaches the Bible. He says, *"We must come to the Bible with the purpose of self-exposure consciously in mind."*[34] (Emphasis his.) This technique of self-exposure with its underlying psychology is intended to perform the very work which the Lord has assigned to the Holy Spirit and the Word itself.

The Bible does more than simply set forth principles. It is activated in our lives by the Lord Himself. Psalm 19 clearly outlines what the Word of God can do:

> The law of the Lord is perfect, converting the soul; the testimony of the Lord is sure, making wise the simple.
>
> The statutes of the Lord are right, rejoicing the heart; the commandment of the Lord is pure, enlightening the eyes.
>
> The fear of the Lord is clean, enduring for ever; the judgments of the Lord are true and righteous altogether.
>
> More to be desired are they than gold, yea, than much fine gold; sweeter also than honey and the honeycomb.
>
> Moreover by them is thy servant warned; and in keeping of them there is great reward.
>
> Who can understand his errors? cleanse thou me from secret faults.
>
> Keep back thy servant also from presumptuous sins; let them not have dominion over me; then shall I be upright, and I shall be innocent from the great transgression.
>
> Let the words of my mouth, and the meditation of my heart, be acceptable in thy sight, O Lord, my strength, and my redeemer. (Psalm 19:7-14.)

This Psalm says that the Word works deep change in a person. However, it is important to remember that the Word cannot be separated from the One who spoke the Word. Whenever the Word operates in a person's life, it is the Lord working through His Word. It is the Lord who converts the soul through His Word. It is the Lord who cleanses from sin and makes a person pure. It is the Lord who enlightens the eyes through His Word, who enables a person to understand his errors, and who cleanses that person from secret faults.

The direct involvement of the Lord in the ministry of the Word is further emphasized at the end of the Psalm when David prays that the Lord will enable him to think, say, and do what is right.

In all of his books Crabb has neither explained nor exalted the role of the Holy Spirit in the process of change. Instead, he downplays the unique work of the Holy Spirit's activities in the heart of a person who is earnestly reading the Word of God for the purpose of sanctification and obedience. He says,

> It's wrong to handle a text like an authorized Ouija board. We are not to read a passage and expect the Spirit of God to mystically impress on our consciousness whatever self-knowledge He wants us to have.[35]

This is a denial of 2 Timothy 3:16-17 as well as being contrary to the plain biblical teaching on the work of the Holy Spirit.

Passages such as Romans 8 and Galatians 5 emphasize the work of the Holy Spirit in sanctification. How can one purport to promote the biblical view of change, and yet fail to include the character and ministry of the Holy Spirit? How can one believe Crabb's notions about real change when he emphasizes and exalts theories like the unconscious with its supposed contents and powers, rather than the Holy Spirit? How can he ignore what the Word of God says about itself in regard to change and growth? Where is the emphasis on walking according to the Spirit? Where is the confidence in the profound reality of new life, which Paul declares in Galatians 2:20?

> I am crucified with Christ: nevertheless I live; yet not I, but Christ liveth in me: and the life which I now live in the flesh I live by the faith of the Son of God, who loved me, and gave himself for me.

Crabb's directions for change do not reflect the doctrine of change contained in those passages.

Crabb presents a view of sanctification that differs radically from the historic position of the church. It represents psychological doctrine. The same theories about needs and the unconscious can be found in psychology texts. The only difference is that Crabb has added the framework of biblical references, so-called categories, and biblical-sounding language to his psychological doctrine, which of course makes him an integrationist.

Is it possible that secular psychologists and psychiatrists who spurned God could ever have produced an interpretation of man's innermost nature and the method of change which stands in full accord with the Scriptures? It would be difficult to square such an idea with I Corinthians 1:18-2:14:

> For after that in the wisdom of God the world by wisdom knew not God, it pleased God by the foolishness of preaching to save them that believe . . . . For I determined not to know any thing among you, save Jesus Christ, and him crucified. . . . And my speech and my preaching was not with enticing words of man's wisdom, but in demonstration of the Spirit and of power; that your faith should not stand in the wisdom of men, but in the power of God. . . . But the natural man receiveth not the things of the Spirit of God: for they are foolishness unto him: neither can he know them, because they are spiritually discerned. (1 Cor. 1:21 and 2:2, 4, 5, 14.)

Crabb's doctrine of change falls significantly short of the doctrine of change as expounded by Paul in Romans 6-8. If real change only involves reprogramming the unconscious to read, "Christ has met my two needs/longings," then Paul could have finished off his presentation on sanctification in the equivalent of three verses. Once Crabb's system is learned, it is a convenient, simplistic way of looking at human nature. His overly simple speculations do not reflect the richness, fullness, and accuracy of biblical teaching on sanctification and change.

15

ENSLAVING THE GOSPEL TO PSYCHOLOGY

Crabb reveals his approach to Scripture in his discussion "Spoiling the Egyptians." He begins with a commitment to the value of psychological theories and hopes to use the Bible as a screening device to determine what to keep and what to toss. The problem begins immediately with the belief that psychological theories about the nature of man have something useful to add to the Bible, which supposedly does not directly address all issues of life and godliness. This beginning assumption eliminates the Bible as the sole judge and standard. It cannot be the sole standard when a person has already decided that psychological theories, devised by darkened minds of the unredeemed, have something essential to add. There is an immediate bias which becomes either the standard itself or severely limits the use of the Bible as the true standard.

The Bible claims to be the authoritative treatise on the doctrine of man, including the fallen nature, salvation, sanctification, faith, and obedience. Therefore, if one is to study the human condition one must begin with Scripture rather than psychology. The commitment must be, first of all, that the Bible is in and of itself completely sufficient for matters of life and conduct. That does not mean that it is merely a sufficient framework on which to suspend unproven psychological theories. One who is committed to the sufficiency of the Word of God and the Work of the Holy Spirit will prayerfully and carefully study the Bible to seek understanding and insight into the nature of man and how God plans to change him. He will not be distracted by "valuable insights" hidden in the morass of theories and therapies devised by those who neither acknowledge God nor seek Him as their source of life and godliness. He will not be biased by psychological theory or interpret the Bible according to preconceived notions. Instead he will believe that the Bible is both fully sufficient and the only standard of truth in matters concerning the doctrines of God and man.

Crabb verbally agrees that the Bible is the only adequate standard and says that the Scriptures are sufficient—with certain qualifications. However, he begins with the assumption that there are valuable insights to be gleaned from psychology. This puts an immediate bias on his approach to Scripture. Although Crabb has noted certain psychological theories that contradict the Word of God, he has demonstrated a keen commitment to find agreement between psychology and the Bible. Thus he approaches Scripture with a bias to confirm and defend his cherished beliefs in the psychological theories of his choice.

Such an approach to Scripture often leads to subjective and imaginative eisegesis rather than sound exegesis. Exegesis is the attempt to establish the meaning of statements and passages of the Bible. In *Baker's Dictionary of Theology*, Everett Harrison says:

> Exegesis is predicated on two fundamentals. First, it assumes that thought can be accurately conveyed in words, each of which, at least originally, had its own shade of meaning. Second, it assumes that the content of Scripture is of such superlative importance for man as to warrant the most **painstaking effort to discover exactly what God seeks to impart through his word**.[1] (Emphasis added.)

Eisegesis, on the other hand, refers to coming to a biblical text with preconceived ideas and making the passage appear to confirm those preconceived ideas. It is similar to what people call "proof-texting," using the Bible to prove whatever notion one has in mind. This is an easy thing for all of us to do. When we have favorite ideas it is extremely easy to find all kinds of passages that seem to fit them. The only way to prevent that from happening is to let the Bible speak for itself. That involves adhering to what the passage is actually saying in reference to the context, the intent and purpose of Scripture, and an accurate understanding of words.

Crabb's treatment of Scripture consistently disregards the rules of proper exegesis. Crabb fails to demonstrate in any of his published books sufficient adherence to the rules of proper Bible interpretation. The overwhelming majority of Scripture passages quoted in his books are interpreted in such a way as to fit his own ideas. They are reduced to biblical paint used to coat psychological views.

Christ and the Cross in Crabb's Integration Model.

Crabb's amalgamation of psychology with the Bible even affects the gospel message. In attempting to integrate the power of the gospel with the powerlessness of psychology, he ends up with a psychological gospel. Even his theologically correct statements feed into his Need Theology. For example he says,

> The gospel really is good news. When the internal troubles of people are exposed, when unsatisfied longings are felt in a way that leads to over-whelming pain, when self-centeredness is recognized in every fiber, then (**and not until then**) can the wonder of the gospel be truly appreciated.[2] (Emphasis added.)

The first sentence is true. However, the next sentence is

totally dependent upon his Need Theology.

Crabb interprets the message of the cross in light of his psychological theory of unconscious needs/longings. In Crabb's system the purpose of the cross is to fill the void of the two unmet needs/longings so that people will not have to look elsewhere to have them filled. He seems to suggest that understanding the two deep needs/longings of the unconscious brings the deepest possible understanding of the gospel. In fact, one gets the distinct impression that unless Christians understand the Hollow Core and recognize their thirst they will limit the power of the gospel in their lives.[3] Hence, the gospel message itself is directly tied to a psychological proposition even though that proposition is not in agreement with Scripture.

This is not a minor matter in Crabb's books, for he regularly promotes the concept that Christ fills the emptiness of the two unmet needs, or that only Christ can relieve the excruciating pain of our two unmet longings. By this mindset, Christology is interpreted directly in light of his theory. Crabb subsumes the person and work of Christ under a psychological theme that has never been shown to be in accord with the Word. The emphasis shifts from God's sovereignty, righteousness and grace to man's supposed need to be worthwhile through security and significance.

One can note the joining together of Crabb's Need Theology and Jesus Christ throughout his books. For instance, the *Marriage Builder* includes numerous phrases linking Christ and Crabb's psychological concept of the unconscious with its two substantive needs.[4] In his other books he relates Christ to his psychological theories of two longings, of thirst in the Hollow Core, and of denial/self-protection. Thus, he interprets the doctrine of Jesus Christ in light of his Need Theology. Yet no biblical data indicates that the Lord desires to have His person and work reinterpreted in this manner. Before linking Jesus to a psychological theory of the unconscious, Crabb must first show firm and convincing biblical proof of its truthfulness. He must demonstrate that the living and written Word stands in full and hearty agreement with his doctrine.

Subsuming Biblical Doctrines under Psychological Theory

Christian doctrines which are taught in Crabb's books all come under the umbrella of his psychological theories. Nothing escapes his explanations about the nature of man and his relationship to God and others. Everything is explained in terms of the unconscious. The problem with trying to employ Crabb's material is that one cannot borrow from his program without affirming that its psychological foundations are true. For instance, if one rejects Crabb's theory of the unconscious, he cannot fully accept the rest of what Crabb proposes since that too rests upon this basic foundation. Thus there can be no such thing as a partial rejection of Crabb's psychological model of counseling. If one rejects the veracity of his borrowed theories on the unconscious, then he must reject the rest of the system.

Every person and every doctrine mentioned are subsumed under Crabb's psychological theories. Not only is the doctrine of man reduced to a psychological construct, but the Father, the Son, and the Spirit are made subservient to his counseling model. By psychologizing doctrines and redefining terms such as *thirst*, Crabb has given us a new way to interpret and understand Scripture. One person observed :

> Since Crabb has redefined all the terms, to really understand the Scripture from his viewpoint you have to read the Bible with his definitions (guidebook) at your side in the same way that *Science and Health with Key to the Scriptures* is the necessary tool to understand the Bible from a Christian Scientist perspective. . . . [5]

For example, the *gospel* becomes the good news that Jesus meets the two needs which motivate all behavior from the unconscious. *Sin* becomes strategies for meeting needs for significance and security. *Confession* is reduced to gaining insight into those wrong strategies. And *full repentance* comes only through getting in touch with the pain of the past. Every personal problem and every case history are interpreted in light of his psychological model of counseling, even though the model cannot be shown to be biblical.

Because Crabb promotes his counseling model as "biblical," because he criticizes aspects of psychology, and because he assures his readers that he biblically screens all material from psychology before he uses it, many **assume** that his model of counseling is biblical. His attempt to use the Bible to screen only the best from psychological counseling systems illustrates the fact that one cannot remain true to the Word of God while mixing it with the unproven, unscientific psychological wisdom of men. He even recognizes inherent dangers in integration and warns:

> In spite of the best of intentions to remain biblical, it is frighteningly easy to admit concepts into our thinking which compromise biblical content. Because psychologists have spent up to nine years studying psychology in school and are pressed to spend much of their reading time in their field in order to stay current, it is inevitable that we develop a certain "mind set." **The all-too-common but disastrous result is that we tend to look at Scripture through the eyeglasses of psychology when the critical need is to look at psychology through the glasses of Scripture.**[6] (Emphasis added.)

Yet, in spite of his own recognition of danger and his sincere effort to remain biblical, Crabb also looks at Scripture "through the eyeglasses of psychology." If he had truly looked "at psychology through the glasses of Scripture," he would have turned away from the myths of psychology and back to the Word of God as the sufficient means of understanding people and helping them change and grow.

PART THREE

COMMENTS

by Hilton P. Terrell

The fondness of Christians for the prolific spawn of popular psychotherapies should be a cause for embarrassment and admonition from Church leaders. Instead, Christian psychiatrists and psychologists who rework alien dogmas into facsimiles of biblical truth are immunized against needed criticism. The vaccine is composed of their undeniable personal zeal for Christ, a generous use of Bible passages (albeit of dubious relevance to their desired points) and the Church's ignorance of the true nature of psychotherapy. A Trojan horse full of dangerous psychofantasies has been professionally prepared for us by Christian psychiatrists and psychologists. The hollow idol has been dragged into the Church by non-professionals, whose eagerness to have the world's psychological teachings accounts for their acceptance more than does the professional's handiwork.

In our early post-Christian culture Christians are increasingly required to stand apart. It is uncomfortable. We want someone to lower our profile by "Christianizing" competing secular doctrines the way Darwinism was managed. We tell ourselves that Christians should use the best knowledge available in Christ's service. Apologists for the syncretism of biblical truth and psychological "truth" often say, "All truth is God's truth." The issue is precisely there. In *Happiness Is a Choice*, Drs. Minirth and Meier presuppose that their discipline offers some truth regarding the hidden, non-material aspect of human nature and that their psychotherapy offers a legitimate means of fleshing out biblical truth for application. It is not so. Whereas observational sciences can build upon biblical presuppositions to our aid, observation offers no brief on issues of the inner man. Only the trappings, the lingo, the aura of science attend psychoanalytic practices. Frequent references to "health" or biochemistry do not verify medical pronouncements on matters of the spirit. At base, such therapies stand upon dogma, not scientific observations, and the dogma is the odious one of Freud and his followers who were some of the century's most anti-Christ teachers.,

No amount of well-intentioned refinement of deadly doctrines will make them clean for use by Christians. Though gems are occasionally found in coal mines, Christians who go fossicking for gems of God's truth in psychoanalytic coal mines will usually emerge empty-handed and filthy. Professional and non-professional Christians of discernment should avoid the dangerous system completely.

PART THREE

FELLOWSHIP WITH FREUD

Psychiatrists Dr. Paul Meier and Dr. Frank Minirth are well-known for their best-selling books, nation-wide radio and television programs, and clinic, which is one of the largest private psychiatric clinics in America. In addition, they have taught for years at Dallas Theological Seminary. They are certainly among the ranks of the most popular psychologizers of Christianity in the contemporary church.

In this critique we examine Meier and Minirth's writing and speaking. Although some of what they have written has been coauthored with others, we do not refer to them, since we are only critiquing Meier and Minirth in this section. We assume that (even if one of the other authors had written what we quote) it represents Meier and Minirth's view or they would have rejected it. Also, we assume that since the radio program features both Meier and Minirth, if one speaks on a subject the other is in agreement unless a contrary opinion is given. Thus, in this critique, when we quote Meier from a radio broadcast, we assume that Minirth is in agreement.

We quote from their earlier books as well as their most recent ones, since we do not see a significant change in their teaching. In fact, they have repeated much of the content of their earlier books in later books, tapes, and recent broadcasts. For example, their very popular book *Happiness is a Choice* was copyrighted in 1978.[1] However, the tape series with the same title, which is based on that book and which contains much of the same teachings, was copyrighted in late 1986.[2] They also promote many of the same themes on their radio and television programs and continue to promote their earlier books.

Because Meier and Minirth have written so many books together and individually and also because of their extensive media work and public speaking, it is not possible to critique all that they have said and written. For example we do not address their unbiblical position on self-esteem, self-image, and self-worth. (We may do that in a future volume.) Much more research and exegesis of Scripture could have been included on each of the topics in this section. However, we wanted to include just enough to build our case. The footnotes provided will give more exhaustive research information for those who are interested.

16

FREUDIAN FOUNDATIONS

Brain Amine Theory.

Depression is one of Meier and Minirth's major writing
and speaking themes. They proclaim a very specific scientific-
sounding view of depression. Their idea of depression has two
parts. The first has to do with brain chemicals and the second
has to do with repression and denial. The scientific basis for
their ideas about brain chemicals is obsolete. And their ideas
about repression and denial are based primarily on unsubstantiated Freudian theory, although they do not identify
them as such.

Meier and Minirth repeatedly claim that holding grudges
causes depletion of certain brain chemicals and therefore
results in depression. The following was stated on their
popular radio program:

> Other than medical causes, holding grudges is the
> only thing I know that causes serotonin and
> norepinephrine to get depleted unless you're in the
> one percent that have manic depressive, bipolar
> disorder or something like that. . . . If your physical
> exam is normal there's a ninety-nine percent
> probability that you're holding grudges.[1]

On another program the following was said in reference to the grudge-chemical-depletion-depression statement: "We have said this a thousand times in the last two or three years on this program."[2] Meier says in their publication, *Christian Psychology for Today* :

> One truth that psychiatric and psychological research has discovered in the last twenty to thirty years is that, when we hold grudges, the chemicals serotonin and norepinephrine are depleted in the brain and this is the cause of clinical depressions. When a person forgives, that helps bring these chemicals back into balance.[3]

That idea is repeated in their books, such as *Happiness is a Choice* [4] and *Introduction to Psychology and Counseling.* [5] In their latest book they say, "When a person holds in her rage, the brain's supply of two key chemical—serotonin and norepinephrine—is depleted, and symptoms of depression result."[6]

In order to evaluate Meier and Minirth's statements about brain chemicals in relation to depression, it is necessary to look briefly at some of the research. There is a unique group of chemicals that occur naturally in the human brain. These chemicals, called *neurotransmitters*, help pass messages along within the brain. In fact there are approximately 100,000 chemical reactions per second occurring in the brain.[7] Their involvement in human behavior has been the focus of much recent research.

One group of these chemicals is known as *monoamine neurotransmitters*. The three key transmitters are called *norepinephrine, serotonin*, and *dopamine*. Some research has indicated that major depression **may** be caused by a deficiency of serotonin and norepinephrine.[8] This is a tentative statement because there is not enough conclusive evidence to support the hypothesis. However, Meier and Minirth take tentative suggestions from research and turn them into authoritative statements. They declare that "the chemicals serotonin and norepinephrine **are** depleted in the brain and this **is** the cause of clinical depressions."[9] (Emphasis added.) But there is a huge difference between *may* (according to research) and *are* and *is* (according to Meier and Minirth). As medical doctor, researcher Nancy Andreasen says in her book *The Broken Brain*, the neurochemical hypothesis is "theory rather than fact."[10] The Mayo Clinic Health Letter also raises this important question: "Are the chemical changes a cause or a symptom of the problem?"[11] In other words, what came first? The depression or the brain neurochemical depletion?

Meier and Minirth treat hypotheses as proven facts, but there is a huge difference between a scientific hypothesis and a proven fact. One is a statement leading to investigation; the other is a conclusion which has been repeatedly proven through scientific rigor. In the area of brain chemicals, we see great caution in the research. Dr. Athanasios Zis and Dr. Frederick Goodwin present a very balanced research-based view of what is known as the "amine hypothesis." (Serotonin and norepinephrine, as well as the other neurotransmitters, are known as *amines*.) Zis and Goodwin review the various research studies having to do with the amine-depletion hypothesis and reveal that earlier formulations of the amine hypothesis are too simplistic to explain all of the research results. They quote recent investigations which indicate that "the initial formulations involving too little or too much neurotransmitters have not been very well substantiated."[12]

Three medical researchers, Joseph Schildkraut, Alan Green, and John Mooney, also contend that accumulating information from research studies requires more than a simple hypothesis, such as the brain amine one. In addition they say:

> At the present time the field seems to be in a new phase characterized by the broad-ranging accumulation of empirical data, much of which cannot be encompassed within any one theoretical framework.[13]

Meier and Minirth connect neurotransmitter depletion and depression in a direct, affirmative, and even dogmatic manner, while researchers (who are actually investigating the data) use caution and question the hypothesis. Meier and

Minirth not only accuse grudges of lowering the brain chemicals and making one depressed; but they also accuse anger and guilt of doing the same.[14]

Whether one accuses grudges or anger or guilt of lowering the neurochemical levels, the problem is still the same. It is a theory, not a fact, and a theory that is too simplistic when viewed through the accumulated research. But above and beyond their over-confidently-stated and over-simplified statement, there is another issue involved that is more serious than the obsolete information they repeatedly recite, and that is their use of Freudian theory. The most serious issue concerning their use of a brain neurotransmitter theory is that it serves as a scientific facade for their Freudian doctrine.

Freudian Theory.

Meier and Minirth reveal their love for Freudian ideas throughout their books. In *Happiness Is a Choice* they present five stages of grief. Stage one is denial, which they say "usually does not last very long."[15] They label the second stage as "Anger Turned Outward" and say:

> The second stage that **all** of us experience whenever we suffer a significant loss is an angry reaction toward someone other than ourselves. We even feel anger toward the person who died, even though he had no choice in the matter. This *always* happens when a young child loses one of his parents due to death or divorce.[16] (Bold emphasis added; italics theirs.)

They also repeat this idea in other sections of the book.[17] They identify stage three as "Anger Turned Inward." They contend that following anger turned outward, "the grieving person begins to feel guilty,"[18] and then, because of the guilt, the person turns his anger inward. They recommend "genuine grief" or weeping (stage four) to bring the person to a resolution (stage five). And finally, they say, "**Every** normal human being, after suffering a significant loss or reversal, goes through all five stages of grief."[19] (Emphasis added.)

Before we address the psychological framework behind their presentation of the five stages of grief, please notice Meier and Minirth's use of the words *every, all,* and *always.* On the one hand, there is no footnote to support the above statements; on the other hand, they do not say that it is just their own personal opinion. Human behavior is so complex and varied that statements about it that employ such superlatives as *every, all,* and *always* are usually wrong. And the above is definitely wrong.

Contained within their theory of grief (sprinkled with superlatives) is their Freudian theory of depression. In fact, the Freudian theory of depression is seen throughout *Happiness Is a Choice* as well as their other writing and speaking. Throughout *Happiness Is a Choice* we read over and over again about anger turned inward, pent-up anger, stuffed anger, and grudges.[20] In its three-part series on depression, the *Harvard Medical School Mental Health Letter* describes the Freudian psychodynamic theory of depression. After explaining the dynamics involved, the authors say that according to Freud "depression is anger turned inward."[21]

The *Letter* mentions that Freud believed that depression is "an expression of unconscious hostility."[22] Meier and Minirth repeatedly use the words *unconscious* and *subconscious* throughout *Happiness Is a Choice* and on their daily broadcast. They say, "Anxiety is the underlying cause of most psychiatric problems," and that anxiety is the result of unconscious conflicts.[23] Elsewhere, Minirth says that "scientific data has shown the importance of the unconscious mind."[24]

Meier and Minirth's idea of anger turned inward from loss of a parent is psychoanalytic. Dr. E. S. Paykel says in the *Handbook of Affective Disorders* :

> Traditional views suggest that depression is particularly induced by certain types of events. Most prominent in the literature is the role of loss. The psychoanalytic concept of loss is a broad one,

including not only deaths and other separations
from key interpersonal figures, but also losses of
limbs and other bodily parts, loss of self-esteem and
of narcissistic self-gratification.[25]

We see then that the loss concept is psychoanalytic and has a
variety of possibilities. The main area of loss seen in the
literature is primarily that of "loss of a parent in childhood,
by death or other causes."[26] After reviewing the various
studies, Paykel concludes, "It is difficult to reach clear conclusions regarding the effects of early loss on depression."[27]
Meier and Minirth obviously reached a clear conclusion, but it
is not supported in the research.

According to Freud, the unconscious is not just a place
where thoughts and emotions which we are not presently
consciously aware of reside. He believed that the unconscious
was the place where repressed ideas exist. He further taught
that the prime source of these repressed ideas is early life
experiences. The *Harvard Medical School Mental Health
Letter* says, "In his famous essay 'Mourning and Melancholia,'
Freud suggested that depression is a kind of unconscious
mourning."[28] According to Freud's theory, the unconscious is
the repository for early life grief. That grief is precipitated by
a loss (such as the loss of a loved one) and involves anger
turned outward toward the loved object. The anger then turns
to guilt and is followed by anger turned inward. Meier and
Minirth say, "Guilt is a common cause of depression because
guilt is a form of pent-up anger. Guilt is anger toward
yourself."[29] In speaking of depression, Freud says:

> So we find the key to the clinical picture: We
> perceive that the self-reproaches are reproaches
> against a loved object which have been shifted away
> from it on to the patient's own ego.[30]

The self-criticism and guilt supposedly demonstrate that depression is anger turned inward.[31] According to Meier and
Minirth, "Somehow, pent-up anger is **always** involved in any
genuine clinical depression."[32] (Emphasis added.)

A central element in Freud's psychoanalytic theory is that of repression. The *Dictionary of Psychology* defines *repression* as "Freud's term for the unconscious tendency to exclude from consciousness unpleasant or painful ideas. It is a concept of major importance in psychoanalysis."[33] In the index for *Happiness Is a Choice* there are numerous entries under *repression of anger.*[34] In going to the many pages listed, one finds, in addition to *repressed anger* and *repressed emotions*, other terms, such as *pent-up anger* and *anger turned inward.* It is difficult to escape the conclusion that all of these terms are related to Freud's theory of repression.

In describing the psychodynamics of depression, Dr. Myer Mendelson speaks of the evolution of the Freudian view of depression. He describes Freud's early theory of depression as follows:

> Freud was never more Victorian than when he confidently expatiated the pathological consequences of masturbation. "I am now asserting that *every* neurasthenia is sexual" (italics in the original) and neurasthenia, he felt, was caused by excessive and abnormal sexual discharge through masturbation, resulting in sexual anaesthesia and weakness. Freud saw "striking connections" between this sexual anaesthesia and melancholia. "Everything that provokes anaesthesia encourages the generation of melancholia . . . melancholia is generated as an intensification of neurasthenia through masturbation."[35]

We mention this first aberrational idea of Freud's as an example of how wrong he could be. Science has made a mockery of both his initially outrageous ideas and his theory of psychic repression.

Dr. Adolf Grunbaum, who is the Andrew Mellon Professor of Philosophy and Research Professor of Psychiatry, refers to Freud's idea of psychic repression as the cornerstone of psychoanalysis in his book *The Foundations of Psychoanalysis.*[36] After carefully analyzing Freud's arguments for his theory of personality and therapy, he finds "the cornerstone theory of repression to be clinically ill-founded."[37]

Dr. David Holmes reviewed a large number of research studies having to do with the possible existence of repression. He concludes that concerning repression "there is no consistent research evidence to support the hypothesis."[38] He further comments on the failure of numerous studies to support the reality of this Freudian notion and then says, "At present we can only conclude that there is no evidence that repression does exist."[39]

According to Freud's theory, a later life incident reactivates or triggers the anger, causing a delayed grief.[40] Meier refers to "current day stress" and says:

> When you're over-reacting to current situations it is because there's something else deep within that's unresolved. It's somewhat similar and it triggers those unresolved anxieties.[41]

Meier and Minirth also refer to this in *Happiness is a Choice* and *Introduction to Psychology and Counseling*.[42] They further say:

> A person who becomes clinically depressed for the first time at age forty in all likelihood had some contributing roots to his depression planted at age four.[43]

Grief stages four and five (genuine grief and resolution) also parallel Freudian theory. Freud believed in what he called "grief work," which would be similar to stage four, which leads to the final stage of resolution.[44] The parallel between the Freudian view of depression and the Meier and Minirth view is undeniable.

Grudges, Forgiveness, and Depression.

Although their dated view of brain chemical depletion

and their love of Freudian theory were transparent to us, two of their comments puzzled us. The first is their implication of grudges and depression and the second is their statement: "When a person forgives, that helps bring these chemicals back into balance."[45] We could find no clue in the research to support either of those ideas. Nor were there any footnotes in Meier and Minirth's books to lead us to research related to those two concepts. The absence of support in the research and in their books raises a question as to the source for those ideas.

The closest we could get to the use of the word *grudges* is in the following statements from *Happiness Is a Choice*:

> In Ephesians 4:26, the apostle Paul tells us that we can get angry without sinning, but that we should never let the sun go down on our wrath (that is, we should not hold grudges past bedtime).[46]

> The root problem in nearly all depressions is pent-up anger either toward ourselves (true or false guilt) or toward others (holding grudges). These grudges are usually *unconscious*. . . . [47] (Emphasis theirs.)

They seem to equate anger toward others with grudges. The dictionary defines *grudge* as "a strong or continued feeling of hostility or ill will against someone" and *anger* as "a feeling of displeasure resulting from injury, mistreatment, opposition, etc., and usually showing itself in a desire to fight back at the supposed cause of this feeling."[48] Although the dictionary indicates that these two words are not equivalents, Meier and Minirth's use of them would still fit their Freudian position.

They do not support the forgiveness statement they make. It is certainly appropriate to encourage biblical forgiveness. However, it is not appropriate to relate forgiveness to neurotransmitter balance unless it is at least suggested in the research. It may be that they are assuming, without proof, that forgiveness leading to reduction in grudges or repressed anger prevents the brain amines from being depleted and thereby relieves or prevents depression. With no footnote or evidence, they declare: "An individual needs to forgive in order to prevent depression."[49] But, one should not state an idea as a fact when it is only an opinion, especially when that idea is in the context of some seemingly scientific material. One might hope for a depression to lift through forgiveness, but in all fairness, it should not be stated as axiomatic without research support.

Meier and Minirth take the Freudian notion of pent-up anger, add a dated, yet-to-be-proven hypothesis about brain amine depletion for scientific proof and a Bible verse on forgiveness, and present it as a scientific, biblical remedy for depression. Freud's unproven personal opinion combined with a dated brain amine theory and baptized with a biblical doctrine makes it look palatable to many Christians. However, adding one unproven psychological opinion of one man (Freud) and one dated scientific theory (amine hypothesis) to one biblical doctrine of forgiveness subtracts from Scripture rather than adding to it.

Biblicizing Freud.

Aside from the use of forgiveness in their depression formula, Meier and Minirth also attempt to biblicize the unconscious by quoting Jeremiah. They say:

> Jeremiah 17:9 is the key to Christian psychiatry: "The heart is deceitful above all things, and desperately wicked, who can know it?" The prophet Jeremiah is saying that we humans cannot fathom or comprehend how desperately sinful and deceitful our heart is—our unconscious motives, conflicts, drives, emotions, and thoughts.[50]

Meier and Minirth simply equate *heart* and *unconscious*, without any exegetical reasoning. They just assume that the two are the same. In fact, they quote *The New International Version* of Proverbs 21:2, "All a man's ways seem right to him, but the LORD weighs the heart," as so-called biblical evidence for unconscious defense mechanisms. This is not only using the Bible to promote Freudian ideas; this is a theology based upon the Freudian unconscious.

We have already discussed, in the section on Dr. Lawrence Crabb's psychology, the problem of equating the heart, as used in the Bible, with the unconscious as described by Freud and others. Therefore we will not repeat it here except to say that there is no biblical support for equating the heart with the unconscious. The word *heart* in the Bible refers to the inner man. And, throughout Scripture the heart is the seat of conscious activity, including attitudes, thoughts, choices, desires, and emotions.

Equating the biblical concept of heart with the psychological concept of the unconscious is an example of attempting to biblicize an unproven psychological notion. Notice the ease with which Meier and Minirth equate the heart with the unconscious. Notice also that they give no exegesis of Scripture to support their glib pronouncement. If indeed "Jeremiah 17:9 is the key to Christian psychiatry," it is very important to properly exegete *heart*.

Simply quoting Psalm 139:23-24 does not give support to the notion of the unconscious either. The point of the Psalm is not that the psalmist is referring to any kind of unconscious reservoir of drives and impulses. He is looking to God to look inside him and measure his attitudes, motives, and thoughts and to lead him into right attitudes, motives, and thoughts so that he might please God. The emphasis is on God's ability to know every person, to change him, and to enable him to walk in righteousness.

Since the heart is not the unconscious, there is no biblical basis for Meier and Minirth's Freudian ideas. Unless they can provide accurate biblical support and substantiated scientific research for their ideas they ought to abandon them, or at least discontinue presenting them as truth. Psychology too easily becomes theology when one comes to Scripture with psychological presuppositions.

Unless a person is familiar with Freudian theory, he could easily suppose that Meier and Minirth developed their ideas about depression from scientific research and the Bible.

That is because they do not mention Freud in their major book about depression, except to express one disagreement with his notion of guilt. Aside from this, we find no other reference or footnote to Freud. This is amazing since their theory is undeniably Freudian. Freud should certainly receive the credit for what Meier and Minirth say about depression. Not to give him credit is an enormous oversight, to say the least. What they do say about Freud is:

> Most of the psychiatrists we have studied under and worked with agreed with the Freudian view that guilt is always an unhealthy thing. We disagree strongly.[51]

It seems that if they state so emphatically on what little they disagree with Freud about, fairness would require that they also emphatically state what they do agree with him about and even express their indebtedness to him. And, as we have shown, there is a great amount of agreement and indebtedness.

The Freudian Unconscious.

Once more the central issue with Meier and Minirth is that their position on depression is Freudian, including the use of the Freudian unconscious. The Freudian unconscious turns out to be a good hiding place for all kinds of unproven ideas and can be used to support almost any idea one wishes. For example, Meier says:

> So obsessives not only get angry more often, but they're aware of anger less often than most people are. Most people when they're angry, they say, "Hey, I'm really feeling angry right now." An obsessive feels angry in his gut and doesn't even know he's feeling angry and says, "I'm just hurt; I'm frustrated." They don't even know that it's anger that they're experiencing. So they stuff their anger

and they hold their anger in. They hold in
unconscious, vengeful motives. Deep down they
want to get even with themselves for not being
perfect enough and with their parents for expecting
them to be and with others, bosses at work, pastors
and other people in their environment. And they
want to get even but they don't even know they
have these unconscious sins. They're not the type
that would consciously, willfully sin very often.
They're very conscientious Christians and yet they
unconsciously , accidentally have a lot of secret sins
that they don't even know they're committing.[52]

Unconscious sins. Imagine that! This is a prime example of
how psychology not only excuses a person from being
responsible for willful rebellion against God; but also of how
psychology becomes theology. If the sins are unconscious, by
definition the person is unaware of what he is doing when he
commits them and remains unaware of their existence. This
implies that a person is acting unconsciously. Then it follows
that if he is not conscious of what he is doing when he is
sinning, he cannot be held responsible for those actions. If he
is not responsible for them, how can God hold him
responsible? And if the sins are unconscious, how can the
person repent and stop sinning without the help of a
psychologist or psychiatrist to delve into the unknown,
unproven unconscious which is supposedly responsible for
sin? The very idea of unconscious sins raises a whole host of
questions that psychiatry cannot answer. However, when one
begins with a psychological commitment (Freudian unconscious) and weds it to a biblical concept (sin), it will result in
a spurious conclusion. The biblical teaching of sin is transmo-
grified by joining it to the fallacious Freudian unconscious.

In commenting on this, Dr. Hilton Terrell quotes from the
Westminster Confession, "Sin is any want of conformity unto,
or transgression of, the law of God." Terrell goes on to say:

Ignorance of God's law is no excuse. We may indeed
be guilty of sins of which we are unaware. . . . The

existence of things of which we are *unaware* in no way substantiates the phantasmagorical construct of an unconscious mind. "Unconscious mind" is definitely an unbiblical black hole which swallows guilt, producing an ever larger gravitational pull on more and more of our formerly culpable behaviors. To admit to "unawareness" of God's standards, however, is biblical. Unawareness is not a "white hole" which flings out excuses for irresponsibility. It is, rather, merely reason for us to study and pray for awareness of His law so that we may be cleansed of evil practices and learn righteous ways, as the Psalmist prays.[53]

What the Research Says.

Researcher Dr. Judy Eidelson says, "The traditional approach to depression has been psychoanalytic [Freudian], which is based on the concept of 'anger turned inward.'" But she says that the research does not support that concept and declares, "There are different causes of anger and different causes of depression; neither necessarily 'causes' the other."[54] In discussing causes of depression, Eidelson says, "There is a tremendous amount of disagreement currently in psychiatry and psychology about the 'real cause' of depression."[55] This was confirmed to us by reading various research articles, professional journals and books on depression. The Mayo Clinic reports, "Depression has no single cause."[56] Eidelson explains:

> Although we know very little about what causes depression, the forms of treatment that practi-tioners offer have typically been determined by what each clinician believes is the cause of the problem.[57]

She then gives examples:

Using a medical analogy, we might conclude that a feverish patient who recovers after taking antibiotics was suffering from a bacterial infection. By the same reasoning, a depression that subsides after exploration of unconscious conflicts might be thought to be *caused* by unconscious forces. A patient who feels better after taking drugs that alter the levels of certain chemicals in the brain might be thought to be suffering from a chemical or hormonal depression. A therapist who sees patients recover after behavior therapy might conclude that depression is caused by insufficient rewards in life. A cognitive therapist who observes patients recovering from depressions after modifying irrational beliefs might conclude that these distorted thoughts *caused* the depression.[58] (Emphasis hers.)

Dr. Nancy Andreasen also points out how presuppositions determine how therapists view depression. She says on the one hand, "Those who operate from a medical model see the disorder [depression] as a disease that is physically based." On the other hand, she says, "Psychiatrists who have a more psychodynamic orientation tend to use the term more broadly, so that some may observe depression in a majority of the patients they see."[59]

Robert Hirschfeld, a psychiatrist in Bethesda Maryland, specializes in researching and treating depression and has written extensively on the subject. He says;

One can only describe many of the causative theories of depression as creative. They have ranged from humoral imbalances to religious possession to sluggish circulation of blood in the brain to psychological predisposition resulting from adverse childhood experience to abnormalities in chemical neurotransmitter function.[60]

Meier and Minirth should heed Hirschfeld's warning. He says:

We must stop thinking causally about depression except when the cause has been scientifically established.[61]

17

FREUDIAN FALLACIES

Ventilating Anger.

Because Meier and Minirth believe that repressed anger causes depression, they give advice for dealing with pent-up anger. Their antidote is ventilation. They recommend ventilating anger,[1] verbally expressing anger,[2] and talking about anger.[3] On one of their programs they say, "Forgive everybody and ventilate your feelings."[4] In *Happiness Is a Choice* they recommend verbalizing anger, ventilating anger, and ventilating feelings.[5] And they contend that the failure to do so can lead to depression.[6] Elsewhere, Minirth says:

> It is important to let the counselee ventilate and talk out his feelings; this helps to deal with the internalized anger that has caused the depression, and helps to bring the anxiety from the subconscious (where it cannot be dealt with appropriately) to the conscious.[7]

In their latest book they repeat the same ventilation advice.[8] Prior to the last twenty-five years, people were encouraged to use self-control. The advice and encouragement was for internalizing rather than externalizing anger. Now, however, everyone seems bent on self-expression rather than self-restraint. And, psychologists have supplied reasons, justifications, and just plain excuses for letting it all hang out. One of the most prevalent reasons they give is that it is good for you. Thus, our society has moved from an era of restraint to one of release under the rubric of health and personal happiness.

Where did Meier and Minirth discover this solution to the problem of so-called pent-up anger? Once again, they are indebted to Freud. Dr. Carol Tavris, who has written a book titled *Anger: The Misunderstood Emotion* refers to this "hydraulic model." She says:

> Borrowing heavily from Hermann von Helmholtz's principle of the conservation of energy, Freud imagined that the libido [sexual energy] was a finite amount of energy that powers our internal battles. If the energy is blocked here, it must find release there.[9]

But on the basis of research, Tavris declares: "Today the hydraulic model of energy has been scientifically discredited."[10] She also says:

> Our contemporary ideas about anger have been fed by the anger industry, psychotherapy, which too often is based on the belief that inside every tranquil soul a furious one is screaming to get out. Psychiatric theory refers to anger as if it were a fixed amount of energy that bounces through the system: if you pinch it in here, it is bound to pop out there—in bad dreams, neurosis, hysterical paralysis, hostile jokes, or stomachaches.[11]

Studies on both adults and children do not support the idea of hold-it-in-and-it-will-hurt-you and let-it-out-and-it-will-help-you. For example, research on heart disease and anger does not suggest suppressed anger as a contributor to heart disease. If anything, the men at highest risk are expressing their anger.[12]

Dr. Leonard Berkowitz, who has extensively studied violence and aggression, disagrees with the idea that it is desirable to let out one's aggressive feelings. Those therapists who encourage such active expressions of negative emotions are referred to as "ventilationists." Their therapies, according to Berkowitz, stimulate and reward aggression and "heighten the likelihood of subsequent violence." He declares:

> The evidence dictates now that it is unintelligent to encourage persons to be aggressive, even if, with the best of intentions, we want to limit such behavior to the confines of psychotherapy.[13]

Tavris says:

> The psychological rationale for ventilating anger does not stand up under experimental scrutiny. The weight of the evidence indicates precisely the opposite: Expressing anger makes you angrier, solidifies an angry attitude, and establishes a hostile habit.[14]

Dr. Redford Williams, Jr., of Duke University Medical Center, has researched the area of anger and its relationship to heart disease. He points out that those individuals who are at high risk for heart disease tend to harbor a cynical mistrust of other people. They get angry often, and most critical is the fact that they openly express their displeasure rather than holding it in. Williams' research indicates that **no evidence** supports the common belief that a person benefits from expressing his anger instead of keeping it to himself.[15]

It would seem that the idea of ventilating anger, as Meier and Minirth suggest, would **not** be a good one. There is an alternative to the current rage to express anger. The alternative is to suppress it, not to repress it, but to suppress it. Tavris says, "There's little evidence that suppressing anger is dangerous to health."[16] The Japanese suppress such feelings as anger. They are aware that such feelings exist. However, they do not act upon them. We know that the Japanese health is far better than the American. Could it be that emotion suppressed is one factor that helps?

Biblical Basis for Verbalizing or Ventilating Anger.

Meier and Minirth continually promote verbalization of anger.[17] In a section on verbalizing anger, they quote Matthew 5:21-24:

> Ye have heard that it was said of them of old time, Thou shalt not kill; and whosoever shall kill shall be in danger of the judgment: But I say unto you, That whosoever is angry with his brother without a cause shall be in danger of the judgment: and whosoever shall say to his brother, Raca, shall be in danger of the council: but whosoever shall say, Thou fool, shall be in danger of hell fire. Therefore if thou bring thy gift to the altar, and there rememberest that thy brother hath ought against thee; Leave there thy gift before the altar, and go thy way; first be reconciled to thy brother, and then come and offer thy gift.

In explaining the section of Scripture, they discuss anger and its resolution. However, they go dramatically beyond the Word when they ask, "Why does Christ want us to verbalize our anger?"[18] Search the section above to see if Christ wants us "to verbalize our anger." The section admonishes us to "be reconciled," **not** "to verbalize our anger." We searched a number of well-known commentaries regarding this section and found none that agree with Meier and Minirth's extrapolation from "be reconciled" to "verbalize our anger." Nor could we find any that asked, "Why does Christ want us to verbalize our anger?"

The exhortation to "be reconciled" means to make amends. How can one verbalize or ventilate anger and at the same time make amends? In addition, the next verse in this section of Scripture says:

> Agree with thine adversary quickly, while thou art in the way with him; lest at any time the adversary deliver thee to the judge, and the judge deliver thee to the officer, and thou be cast into prison.
> (Matthew 5:25.)

How can one agree with an adversary while at the same time verbalizing or ventilating anger?

While the Bible says to speak to brothers concerning offenses and disagreements for the purpose of forgiveness and restoration (such as Matthew 18 and James 5:19-20), the Bible does not direct a person to verbalize or ventilate his anger. The verses in Scripture that have to do with anger point in the opposite direction. The verse Meier and Minirth constantly use to support verbalization and ventilation of anger is "Be angry, and sin not" (Ephesians 4:26). However, the context of that verse puts the emphasis on not sinning, rather than on being angry. What God is saying through Paul is that when the feelings of anger come, do not sin through expressing that anger in sinful ways. While anger may or not be justified, the situation prompting the emotion of anger may also tempt a person to sin or harbor thoughts that continue to fuel the anger. Paul is not directing believers to either verbalize or ventilate. In fact, people usually end up sinning against others through those activities. Thus we have other Bible passages telling us to wait and cool down rather than to ventilate:

> Wherefore, my beloved brethren, let every man be swift to hear, slow to speak, slow to wrath: For the wrath of man worketh not the righteousness of God.
> (James 1:19-20.)

> He that is slow to wrath is of great understanding: but he that is hasty of spirit exalteth folly.
> (Proverbs 14:29.)

A wrathful man stirreth up strife: but he that is slow to anger appeaseth strife. (Proverbs 15:18.)

Be not hasty in thy spirit to be angry: for anger resteth in the bosom of fools. (Ecclesiastes 7:9.)
The discretion of a man deferreth his anger; and it is his glory to pass over a transgression. (Proverbs 19:11.)

Let all bitterness, and wrath, and anger, and clamour, and evil speaking, be put away from you, with all malice: And be ye kind one to another, tenderhearted, forgiving one another, even as God for Christ's sake hath forgiven you. (Ephesians 4:31-32.)

Proverbs 15:1 raises a question as to how one can verbalize or ventilate anger without it sounding like grievous words:

A soft answer turneth away wrath: but grievous words stir up anger. The tongue of the wise useth knowledge aright: but the mouth of fools poureth out foolishness. (Proverbs 15:1-2.)

The Proverbs continually relate expression of anger to foolishness rather than to health and happiness. No matter how quietly one verbalizes or ventilates anger, it is still anger and will be recognized as such.

After exhaustively studying Matthew 5:21-25 (quoted above) from commentaries, we conclude that Christ does **not** want us to verbalize our anger simply to get it out of our system so that we will not be depressed. There may be occasions to express righteous indignation and even holy anger, as did Jesus, Moses and the prophets. However, we see no glorification of Christ in a generalized statement that Christ wants us "to verbalize our anger." Also the research seems to contradict what Meier and Minirth are recommending.

Another example of reading a psychological opinion into

Scripture is found in their book *How to Beat Burnout*, which was written with two other people. In this book, they discuss the prophet Elijah and how he reached a place of "burnout." They describe the symptoms and then what they call "God's Remedy for Burnout." Central to what they regard as "God's remedy" is the following: "God prompted Elijah to ventilate his intense feelings."[19] The section of the Old Testament to which they refer is 1 Kings 19. The particular verses of importance are 4, 10, and 14. We list here only verses 4 and 10 since verse 14 is a virtual repeat of 10.

> But he [Elijah] himself went a day's journey into the wilderness, and came and sat down under a juniper tree: and he requested for himself that he might die; and said, It is enough; now, O Lord, take away my life; for I am not better than my fathers.

> And he [Elijah] said, I have been very jealous for the Lord God of hosts: for the children of Israel have forsaken thy covenant, thrown down thine altars, and slain thy prophets with the sword; and I even I only, am left; and they seek my life, to take it away.

In reading these verses and the entire chapter we find no support for Meier and Minirth's statement that "God **prompted** Elijah to ventilate his intense feelings." (Emphasis added.) In addition we find no such statement in any of the commentaries. The idea that "God prompted Elijah to ventilate his intense feelings" is a conclusion on Meier and Minirth's part that relates more to their psychological bent than to biblical intent.

Brain as a Computer Myth.

The neurotransmitter depletion idea is not the only theory about the brain that Meier and Minirth espouse as fact. Nor is it the only seemingly scientific idea to which they give a Freudian twist. Another example of theory made fact and Freudianized is their brain-as-a-computer statements. They say:

> Our brains are just like computers, *except* for the fact that they have a *will* and computers have no will of their own.[20] (Emphasis theirs.)

They also say, "The brain functions as a computer with memory banks. Stressful memories are recorded and stored and can be replayed today in as vivid a form as when they initially occurred."[21] In their latest book they say, "As we shall see throughout this book, memories are indelibly etched in the biochemical pathways of our brains."[22] They speak of the brain recording memories and/or feelings much like a computer. They also use the computer terminology of programming. And they even erroneously invoke research support. They say, "Our brains are very much like complex computers, as behavioral research is demonstrating today."[23] However, Dr. John Searle, in his Reith Lecture "Minds, Brains, and Science," said:

> Because we don't understand the brain very well we're constantly tempted to use the latest technology as a model for trying to understand it.
>
> In my childhood we were always assured that the brain was a telephone switchboard. ("What else could it be?") And I was amused to see that Sherrington, the great British neuroscientist, thought that the brain worked like a telegraph system. Freud often compared the brain to hydraulic and electro-magnetic systems. Leibniz compared it to a mill, and now, obviously, the metaphor is the digital computer. . . .
>
> The computer is probably no better and no worse as a metaphor for the brain than earlier mechanical metaphors. We learn as much about the brain by saying it's a computer as we do by saying it's a telephone switchboard, a telegraph system, a water pump, or a steam engine.[24]

What Searle is getting at is the fact that the brain is not a mechanical piece of technology.

In his book *Remembering and Forgetting: Inquiries into the Nature of Memory*, Edmund Bolles says, "The human brain is the most complicated structure in the known universe."[25] In introducing his book he says,

> For several thousand years people have believed that remembering retrieves information stored somewhere in the mind. The metaphors of memory have always been metaphors of storage: We preserve images on wax; we carve them in stone; we write memories as with a pencil on paper; we file memories away; we have photographic memories; we retain facts so firmly they seem held in a steel trap. Each of these images proposes a memory warehouse where the past lies preserved like childhood souvenirs in an attic. This book reports a revolution that has overturned that vision of memory. Remembering is a creative, constructive process. There is no storehouse of information about the past anywhere in our brain.[26]

After discussing the scientific basis for memory and how the brain functions, he says:

> The biggest loser in this notion of how memory works is the idea that computer memories and human memories have anything in common.

He goes on to say, "Human and computer memories are as distinct as life and lightning."[27]

Medical doctor and researcher Nancy Andreasen says in her book *The Broken Brain* that "there is no accurate model or metaphor to describe how [the brain] works." She concludes that "the human brain is probably too complex to lend itself to any single metaphor."[28]

The current research demonstrates that computer memory and biological memory are significantly

different. It is puzzling that Meier and Minirth give the impression that they are aware of the complexities of the brain, as indicated in their references to biochemistry, and yet have resorted to the inaccurately simplistic notion of the brain functioning like a computer.

Meier says, "Eighty percent of our thoughts, feelings, and motives are out of our awareness. They're in our subconscious."[29] Let us consider the eighty percent part of what he says. We are just , so to speak, scratching the surface of knowledge about the brain. In the midst of all the theories about the functioning of the brain and discoveries about the brain itself, Meier injects a fixed percentage, which raises many questions. Why eighty percent? Why not seventy percent or seventy-five percent or ninety percent or fifty-five percent?

With the accumulating and yet comparatively sparse knowledge that brain researchers have of the brain, Meier and Minirth's percentage applied to "thoughts, feelings and motives" is most incongruous. What do they even mean? How would one even measure eighty percent of our "thoughts, feelings, and motives"? It is a contrived figure at best, based upon what we are not told.

To then take the eighty-percent figure and say that "eighty percent of our thoughts, feelings, and motives . . . are in our subconscious" stretches the error. Not even by a microscopic postmortem could anyone tell which part of the mind is subconscious, let alone the attribution of "thoughts, feelings and motives" at a fixed percentage level. The idea that "eighty percent of our thoughts, feelings, and motives. . . are in our subconscious" is a fiction made to sound factual and falsely attached to a Freudian fallacy (the unconscious).

Here again the problem is not just theory made to sound as fact, but rather the twisting of the brain-as-computer technology idea to fit Freudian psychology. Meier and Minirth begin by speaking of the brain as a computer and then explain how the personality is formed at a very early age. Following this is the idea of repressed anger, which surfaces later in life when precipitated by an incident which arouses anger. They say, "Thus, *bad programming from the past* can affect our present-day attitudes."[30] (Emphasis theirs.)

In discussing "Causes of Anxiety," they mention early childhood anxiety that is "repressed into the subconscious." They refer to the brain-as-a-computer idea and say, "When an individual encounters current-day situations and experiences that cause anxiety, his anxiety from his early childhood is also aroused."[31] They make such assertions, in spite of the fact that the brain does not operate as a computer any more than it operates like any other piece of technology. But, using the latest metaphor and particularly the latest technological metaphor does not make a psychological opinion scientific.

Biblical Words Psychologized.

Meier and Minirth say:

> Modern psychoanalytic theory derives primarily from the work of Sigmund Freud, a Viennese neurologist (1856-1939). The theory places major emphasis on the role of the unconscious and of dynamic forces in mental functioning.[32]

Three of the "dynamic forces" in the Freudian system are the id, ego, and superego. Meier and Minirth say of these "dynamic forces":

> In the New Testament, the apostle Paul is an example of a wise counselor. One can see in his writings to early Christians some of the ideas later developed by Sigmund Freud. Freud's "id" roughly corresponds to what Christians call the "old nature." Freud's "superego" corresponds roughly to the conscience. The "ego" corresponds to the will.[33]

They then quote the apostle Paul.

> And the very God of peace sanctify you wholly; and I pray God your whole spirit and soul and body be

preserved blameless unto the coming of our Lord Jesus Christ. (1 Thessalonians 5:23.)

Elsewhere Minirth says, "There are indeed, some similarities between the writings of Sigmund Freud and the teachings of Saint Paul, but there is no doubt, that Saint Paul was the greater analyst of the two."[34]

Please note that Meier and Minirth are not criticizing those elements of Freud's system. On the contrary, those concepts are part of Freud's system which are both acceptable and seemingly biblical to them. But for us, the "rough correspondence" between the id-ego-supergo and biblical truth is like comparing a rat to a man. They both have body appendages and parts (legs, eyes, etc.) and they are both mammals. However, there is a gigantic difference between the two!

According to the *Dictionary of Psychology*, the *id* is:

> . . . that division of the mind, or psyche, which is the seat of the libido. From it arise the animalistic, chaotic impulses which demand gratification. The id is not in contact with the outside world, only with the body, and thus centers its demands on the body. It is governed entirely by the pleasure principle and attempts to force the ego, which is governed by the reality principle, to accede to its wishes regardless of the consequences.[35]

Even though the old nature is sinful, it does not correspond to the id. The old nature is the condition of man under the domination of sin. The old nature is of the flesh rather than of the Spirit. The old nature is not some unconscious realm of hidden drives. It is the very nature of the unredeemed person. The Freudian id and the old nature are entirely different. Their source is different. The id is from the unproven, unscientific, worldly wisdom of one man (Freud), and the old nature is the condition of man as a result of the Fall, according to the truth of God.

The id is a contrivance that Freud came up with because

he rejected God's truth about man. An old sinful nature was entirely unacceptable to him. Thus he attributed to man an id to explain something that Freud could not deny though he had rejected the truth behind it. The id, ego, and superego comprise a false theology that does not "roughly correspond" but rather attempts to usurp the truth of God about man. This is a good example of how psychology denies the truth of God and then gives false answers to the same questions.

Further, Minirth's statement "that Saint Paul was the greater analyst of the two,"[36] is absolutely false. Paul was not an analyst by any stretch of the imagination. An analyst, according to the *Dictionary of Psychology* is "a practitioner of psychoanalysis,"[37] in other words, a follower of Freud. If Paul were alive today, he would not follow such a perverted, unproven, unscientific system of psychoanalysis devised by a man who rejected God. Paul had the truth of God; he refused to use the opinions of men. (1 Corinthians 1 and 2.)

Another example of a good biblical word being psychologized is *guilt*. One Bible dictionary says:

> In Romans, Paul points out man's guilt in the light of the law of God, and the fact that Jesus' death on the cross paid for sinful man's guilt and paved the way for man's forgiveness, his justification.[38]

In contrast, Meier and Minirth say:

> Guilt is a common cause of depression because guilt is a form of pent-up anger. Guilt is anger toward yourself.[39]

They go on to mention that there is a difference between true and false guilt. However, this does not rescue the fact that biblical guilt is not psychoanalytical guilt.

The Freudian Demise.

Dr. Frank Sulloway, author of *Freud: Biologist of the Mind*,[40] says:

But, when it comes to many important aspects of human development that are central to Freud's clinical theories, the extraclinical evidence is already in and has failed to confirm Freud's views.[41]

Dr. Hans Eysenck, a professor at the Institute of Psychiatry in London, in an article titled "The Death Knell of Psychoanalysis," says:

Freud is no longer taken seriously in academic circles and . . . factual destruction of his work by experimentalists and clinicians is now pretty complete.[42]

After reviewing the research, Dr. Frederick Crews, a professor at the University of California, says:

It would scarcely be excessive to conclude . . . that psychoanalysis is little more than a collective contagious delusional system.[43]

He also says of Freud:

. . . we can no longer suppose that he discovered a cure for neurosis or unlocked the secrets of the unconscious. So far as we can tell, the only mind he laid bare for us was his own.[44]

Crews declares that **"the entire Freudian tradition**—not just a dubious hypothesis here or an ambiguous concept there—**rests on indefensible grounds.**"[45] (Emphasis added.)

Research psychiatrist E. Fuller Torrey wrote a book titled *The Death of Psychiatry*. In it he says:

Psychiatry, then, is ultimately dying because it can now be seen as nonfunctional. As a medical model approach to problems of human behavior it produces confusions rather than solutions.[46]

In his book *The Myth of Psychotherapy*, Dr. Thomas Szasz says, "Sigmund Freud's claims about psychoanalysis were fundamentally false and fraudulent."[47] Grunbaum states unequivocally of psychoanalysis: "Its scientific foundations are impoverished."[48]

Nobelist Sir Peter Medawar severely criticizes psychoanalysis in his book *Pluto's Republic*. He concludes a special chapter on psychoanalysis by saying:

> But considered in its entirety, psychoanalysis won't do. It is an end-product, moreover, like a dinosaur or a zeppelin; no better theory can ever be erected on its ruins, which will remain for ever one of the saddest and strangest of all landmarks in the history of twentieth-century thought.[49]

Psychiatrist Garth Wood concludes his book *The Myth of Neurosis* with a chapter titled "The Evidence Against Psychoanalysis and Psychotherapy."[50] He says:

> I hope to show here that what has become big business is in fact a fraud. The evidence does not support the claims of psychoanalysis or psychotherapy.[51]

He also says:

> It is this resistance, this unwillingness or disability to allow that what they do is at best worthless and at worst harmful, which is the chief crime of the psychotherapists.[52]

Wood concludes the book by stating:

> In other words, all the inferiority complexes, the dream interpretations, the Oedipal factors, the collective unconscious, the free associations, are

nothing but red herrings. The vital ingredient is after all merely a caring listener who raises hopes and fights demoralization. . . . But if this is all that is needed, what then of professional training in the intricacies of psychotherapy, what of the huge fees, what of the third-party medical insurance reimbursements, of the pretense and the rhetoric, of all the shams and the charlatans, the sound and the fury signifying nothing? If this is all the great "science" of psychotherapy is, then let us sweep it away now and bother ourselves with it no more.[53]

Szasz contends that, "One of Freud's most powerful motives in life was the desire to inflict vengeance on Christianity for its traditional anti-Semitism."[54] How strange that Christians would turn to the unproven and unscientific ideas of a man who was so anti-religion and particularly anti-Christian.

18

PERSONALITY DISORDERS

Personality Disorders and Types.

One of the major frameworks within which Meier and Minirth see individuals is through personality disorders. The ones to which they often refer are the obsessive-compulsive, the hysteric, and the passive-aggressive. They discuss these as well as other personality disorders in their books and magazines and on their broadcasts. The definition they give for *personality disorders* is: "deeply ingrained maladaptive patterns of behavior, often present throughout life."[1]

One edition of their publication *Christian Psychology for Today* was devoted to personality types.[2] In their books and speaking, they sometimes refer to personality *disorders* and at other times to personality *types*. They delineate personality types by using the names and characteristics of personality disorders. Evidently for them personality types are just milder forms of the personality disorders. Their magazine features articles about the obsessive-compulsive, the hysteric, and the passive-aggressive as personality types. Other types identified with names of disorders are mentioned as well. Such labeling assigns a personality disorder category for everyone. No one escapes the diagnostic label.

Their commitment to the personality disorders/types as a major means of diagnosing and explaining human behavior pervades their writing and speaking. For example, reference is often made to personality disorders on their radio broadcasts.[3] In fact, Meier says, "I love to talk about personality types."[4] But where do these personality types or disorders come from? Are they a valid means of understanding or diagnosing people? And most of all, are they biblical?

A personality type is a classification of an individual into one or more contrived categories based upon an estimate of how well the person fits. For example, Carl Jung classified individuals as introverts or extroverts. Generally the introvert is withdrawn while the extrovert is outgoing. Currently there are literally hundreds, if not thousands, of personality types that are used. Many of them are twofold typologies, such as idea people and feeling people, optimists and pessimists, realists and idealists, loners and joiners, and so on. However, there are threefold, fourfold, and multifold types that have been proposed.

Someone has even contrived a personality typology based upon brain neurotransmitters. In this system "novelty seeking," "harm avoidance," and "reward dependence" are associated with the dopamine, serotonin, and norepinephrine neurotransmitters.[5] One person related personality to blood types. For example Type O would be assertive and straight-thinking; Type A would be conscientious and hardworking; and so on.[6] Another individual related nearsightedness and farsightedness to personality.[7] And finally, not to be outdone by the near-far-sightedness theory, there is an auditory personality typology. This one depends upon sound rather than sight, hearing rather than seeing.[8]

What are we to make of the plethora of personality types? As Dr. Ernest Hilgard and his colleagues have said, "Type theories are appealing because they provide a simple way of looking at personality, but, in actuality, personality is far more complex."[9] A little reflection on all this type theory should lead a person to the same conclusion. Human beings are more complex than the twofold, threefold, fourfold, and even sixteenfold systems that men have contrived. Personality varies from person to person and place to place. People act differently from one person to another and they act differently in different circumstances.

The simplicity of any type theory is its underlying appeal. One can learn the types quite quickly and apply them quite readily. Once learned, they take on a life of their own. It is known from research "that people tend to test theories by looking for information to confirm them."[10] Because of this the success and survival rate of typologies is quite high. This is one of the reasons astrology has lasted so long.

DSM.

The desire to label man is not new. Historical records indicate that the ancient Greeks were fascinated with labeling people. The Greek physician and philosopher Hippocrates developed a typology during the fifth century B.C. He proposed that there were four personality types, each related to one of four body fluids, which he identified as blood, yellow bile, black bile, and phlegm. The four personality types connected to the four fluid types were sanguine, choleric, melancholic, and phlegmatic.[11]

From Hippocrates' time to the present, numerous personality types have been proposed. However, the use of personality labels and types became more systematized around the beginning of this century. Emil Kraeplin, a contemporary of Sigmund Freud, developed a classification system that was the beginning of the present system used by psychiatrists.[12] The present system is known as the *Diagnostic and Statistical Manual of Mental Disorders* (DSM). Psychiatrists regard the *Manual* as the bible of mental disorders. In 1952 the *Manual* officially listed sixty different diagnoses, but today it includes over 230.[13]

Someone has suggested that the American Psychiatric Association would like to have one mental disorder label for each American or at least enough labels to cover the total population. Jay Katz, a professor of psychiatry at Yale, admitted under oath in court testimony, "If you look at DSM-III you can classify all of us under one rubric or another of mental disorder."[14] In his book *The Powers of Psychiatry*, Dr. Jonas Robitscher says that "some psychiatrists have raised the estimate of the incidence of neurosis in our society to 95 percent or more."[15]

The recent editions of the DSM list a number of categories of mental disorders, one of which has to do with personality disorders. As mentioned earlier, the three personality disorders that are very popular with Meier and Minirth are the obsessive-compulsive, the hysteric, and the passive-aggressive. The DSM is a major source of Meier and Minirth's system of labeling.[16]

Because of the psychiatric power of labels, this question must be addressed: Are the categories of personality disorders a reliable or valid means of diagnosing and dealing with people? Since these personality disorders are found in the DSM, it would seem reasonable to ask whether the DSM itself is a reliable or valid classification scheme.

The most important criteria for a test or diagnostic system is its validity. To be valid, a test or diagnostic system must be shown to measure what it claims to measure. Another important criteria is that of reliability. A test or diagnostic system is reliable if the person who takes the test has the same, or close to the same, results on two different test administrations or two different diagnoses.

According to Meier and Minirth, "Christians can certainly utilize the DSM system just as they utilize other advances of modern science."[17] However, researchers have much less confidence in the DSM. Dr. Herb Kutchins and Dr. Stuart Kirk discuss the diagnostic reliability of the DSM in *The Harvard Medical School Mental Health Letter*. They say, "The reliability of a classification is defined as the extent to which clinicians working independently can agree on its application to a series of cases."[18] After reviewing the reliability scores for the DSM, they reveal that "the reliability scores for most of its diagnostic categories were not good."[19] In regard to the personality disorders, they say:

> . . . personality disorders as a class were said to have been evaluated more reliably than ever before, but reliability scores for the individual personality disorders were admittedly quite low (unfortunately,

most of them have never been reported).[20]

Kutchins and Kirk's statement about the latest edition of the DSM is that "it is troubling that DSM-III-R was published without any attempt to determine whether reliability had improved."[21] They suggest that the popularity of the DSM is more related to its "third-party reimbursement for psychotherapy through private health insurance, employee assistance programs, and services for the medically indigent."[22] Based upon surveys, they say that "a majority of psychologists and social workers say that they use DSM **only** because it is required."[23] (Emphasis added.)

If the DSM is not a reliable classification scheme, then it is obvious that it cannot be valid. In other words, if it is not consistent, it cannot have integrity. Therefore, the use of it is questionable at the very least. And furthermore, any typology derived from it is doubly invalid.

A further criticism of the DSM is related to the basis for excluding certain behaviors from the list. We are all familiar with the fact that fifty-eight percent of the psychiatrists voted to delete homosexuality from the DSM list. Obviously human behavior is now subject to votes in deciding what behavior is and what behavior is not appropriate to list. We are told that the DSM excludes those conditions which "have strong cultural or subcultural support or sanctions."[24] This criteria was used to keep homosexuality off the list. In addition, the homosexual's evaluation of his own condition became the criteria for a psychiatric label. If a homosexual does not experience conflict he does not get a psychiatric label.

The lopsidedness of the scheme is apparent with caffeinism and alcoholism on the list but not child abuse, which is described as "not attributable to a mental disorder."[25] In discussing a recent revision a new mental "disease" was recommended. The new category was "paraphilic rapism." However, several feminists were so upset by it that they threatened to sue. Thus it was removed. Dr. Thomas Szasz accuses the committee of "acting like legislators introducing new bills in Congress and supporting or withdrawing them, depending on how the political winds blow."

He points out, "This is not the way real doctors act."[26]

To further compound the ludicrousness of the labeling ritual, the *Comprehensive Textbook of Psychiatry* says that its definition of mental disorder "may need to be changed in future years to correspond with the change in the attitude of society and the psychiatric profession toward certain conditions."[27] But, don't look for the DSM labels to disappear. They are not only required for third-party payments, but, according to Szasz, they are necessary to maintain psychiatric power. Szasz points out that psychiatrists and other mental health workers acquire power over others through labels.[28]

The DSM labels, in spite of their unreliability, give much power to those who use them. One does not even need to be a psychiatrist to gain the power. Just using terms, such as *obsessive-compulsive*, *hysteric* and *passive-aggressive*, gives power and authority to the user. Maybe this is why those terms have become so popular among lay people. They get a taste of the same power that professionals have. However, in spite of the power of labels and payments from insurance companies, the DSM has not established its reliability, let alone its validity. Moreover, no one has ever shown that labels help understand or change anyone. Therefore the use of the DSM labels as disorders or types by Meier and Minirth or anyone else should be ignored.

In comparing diagnostic accuracy between professionals and lay persons, Dr. David Faust and Dr. Jay Ziskin say, "Studies show that professional clinicians do not in fact make more accurate clinical judgments than lay persons." As an example from research, they state, "Professional psychologists performed no better than office secretaries." Probably most damning to the professional is their statement: "Virtually every available study shows that amount of clinical training and experience are unrelated to judgmental accuracy."[29]

The final and most important question is this: Are the personality disorders or types biblical? It is obvious that these labels are not biblical terms. They are nowhere referred to in Scripture. Nor are they inferred in any way in the Bible. They are purely and simply psychological terms that have been imposed upon individuals and even imposed upon the saints in the Bible.[30] Meier and Minirth speak of Peter and say he was "primarily hysteric" and that God "made him into a more godly hysteric." They say that Paul "had probably an obsessive-compulsive disorder" and that God "made him into a healthier obsessive-compulsive Christian." And, "Timothy was a little bit passive-aggressive."[31]

Again these are not biblical terms, but rather psychological terms imposed upon these men of God. Meier and Minirth even admit the source of the labels to be the DSM.[32] Thus we see a use of DSM personality disorders relabeled as personality types and inaccurately and unfairly applied to Christian leaders in the early church.

Personality Types.

In *Happiness Is a Choice*, Meier and Minirth discuss the hysteric personality type in one chapter and the obsessive-compulsive in another. Throughout both chapters the so-called unconscious dynamics are discussed. As we said earlier, little is mentioned of Freud in that book. However, the Freudian theory of depression is the same as discussed earlier. Only now it is used in reference to the hysteric and obsessive-compulsive personality types. Meier and Minirth say:

> The dynamics of obsessive-compulsive (perfectionist) and hysterical (emotional) individuals have been outlined in the preceding chapters. All of these factors predispose a person to depression.[33]

The elements in depression of repression, pent-up anger, guilt and the unconscious are all repeated and related to the hysteric and the obsessive-compulsive personality types. Meier and Minirth also seem to enjoy discussing these on their broadcasts. The following comments, which reveal the way they relate depression to personality types, were made on one of their programs:

> So obsessives not only get angry more often, but

> they're aware of anger less often than most people are. . . . An obsessive feels angry in his gut and doesn't know he's feeling angry. . . . They don't even know its anger that they're experiencing. So they stuff their anger and they hold their anger in. They hold in unconscious vengeful motives.[34]

In order to understand the "unconscious dynamics" of an "hysterical adult female,"[35] Meier and Minirth discuss an hypothetical case. They say:

> She felt, moreover, that special privileges were accorded to men; she reacted with **competitive envy** and developed what is known as **castration behavior**.[36] (Emphasis ours.)

Note the words *competitive envy* and *castration behavior*. The origin for those ideas is Freud's theory of the Oedipus complex. For more details, we suggest reading the section on psychoanalysis in our book *The Psychological Way/The Spiritual Way*.[37]

Freud believed that during what he called the phallic stage of development every boy desires to kill his father and have sexual intercourse with his mother; and every girl desires to kill her mother and have sexual intercourse with her father. Freud attributed those desires to all children between the ages of three and six. Meier and Minirth's version of the Oedipus complex is very interesting. They say:

> During these years most children go through a stage of thinking that somehow they will grow up but the parent of the opposite sex will stay the same age. The idea that they will somehow replace the parent of the same sex by marrying the parent of the opposite sex is known as the Oedipus complex. Although the oedipal stage of development was greatly over-emphasized by Sigmund Freud and others, it has been documented repeatedly as occurring in probably a majority of children.[38]

They obviously believe in the Oedipus complex, but their version of it in contrast to Freud's is amusing.

For Freud, the male sex organ is prized. His sexual system establishes genital superiority for men and genital inferiority for women. Freud said that during a girl's early life development she discovers that the boy has a protruding sex organ while she has only a cavity. According to Freud's theory, the girl holds her mother responsible for her condition, which causes hostility. She thus transfers her love from her mother to her father because he has the valued organ, which she wants to share with him in sex.

In Freud's wild scheme, the girl fears that her mother will injure her genital organ because of her sexual desire directed at her father. But, the girl senses that she has already been castrated and thus ends up desiring the male sex organ. The female castration anxiety results in what Freud called "penis envy." According to Freud, every woman is merely a mutilated male who resolves her "castration anxiety" by wishing for the male sex organ. Thus, the source of Meier and Minirth's diagnosis of "competitive envy" and "castration behavior" is Freud.

In both their books and popular radio programs, Meier and Minirth repeatedly emphasize the importance of early childhood. For example, they say that "the roots of the hysterical personality reach back into childhood."[39] In a special note they say:

> Over one-third of the hysterical females we have treated have had sexual intercourse with their fathers or stepfathers. Usually they claim they were raped by their fathers, denying the obvious fact that they also had a strong hand in the situation by seducing them, either consciously or unconsciously [of course, this in no way diminishes the responsibility of the father or stepfather].[40] (Brackets theirs.)

Our focus here is their statement about the little girls "denying the obvious fact that they also had a strong hand in the situation by seducing them [fathers and stepfathers], either consciously or unconsciously." Since the "hysterical personality" is the terminology used, we consulted the DSM-III-R to see what is said, since Meier and Minirth admit that is their source for personality disorders. The DSM-III-R has a section on the "Histrionic Personality Disorder," which is the equivalent of the "Hysterical Personality."[41] This personality disorder is described as "inappropriately sexually seductive in appearance or behavior."[42] However, nowhere in the DSM-III-R description is there any hint of a little girl seducing her father. It is a cataclysmic leap from describing a woman as being "inappropriately sexually seductive" and saying that women who were sexually abused as young children were seducing their fathers or stepfathers. The source for that repugnant idea is obviously the Freudian Oedipal theory.

One wonders how many women have been betrayed by psychotherapists who have perpetrated this unproven Freudian theory. And then as a result, how many have been submerged in years of analysis to get over the false condemnation of having seductively encouraged the rape? And if a woman becomes outraged at this preposterous indictment, the Freudian-trained therapist accuses her of "castration anxiety," "hysteria," and "penis envy." Although children sing-song the rhyme, "Sticks and stones will break my bones, but words will never hurt me," the word power of psychiatrists has done more damage than breaking bones, which heal more rapidly than unfounded condemnation from trusted authority figures.

While both the male and female hysterics are listed as seducers, Meier and Minirth usually refer to the female. They say, "Many a female hysteric seeks a good man to bring down sexually, so she can tell everyone that he seduced her, thus ruining his reputation."[43] The emphasis on the female seducer fits the Freudian scheme better than that of the male seducer. Dr. Theodore Lidz, a professor of psychiatry whose work is quoted and recommended by Meier and Minirth, says: "Freud recognized that the girl does not usually repress her desire for the father so completely as the boy represses his erotic feelings for his mother."[44] He also says that "the girl is likely to retain fantasies of becoming the father's sexual choice over the mother."[45] This female-hysteric-sex-seducer emphasis amplifies the obviousness of their Freudian Oedipal ideas.

Medical historian E. M. Thornton describes the case of Dora in *The Freudian Fallacy*. Dora was an eighteen-year-old girl who came to Freud with a variety of physical problems, "which he believed to be hysterical."[46] Freud found that a close friend of Dora's father had tried to seduce her and that her father was probably having an affair with this man's wife. After much analysis, Freud believed that Dora's "hysteria" was related to an unconscious desire to have sex with her father. Rather than medically treating Dora's symptoms, he saw them as symbols of deep conflicts in her unconscious. In reviewing Dora's symptoms and even her dreams, Thornton came to the conclusion that Dora actually suffered from epilepsy. However, the perverted mind of Freud interpreted Dora's dreams and concluded that Dora masturbated (though she denied it) and secretly desired to engage in sex with her father. Freud said of Dora:

> The circumstantial evidence for her having masturbated in childhood seems to be complete and without a flaw. In the present case I had begun to suspect the masturbation when she had told me of her cousin's gastric pains, and had then identified herself with her by complaining for days together of similar painful sensations. It is well-known that gastric pains occur especially often in those who masturbate.[47]

Many now believe that Freud's theories of infantile sexuality were the result of his own distorted childhood and his own emotional problems. In a letter to a friend (October, 1897), Freud confessed his own emotional involvement with his mother and his nursemaid in a series of flowing memories and dreams. He said, "I have found, in my own case too, falling in love with the mother and jealousy of the father, and

I now regard it as a universal event of early childhood."[48]
Freud's theory was a projection of his own sexual aberrations
upon all mankind.

For Freud, the dream was the "royal road to the
unconscious." Like Freud, Meier and Minirth also exhibit
great confidence in dreams symbolically revealing unconscious conflicts and desires. They say:

> In our dreams **all** of our current unconscious con-
> flicts are symbolized. **Every dream** has symbolic
> meaning. Dreams are usually **unconscious wish-
> fulfillments** in symbolic form.[49] (Emphasis added.)

If one were to ask a Freudian to use one word to describe his
theory of dreams it would be *wish-fulfillment*. A symbolic
approach to dream content and an emphasis on unconscious
conflicts and desires are central to Freud's thinking. As
Hilgard et al say, "Freud felt that dreams were influenced by
wishes . . . in the dream, forbidden desires were acted out in
disguised form."[50] Freud could imagine all sorts of meanings
from dreams because of the highly subjective nature of dream
interpretation. He gave himself great latitude by insisting
that dreams had both *manifest* and *latent* content. The
manifest content consisted of psychoanalytic images, but the
latent content was the hidden meaning of those images.[51]
Therefore he could create nearly any imaginative meaning,
and for Freud the meanings were highly sexual to fit into his
Oedipal theory.

Meier and Minirth say: "It has been theorized, probably
correctly, that in dreams one symbolically reduces emotional
tensions, satisfying unconscious conflicts."[52] Conversely, Dr.
J. Allan Hobson, who is professor of psychiatry at Harvard
Medical School, says:

> . . . dreaming is not a response to stress but the
> subjective awareness of a regular and almost
> entirely automatic brain process. That is one of
> many reasons for doubting Freud's theory that
> dreams are caused by the upsurge of unconscious

wishes.[53]

According to Hobson, the research suggests that dreams have "causes and functions that are strictly and deeply biological."[54] He asks the question, "But why are dreams so intensely visual, and why do they produce a sense of constant movement?" He then relates the Freudian explanation:

> Freud thought that the source of these pseudosensory stimuli was a mechanism of disguise and censorship by which "dream work" transformed an unacceptable or latent unconscious wish into images and linked them in a story.[55]

However, Hobson gives a different explanation:

> . . . dream stories and symbols are not a disguise, and the interposition of "defensive modifications" to disguise their origins, as postulated by Freud, is unnecessary. The nonsensical features of dreams are not a psychological defense, any more than the disoriented ramblings of a patient with Alzheimer's disease are.[56]

Meier and Minirth mention EEG patterns and REM sleep (both scientific) but add the Freudian notions of the unconscious and wish-fulfillment (both unscientific). They add:

> God somehow uses dreams each night to help us resolve unconscious conflicts, or at least to dissipate some of the emotional pain tied to unconscious conflicts.[57]

Unfortunately God has been dragged into supporting Freudian theory, completely without scientific or biblical justification. There is no biblical basis for the unconscious or the Freudian notion of dreams as wish-fulfillment. Adding nonscience to science does not add up to science. And adding to this nonscientific conclusion that "God somehow uses dreams to resolve unconscious conflicts" does not add up to biblical truth.

Battered Women.

Meier and Minirth's view of battered women fits into their Freudian ideas of women's so-called unconscious sexual desires. This is important to look at because of the vast numbers of battered women and the research dealing with this serious problem.

Any attempt to estimate the prevalence of battered women in our society is difficult simply because many abused women refrain from reporting the assault. Dr. Lenore Walker, who has studied the phenomenon of battered women says, "It is estimated that only one out of ten battered women has reported her abuse to the police."[58] In addition she says, "From my research, I estimate that 50% of women will be battered by men who love them at sometime in their lives."[59] Regardless of the figures used, the prevalence is higher than one might think. Therefore it is a serious problem needing careful appraisal and sensitive remedies.

Dr. Irene Frieze and Dr. Maureen McHugh say:

> As we reviewed the research dealing with the reactions of *all* types of victims, we found a general tendency for victims to blame themselves. It is not uncommon, for example, for victims of unprovoked sexual assaults or of battering to take personal responsibility for the crime.[60] (Emphasis theirs.)

Frieze and McHugh say that even when battered women try very hard to avoid the violence, "these efforts are rarely successful in stopping the battering." In fact, they say that "it is more common for the violence to become more severe and frequent over time."[61]

What do Meier and Minirth have to say about this serious and extensive problem? They say:

> On the other hand, whenever a battered wife comes

seeking advice and consolation because her husband beats her up twice a week, **our usual response is, "Oh, really? How do you get him to do that?"** In all the scores of cases of this nature that we have analyzed in depth, there was only one case in which the battered wife was not provoking (usually unconsciously) her explosive husband until he reached the boiling point (of course, this does not diminish the husband's responsibility). After a beating, the husband usually feels very guilty and spoils his wife for several weeks. In the meantime, she is getting from people around her the sympathy which she craves, and **she is satisfying her unconscious needs to be a masochist**.[62] (Emphasis added.)

When they say that "she is satisfying her unconscious needs to be a masochist," they are demonstrating their attachment to Freudian ideas. Freud's ideas about sex also related masochism to sexual energy. The *Dictionary of Psychology* defines *masochism* as "a sexual disorder in which the individual derives satisfaction from the infliction of pain upon himself."[63]

It is difficult to tell how much Meier and Minirth relate masochism to sex, but it was Freud who coined the term *masochism*. Coupled with the fact that Meier and Minirth refer to "her **unconscious** needs to be a masochist," it becomes transparent that they are using Freudian theory again. (Emphasis added.) Dr. Irene Gilman explains the traditional psychoanalytic view of masochism in women:

> According to the classic Freudian view of the neurotic female masochist, the woman unconsciously engages in self-destructive behavior because of a failure to resolve her oedipal complex. The theory asserts that the girl develops competitive strivings in relation to her mother, but avoids this competition because of a fear of losing her mother's love. Thus, the young female needs to show her mother that she is not interested in the male (father). The

> unconscious provocation of male aggression by the
> young female serves both to assure her mother that
> the daughter has forsaken her wish to possess the
> male and to reduce the guilt feelings she had
> originally developed surrounding her oedipal wish.[64]

It seems to us that placing the blame on a woman for being battered because of "her unconscious needs to be a masochist," encourages self-blame for a woman and diminishes full responsibility on the part of the man.

Walker says, "Numerous theories of causation of spouse abuse have been proposed in the literature." She continues, "These theoretical orientations develop different approaches that often reflect the biases and training of their proponents."[65] Meier and Minirth's approach to the problem of the battered woman obviously reflects their Freudian bias and their psychoanalytic training. And that Freudian bias is a matter of personal opinion, not fact. One might even add that it is poor personal opinion which is becoming poorer as the contemporary attacks on Freudian theory increase.

It is extremely unfortunate when women who are battered reach out for help and are slapped down again, not with clubs and fists, but with a defunct theory that causes further degradation. It is surprising that women have not risen up in outrage over Meier and Minirth's reference to a battered woman's "unconscious needs to be a masochist." Perhaps Meier and Minirth would say that this very fact proves that women are masochists after all. There is certainly a great incongruity between what Meier and Minirth say about battered women and what recent researchers have said about this tragedy.

The typical psychoanalysts' views will present women as masochists because they see women through Freudian theory. Individuals such as Dr. Paula Caplan,[66] Dr. Richard Gelles,[67] Dr. Harriet Lerner,[68] Dr. Jeffrey Masson,[69] Dr. Florence Rush,[70] Dr. Murray Straus,[71] and many others would see it otherwise. Dr. Paula Caplan begins her book *The Myth of Women's Masochism* by saying:

When the man in my life hurts my feelings, or when I've put on weight, or when I'm frustrated about my children or my job, people sometimes ask me, "Why do you *do* this to yourself?," suggesting that I set out to put myself in unhappy situations. Such words are the most common expression of the myth of women's masochism, the myth that is responsible for profound and far-reaching emotional and physical harm to women and girls.[72] (Emphasis hers.)

She quotes the *Random House Dictionary of the English Language* as defining *masochism* as:

. . . the condition in which sexual gratification depends on suffering, physical pain, and humiliation . . . gratification gained from pain, deprivation, etc., inflicted or imposed on oneself, either as a result of one's own actions or the actions of others, esp. the tendency to seek this form of gratification.

She then says:

Often women's behavior is used as evidence of our innate masochism, our sickness, while men's similar behavior is used as evidence that they are real men and good providers.[73]

She also says:

When a theory causes serious harm, it is time to ask, "Are there other, reasonable ways to explain the behavior in question?" As we shall see, the behavior in women that has been called masochistic actually has other explanations, all of which reflect a healthier view of women, justify optimism about women's potential for happiness, and point the way to changes that will improve women's lives. The belief that females seek out pain and suffering, that we have an innate *need* for misery, poisons every aspect of women's lives.[74] (Emphasis hers.)

We give this as one of numerous examples to show that others view the idea of women's masochism as a monstrous myth rather than a reality and that others read and conclude from the research that the idea of women's masochism is a tragic farce rather than a truthful fact.

Why didn't Meier and Minirth develop a theory of the battered woman based upon (to reverse their theory) "**he** is satisfying his unconscious needs to be a sadist"? It would be just as simple to develop and support such a theory. However, it would not fit into what one well-known social psychologist calls "a typically misogynist psychoanalytic point of view."[75]

Dr. Theodor Reik says in his book *Masochism in Modern Man* that "masochism as a perversion is rare among women."[76] He also says that "the suffering of pain, being beaten or tied up, disgrace and humiliations, do not belong to the sexual aims of the normal woman."[77] We think Reik accurately portrays women when he says, "A woman does not want to be punished, abused, tormented or flagellated, but wants to be loved."[78] It is because of love, not masochism, that women endure suffering.

In her writing about "Women as Victims of Violence," Caplan says:

> One more form of violence against women that warrants examination is father-daughter incest. The traditional clinical interpretation involved blaming both of the females involved: the mother and the daughter.[79]

She goes on to say:

> It has not been unusual to hear clinicians claim that the daughters who are victims of incest with their fathers, in addition to being "seductive," were also masochistic and thereby precipitated the incest. Understanding how these families really operate,

however, makes it clear that for many of these girls, putting up with the pain and shame of their fathers' sexual assaults on them is less fearful than taking the risk of destroying their families altogether.[80]

The recent book *Intimate Violence*, by Dr. Richard Gelles and Dr. Murray Straus, "represents the results of more than fifteen years of research and study of family violence."[81] In this book Gelles and Straus explode the myth that "Battered Women Like Being Hit." They say, "Perhaps the cruelest of all the myths surrounding family violence is the one that claims that battered women like being hit."[82] In summarizing the research, they say:

> The research on the factors that determine whether women stay or leave violent relationships effectively explodes the myth that wives who remain with violent men are masochistic. The weight of the collected evidence points more to social factors entrapping women in violent marriages.[83]

At one time Sigmund Freud presented a paper which dealt with the sexual seduction of children. In fact at that time he believed that sexual seduction of children was the source of adult mental problems. However, Freud abandoned his seduction theory in favor of his theory of childhood sexual fantasy, which became the cornerstone of psychoanalysis. Dr. Jeffrey Masson, former archives director for the Sigmund Freud Archives wrote a book titled *The Assault on Truth: Freud's Suppression of the Seduction Theory*. In it he documents Freud's evolution from the seduction theory to the childhood sexual fantasy theory. Masson says:

> The issue that most intrigued me was Freud's abandonment of the so-called seduction theory. As a psychoanalytic student I had been taught that Freud initially believed the women who came to him for therapy when they said they had been sexually abused as children, often by members of their own

family. Then he made what he thought to be a momentous "discovery": What he heard from these women were not genuine memories; they were, Freud said, fabricated stories, or made up fictions.[84]

Masson also says:

> We know that [Freud's] insistence (in 1896) that women were telling him the truth about having been sexually abused in early childhood did not last, and that, by 1903, he had retracted this statement.[85]

In discussing Freud's Dora case (which we mentioned earlier), Masson says:

> The Dora case stands at the threshold of Freud's change of theories (the abandonment of the seduction hypothesis). It is his declarations to his colleagues, as if he were telling them: "Look, Dora was suffering from internal fantasies, not external injuries. The source of her illness was internal, not external; fantasy, not reality; libido, not rape."[86]

Masson contends that Freud suppressed his seduction theory for intellectually dishonest reasons. Masson wrote to Anna Freud and expressed to her that Freud was wrong to abandon the seduction hypothesis. In response she replied:

> Keeping up the seduction theory would mean to abandon the Oedipus complex, and with it the whole importance of fantasy life, conscious or unconscious fantasy. In fact, I think there would have been no psychoanalysis afterwards.[87]

The idea of women's masochism is built on a Freudian myth. And the fake Freudian myth is dishonestly built on a real Greek myth, the myth of Oedipus. Szasz says, "By dint of his rhetorical skill and persistence, Freud managed to transform an Athenian myth into an Austrian madness." He calls this "Freud's transformation of the saga of Oedipus from legend to lunacy."[88] But the real losers in all of this psychology-based-on-mythology are the women who are found guilty of masochism without a jury, a trial, or even a hearing.

Scripture and the Hysteric.

Meier and Minirth also see Scripture through the lens of Freudian theory. They say, "The Book of Proverbs describes hysterical females and males better than any book on psychiatry we have read."[89] They cite Proverbs 5:3-21 and 6:12-14 for proof. Those verses do describe sinful, wicked people. However, the Bible does not refer to them as being hysterical. It is Meier and Minirth who say the Bible "describes hysterical females and males better than any book on psychiatry we have read."[90] The point is that Meier and Minirth are taking a DSM personality disorder called *histrionic* (*hysteric*) and making it sound as if the Bible supports the DSM categories of personality disorders.

The diagnostic criteria for the Histrionic Personality disorder (hysteria) from the DSM are:

> A pervasive pattern of excessive emotionality and attention-seeking, beginning by early adulthood and present in a variety of contexts, as indicated by at least four of the following:
>
> (1) constantly seeks or demands reassurance, approval, or praise
> (2) is inappropriately sexually seductive in appearance or behavior
> (3) is overly concerned with physical attractiveness
> (4) expresses emotion with inappropriate exaggeration, e.g., embraced casual acquaintances with excessive ardor, uncontrollable sobbing on minor sentimental occasions, has temper tantrums
> (5) is uncomfortable in situations in which he or

she is not the center of attention

(6)   displays rapidly shifting and shallow expression of emotions

(7)   is self-centered, actions being directed toward obtaining immediate satisfaction; has no tolerance for the frustration of delayed gratification

(8)   has a style of speech that is excessively impressionistic and lacking in detail, e.g., when asked to describe mother, can be no more specific, than "She was a beautiful person."[91]

Does that sound like Proverbs 5:3-21 and Proverbs 6:12-14 that Meier and Minirth cite as evidence? We have already established the lack of appropriate reliability for the DSM. But even though it is not reliable, try to apply "at least four" of the DSM criteria to either of the two sections of Proverbs. We tried and could not do it. It may be that a reader or two will have more imagination than we do but we doubt it.

Another problem with their conclusion is that under ordinary circumstances, diagnosis is highly unreliable. Even after seeing an individual for hours and interacting with him or her, there are still enormous errors in diagnosis that occur. How can Meier and Minirth come to the hysterical conclusions they have come to with each short section of Proverbs?

Research.

Finally, some of Meier and Minirth's applications of the personality disorders are quite questionable from a research point of view. For example, Meier says:

They're [the obsessive-compulsives] conscientious about time. They show up exactly on time. They go to a class or anything— they're right on the button. They're not more than a minute early or a minute late. . . . The hysteric likes to show up early because he or she likes to get extra attention. The passive-aggressive shows up late and the sociopath skips and doesn't show up at all.[92]

Where is the research to support such a relationship? Whether we view these as DSM personality disorders, which lack validity, or merely personality types, which lack complexity, there is a faulty basis in either case from which to research the relationships mentioned.

Meier relates personality disorders to certain problems such as panic attacks. He says, "Most of the people who get panic attacks are obsessive-compulsive."[93] To begin with, there is a variety of panic attacks. If he is suggesting that most of those who have panic attacks, regardless of type, experience obsessive-compulsive thoughts, he needs to provide research support. He also suggests that agoraphobics have "obsessive-compulsive thinking."[94] In checking a standard text on agoraphobia, we find that obsessional thoughts are **sometimes**, **not always** involved.[95] But Meier says that most are obsessive-compulsive. It is more complex than that, because though **some** may have obsessional thoughts **sometimes**, this is a far cry from **most**. One should exercise care in extrapolating information contained in the research.

One wonders why patients, or even non-patients, believe in such unsubstantiated personality terms. Faust and Ziskin say:

> . . . research shows that individuals believe in overly general personality descriptions of dubious validity, a form of suggestibility that provides a livelihood for astrologers and palm readers and misguides clinicians.[96]

Psychiatrist Lee Coleman in his book *The Reign of Error* says, "The mode of labeling in psychiatry becomes a serious concern only when the labels are treated as scientific." The theme of Coleman's book is psychiatric authority. He says, "Lack of scientific tools should be reason enough to rescind psychiatry's immense legal authority."[97] He also says:

I have testified in over one hundred and thirty criminal and civil trials around the country, countering the authority of psychiatrists or psychologists hired by one side or the other. In each case I try to educate the judge or jury about why **the opinions produced by these professionals have no scientific merit.**[98]

19

DEFENSE MECHANISMS

Meier and Minirth speak and write about defense mechanisms. In their book *Introduction to Psychology and Counseling*, they say:

> Psychological defense mechanisms are defined by Charles Morris as "the ways people react to frustration and conflict by deceiving themselves about their real desires and goals in an effort to maintain their self-esteem and avoid anxiety."[1]

In addition they say:

> The most basic defense mechanism is repression, which Theodore Lidz defines as "the barring or banishment of memories, perceptions or feelings that would arouse the forbidden." Lidz adds that "in order to prevent rearousal of some childhood sexual experiences or the discomfort of remembering sexual desires for a parent, the entire period of early childhood may be repressed."[2]

Meier and Minirth refer to these defense mechanisms as being "unconscious" and "self-deceiving."[3]

There is a great deal of similarity between what Meier and Minirth say about defense mechanisms and the Freudian theory of defense mechanisms. The strong influence of Freud can be seen by comparing the above quotes with the following description of Freud's theory. Further comparison can be made by reading Dr. Theodore Lidz's book, which Meier and Minirth quote and recommend. In that book one can see the application of Freudian psychology to its fullest.

Freudian Theory of Defense Mechanisms.

Freud names three parts of the personality as the *id*, *ego*, and *superego*.[4] Dr. Ernest Hilgard et al say:

> Freud believed that the conflict between id im-
> pulses—primarily sexual and aggressive instincts—
> and the restraining influences of the ego and
> superego constitutes the motivating source of much
> behavior.[5]

According to Freud's system, anxiety is the result of restraining the "sexual and aggressive instincts." Freud called the method of reducing the resultant anxiety *repression*. According to Hilgard et al, "Those methods of anxiety reduction, called *defense mechanisms*, are means of defending oneself against painful anxiety."[6] They additionally state:

> Freud used the term *defense mechanisms* to refer to
> unconscious processes that defend a person against
> anxiety by distorting reality in some way. . . they all
> involve an element of self-deception.[7]

In describing *repression*, Hilgard et al say:

> In repression, impulses or memories that are too
> threatening are excluded from action or conscious
> awareness. Freud believed that repression of certain
> childhood impulses is universal. For example, he
> maintained that all young boys have feelings of

sexual attraction toward the mother and feelings of
rivalry and hostility toward the father (the Oedipus
complex); these impulses are repressed to avoid the
painful consequences of acting on them. In later
life, feelings and memories that would cause anxiety
because they are inconsistent with one's self-concept
may be repressed. Feelings of hostility toward a
loved one and experiences of failure may be
banished from memory.[8]

One last part of the picture of defense mechanisms has to
do with the individual's desire "to maintain self-esteem."
Freud believed that "self-reproaches" diminish self-esteem.
He said, "So we find the key to the clinical picture: we
perceive that the self-reproaches are reproaches against a
loved object which have been shifted away from it on to the
patient's own ego."[9] Thus, he proposed that people develop
defense mechanisms as a means of self-deception "to maintain self-esteem."

From the evidence cited above, it is obvious that the
theory of defense mechanisms used by Meier and Minirth is
Freudian. They devote a full chapter to defense mechanisms
in *Introduction to Psychology and Counseling*, but they do not
even mention Freud in the chapter.[10] It seems strange that
they would not give credit where credit is due. In addition,
they refer to defense mechanisms in other books and on their
radio program.[11] They use Freudian defense mechanisms to
describe, understand and explain behavior.

In *Happiness Is a Choice*, they make a number of
statements using one or more of the defense mechanisms,
which they simply call *defenses*. For instance they say, "There
are several major defenses that John P. Workaholic uses to
deceive himself."[12] In reference to an hysteric they say, "Her
chief defense is denial."[13] In discussing "Personality Traits of
the Depressed," they list: "Defenses of denial, displacement,
introjection, projection, and somatization."[14]

There is no question that the use of the Freudian defense
mechanisms with his underlying theory of repression is a
major means by which Meier and Minirth view people. As we

said earlier, Dr. Adolf Grunbaum, in his book *The Foundations of Psychoanalysis*, discusses Freud's psychoanalytic theory and "finds the cornerstone theory of repression to be clinically ill-founded."[15] Grunbaum faults Freud's theory for failing the test of science. Individuals should be aware that the defense mechanisms are both unscientific and unsubstantiated.

Rather than revealing the Freudian source of defense mechanisms, Meier and Minirth attempt to validate them with the Bible and their own personal opinion. On one of Meier and Minirth's broadcasts it was said, "There are forty defense mechanisms that we know about and nearly all of these are described in Scripture as well as in the psychiatric research."[16] In their book *Introduction to Psychology and Counseling*, they list the forty "Unconscious Defense Mechanisms Frequently Seen in Counseling."[17] In certain cases they offer a biblical source. In our earlier discussion of Meier and Minirth's attempt to use Psalm 139:23-24, Proverbs 21:2, and Jeremiah 17:9 to support their belief that the Bible refers to the unconscious, we showed that the Scriptures which they cite as evidence do **not** support the unconscious as being equivalent to the biblical word *heart*. Also, there is no biblical support anywhere for the Freudian unconscious. And since the defense mechanisms depend upon the Freudian concept of the unconscious, there can be no support for them in Scripture either. However, we will nonetheless deal with two of their examples.

Projection.

Meier and Minirth describe the use of the unconscious defense mechanism of projection this way:

> An individual who is so afraid of his own feelings, perhaps anger or lust, projects (like a slide projector on a screen) his feelings onto the other persons in his environment, thus convincing himself that others are the possessors of those feelings and are

plotting to use those feelings against him.[18]

They give one example from the Old Testament for delusional projection and three references from the New Testament for primary projection. They indicate that primary projection is: "The same as delusional projection but not of such psychotic proportions."[19]

Meier and Minirth use 1 Samuel 18:31 as an example of delusional projection. They say, "King Saul . . . developed the delusion that David was plotting to kill him. He projected his own wishes to murder David onto David."[20] A careful reading of this section of Samuel will reveal no verse that indicates that Saul's reason to chase David was because of a delusion that David was out to kill him. He was wildly jealous of David. And he feared that David would someday replace him as king, because the Lord had removed His favor from Saul. Nor was Saul repressing his desire to kill David (which would be necessary to fill the requirements for a diagnosis of projection). If we read carefully the events in 1 Samuel 18-31 we see instances in which Saul attempted to kill David, but none in which David attempted to kill Saul and none in which Saul indicated that he even thought (consciously or unconsciously) that David was attempting to kill him.

The Old Testament tells us a lot about Saul. Read once more the description of delusional projection (quoted above). Then read 1 Samuel to see if any of those characteristics apply to Saul. A sincere and honest effort to apply those characteristics will show that there is nothing obvious in 1 Samuel to support the description of delusional projection, only guess work. Nothing in 1 Samuel reveals what was going on at any unconscious level with Saul. Nor does it even come close to hinting that projection could be going on.

Rather than unconscious projection, there was conscious response to what was being said. After David cut off a part of Saul's robe when he could have killed him (1 Samuel 24:4), David called out to him and said, "Wherefore hearest thou men's words saying, Behold David seeketh thy hurt?" (1 Samuel 24:9.) This was not any kind of unconscious delusion. This was the talk of Saul's men. There was nothing repressed into any so-called unconscious about Saul's intent to kill David, and there was every reason to fear retaliation. Furthermore, in checking the original for the word *hurt*, we find nothing to indicate death, only harm.

Now let's examine the three references in the New Testament that Meier and Minirth use as examples of primary projection.[21] The first is Matthew 7:1-5, particularly verses 3-5.

> Judge not, that ye be not judged. For with what judgment ye judge, ye shall be judged: and with what measure ye mete, it shall be measured to you again. And why beholdest thou the mote that is in thy brother's eye, but considerest not the beam that is in thine own eye? Or how wilt thou say to thy brother, Let me pull out the mote out of thine eye; and, behold, a beam is in thine own eye? Thou hypocrite, first cast out the beam out of thine own eye; and then shalt thou see clearly to cast out the mote out of thy brother's eye. (Matthew 7:1-5.)

There is no hint in these verses that anything is involved at the unconscious level. The plain meaning of the passage is that one needs to be careful in judging others. On the one hand, we know that believers are not to refrain from all judging (7:6, 16), since Christians need to judge words and actions of themselves and others (1 Cor. 5:3-5, 12, 13). But on the other hand, one must not have a censorious spirit.[22]

There is nothing in this section to infer that the beam is unconscious. Nor is there any hint that the mote is necessarily directly related to the beam. They could be a "reflection" of one another. However, they need not be. The one with the beam could be stealing large amounts of money from his work while at the same time judging another person for missing church. Reading this entire section of Matthew 7:1-12 we find that the main subject is neither the beam or the mote. It has nothing to do with unconscious projection. The main subject is found in Matthew 7:1: "Judge not that ye be not judged."

They also use Romans 2:1-3 in attempting to make the Bible appear to support their Freudian theory of projection.[23]

> Therefore thou art inexcusable, O man, whosoever thou art that judgest: for wherein thou judgest another, thou condemnest thyself; for thou that judgest doest the same things. But we are sure that the judgment of God is according to truth against them which commit such things. And thinkest thou this, O man, that judgest them which do such things, and doest the same, that thou shalt escape the judgment of God? (Romans 2:1-3.)

This is not a statement about unconscious projection, but rather an admonition concerning judging others for those sins listed in Romans 1:18-32. This is indicated by the word *therefore* at the beginning of the passage and words such as *the same things* and *such things.* Romans 1:18-32 includes both obvious gross sins and sins that people may overlook in themselves. Thus a person may be tempted to judge another person for fornication while himself being disobedient to parents or unmerciful. The warning is that we will be judged by the same standards we apply in judging others. Paul was leading up to the fact that "all have sinned, and come short of the glory of God" (Romans 3:23). Rather than this passage supporting the idea of the Freudian unconscious defense mechanism of projection, Paul was speaking of the human tendency to criticize and condemn others while minimizing personal sin and excusing oneself. This is the bias of the sinful self nature which must be brought to the cross of Christ.

The third scriptural reference they use in trying to prove Freud's theory of the unconscious defense mechanism of projection is James 1:13-17.[24]

> Let no man say when he is tempted, I am tempted of God: for God cannot be tempted with evil, neither tempteth he any man: But every man is tempted, when he is drawn away of his own lust, and enticed.

> Then when lust hath conceived, it bringeth forth
> sin: and sin, when it is finished, bringeth forth
> death. Do not err, my beloved brethren. Every good
> gift and every perfect gift is from above, and cometh
> down from the Father of lights, with whom is no
> variableness, neither shadow of turning. (James
> 1:13-17.)

None of the above passage supports faith in Freudian unconscious drives or defenses. Though a person may blame God or
others for tempting him to sin, that blame is a conscious
activity. James appeals to conscious volition. He does not
explain or excuse behavior by saying that people sin because
of unconscious drives or defenses. They sin because of their
own lust, which is a self-pleasing activity of the flesh. Freud
created the idea of defense mechanisms to explain the
condition of man because he refused to believe what the Bible
says about God's sovereignty, His law, the sinful condition of
man, and God's provision for salvation and sanctification
through Jesus. To attempt to equate the two will always
diminish a person's view of the Bible.

Denial.

Another unconscious defense mechanism which Meier
and Minirth attempt to support with the Bible is denial.
They describe *denial* this way:

> Thoughts, feelings, wishes, or motives are denied
> access to consciousness. It is the primary defense
> mechanism of histrionic personalities, who deny
> their own sinful thoughts, feelings, wishes, or
> motives even when they become obvious to those
> around them.[25]

They use Proverbs 14:15 and Proverbs 16:2 in their attempt
to biblicize the unconscious defense mechanism of denial.
Proverbs 14:15 says, "The simple believeth every word: but
the prudent man looketh well to his going." This proverb can

be taken at face value without trying to read in any kind of hidden meaning such as unconscious denial. There are people who simply believe what they read or hear, because they fail to evaluate what has been written or said. Someone who is wise, on the other hand, will want to find out if something is true before he will believe it. In fact, one of the serious problems in the church today is that of believing what teachers and preachers say without prayerfully looking into the Word of God to see if what is said is true.

The other proverb they cite is Proverbs 16:2. "All the ways of a man are clean in his own eyes; but the LORD weigheth the spirits." The unconscious defense mechanism of denial is not simply not facing the truth about oneself. Simply ignoring our own faults or excusing our sin or even forgetting about it does not make it an unconscious denial. The human tendency according to the Bible is for people to see themselves in a biased manner. Furthermore, one cannot equate the spirit of man with the unconscious. Paul made this clear when he wrote: "For what man knoweth the things of a man, save the spirit of man which is in him? Even so the things of God knoweth no man, but the Spirit of God." (1 Corinthians 2:11.) This verse compares the relationship of the spirit of man with man himself and the relationship of the Spirit of God with God Himself. Therefore, if one were to equate the spirit of man with the unconscious, one would also be saying that the Spirit of God is His unconscious, which would be perfectly ridiculous.

Conclusion.

Through their writing and speaking, Meier and Minirth attribute great importance to the Freudian theory of defense mechanisms. In addition, they unsuccessfully attempt to support those unproven, unscientific Freudian inventions with Scripture. The defense mechanisms are without Scriptural or scientific support.

20

PERSONALITY FORMATION

Early Life Determinants.

It is often difficult to find out whether or not Meier and Minirth have research backing for their statements. They sometimes expound their ideas completely without footnotes to indicate the source of their statements. For example they say:

> In exploring possible causes for the counselee's present difficulties, the counselor must consider early childhood. If the parents were absent and the child's dependency needs were not met, then the individual is more prone to depression or sociopathy, depending on how he handles the conflict. If the parents would not allow the child to be an individual but were symbiotic with him, then he is more prone to schizophrenia. If the parents were harsh, then the individual may be a guilty compulsive, a critical paranoid or an acting-out sociopath, depending on how he handles the conflict. If the parents were seductive or rewarded overly dramatic behavior, then the individual is more likely to have hysterical problems. If both parents were in constant conflict, the individual is more prone to deep-seated insecurity and anxiety or neurosis.

Thus man can have unresolved conflicts from childhood, and those conflicts can intensify his present problems. Man does have conflicts. Man is psychological.[1]

The above statement represents their Freudian views and their own personal opinions, which would be seriously questioned by practitioners who are not of their personal and psychoanalytic persuasion.

In *Happiness Is a Choice*, Meier and Minirth say:

In his earlier book (*Christian Child-Rearing and Personality Development*, Baker Book House 1977), Dr. Meier summarized several hundred research articles on personality development to demonstrate that approximately 85 percent of our adult behavior patterns are firmly entrenched by our sixth birthday.[2]

In their book *Introduction to Psychology and Counseling* they say, "By the time children are old enough to go to school, most of their character structure has already been established."[3]

Their statement "approximately 85 percent of our adult behavior patterns are firmly entrenched by our sixth birthday" has been a repeated theme in their writing and speaking. They claim that it is demonstrated by "several hundred research articles." But, their "85 percent" litany is actually related to their Freudian orientation. The research demonstrates change rather than the almost deterministic theory that Meier and Minirth claim. Before turning to the research we will first discuss the Freudian theory that underlies their "85 percent" statement. We begin by discussing the theory of infantile sexuality.

According to Freud's theory of infantile sexuality, the first five or six years of life pretty much determine the rest of a person's life. Freud believed that every human being is confronted with four stages of development: oral, anal, phallic, and genital. He taught that the four stages of infantile sexuality follow one another and occur at certain ages in normal development. The oral stage is from birth to eighteen months; the anal stage is from eighteen months to three years; the phallic stage is from three to five or six years; and the genital stage continues through puberty. All four stages have to do with sexuality, and Freud related adult characteristics and mental-emotional disorders to childhood experiences within the various stages. He believed that if a person failed to pass successfully through each stage or experienced a trauma during one of the stages, there would be inexplicable damage to his psyche.

Freud's theory of infantile sexuality is also related to his theory of psychic determinism, both of which are within his theory of the unconscious. According to his theory of psychic determinism, each person is what he is because of the effect of the unconscious upon his entire life. Freud believed that "we are 'lived' by unknown and uncontrollable forces."[4] He theorized that these forces are in the unconscious and control each person in the sense that they influence all that the person does. Thus, he saw people as puppets of the unknown and unseen unconscious, shaped by these forces during the first six years of life.

Freud contended that as each child passes from one psychosexual stage of development to another, his psyche is shaped by the people in his environment and especially by his parents. Psychic determinism establishes a process of blame that begins in the unconscious and ends with the parents. Freud removed a person's responsibility for his behavior by teaching that everyone has been predetermined by his unconscious, which was shaped by the treatment given him by his parents during the first few years of his life.

Freudian theory is known as psychic determinism. However, we have never seen a percentage of fixedness placed upon the time from birth to age six. Even Freud believed in some hope for the individual. In one of the Meier and Minirth programs, the following was said:

> When we get the responsibility from God to raise our children, He gives us most of that responsibility from their birth til they're six years old. After that

we're just modifying the other 15 percent.[5]

In *Happiness Is a Choice*, they speak of parents bringing in a teenager to them and they say, "All we can do is help the parents to find some ways to modify the 5 or 10 percent of that teen-ager's personality that isn't already formed."[6] Elsewhere Meier says that "what you feed into your child's brain during those first six years is what's going to come out of his brain the next seventy years."[7] While the figure they use of a child after age six is 15 percent, apparently for a teen-ager it drops to 5 or 10 percent. Meier and Minirth say 85 percent by age six and no one knows what percentage Freud would have used. But, the fact that Meier and Minirth give such a high percentage of determinism (85 percent by age six, with only 5 to 10 percent possibility for change during the teen-age years) demonstrates that this too is of Freudian origin.

A little thoughtful reflection on the setting of percentages would lead one to conclude that such use of numbers is not a good idea. Think about what "adult behavior patterns" are. How would one be able to sum up and put down all that constitutes "adult behavior patterns"? Also, a child before age six would be cognitively and behaviorally incapable of performing some "adult behavior patterns." In addition to this, some "adult behavior patterns" would be illegal for a child under six. Even if one could develop this impossible list of behavior patterns, what does it mean when they apply an 85 percent figure? Even if we used an adjective, such as *gregarious*, what is 85 percent of it by age six? While those who create and use such percentages may gain a sense of security, there are too many variables which are beyond investigation to make any sense of such numbers.

Besides a misleading sense of authority in the use of such percentages, there is research which refutes the idea of such iron-clad determinism. In his book *The Psychological Society*, Martin Gross summarizes the work of Dr. Stella Chess, professor of child psychiatry at New York University Medical Center. Gross says that a potent conclusion that evolves from Chess's work is that "*the present psychiatric theory that the first six years of life are the exclusive molders of personality is patently false.*"[8] (Emphasis his.)

Social psychologist Dr. Carol Tavris discusses the idea of constancy versus change in an article titled "The Freedom to Change." She discusses Freud and his psychoanalytic therapy and says:

> Now the irony is that many people who are not fooled by astrology for one minute subject themselves to therapy for years, where the same errors of logic and interpretation often occur. . . . Astrologists think we are determined at birth (or even conception) by our stars; psychoanalysts think we are determined within a few years of birth by our parents (and our anatomy).[9]

Tavris goes on to discuss the research that opposes the idea of Freudian determinism. And, the very same research would stand in opposition to Meier and Minirth's eighty-five percent notion. She cites the work of Dr. Orville Brim of the Foundation for Child Development in New York and says, "Most of Brim's career has been devoted to charting the course of child development and its relation to adult personality." She declares that Brim is convinced that "far from being programmed permanently by the age of 5, people are virtually reprogrammable throughout life." She quotes him as saying, "Hundreds and hundreds of studies now document the fact of personality change in adulthood."[10] She also quotes Brim as saying:

> Social scientists are unable to predict adult personality from childhood or even from adolescence in any important way. We can't blame the methods anymore, and we can't say that people who don't fit the predictions are deviant, unhealthy or strange. They are the norm.[11]

In addition to Brim, Tavris discusses the work of Dr. Jerome Kagan, a professor at Harvard University. Kagan, together with Howard Moss, wrote a classic book in the field titled *Birth to Maturity: A Study in Psychological Development*, which agrees with Meier and Minirth's views. However, after further research, Kagan made an 180-degree turn in his ideas of child development. After taking a second look at *Birth to Maturity*, Kagan and Moss "could find little relation between psychological qualities during the first three years of life . . . and any aspect of behavior in adulthood."[12] According to Tavris, "Kagan now believes that few of a baby's attributes last indefinitely, unless the environment perpetuates them."[13]

Brim and Kagan later wrote a book together titled *Constancy and Change in Human Development*. They say:

> The view that emerges from this work is that humans have a capacity for change across the entire life span. . . there are important growth changes across the life span from birth to death, many individuals retain a great capacity for change, and the consequences of the events of early childhood are continually transformed by later experiences, making the course of human development more open than many have believed.[14]

While writing this section we wrote to Brim and Kagan and asked their current response concerning Meier and Minirth's eighty-five-percent idea. Brim responded:

> The statement that you report about adult personality [Meier and Minirth's eighty-five percent] cannot be substantiated by any scientific research at all. In fact, what evidence there is, and there is a good amount of it, shows a continuing change in personality over the lifespan.[15]

Kagan's reply also indicated disagreement with Meier and Minirth's eighty-five-percent determinism.[16]

We also wrote to Dr. Bernard Rimland, who is the director of the Institute for Child Behavior Research in San

Diego. In his reply about Meier and Minirth's eighty-five percent notion, he says the idea "that the personality is the product of the individual psychosocial experiences . . . is totally unsupportable by any scientific evidence that I've been able to find."[17]

Our greatest concern with the eighty-five-percent statement is that it once more expresses Meier and Minirth's strong Freudian ideology. In addition, their use of a number such as eighty-five percent, even though it is preceded by the word *approximately*, makes no sense when considering the complexity and incomparability of "adult behavior patterns" and those of pre-six-year-olds. And finally, based upon the research, we doubt that Meier, Minirth, or anyone else could "demonstrate that approximately 85 percent of our adult behavior patterns are firmly entrenched by our sixth birthday."[18]

Child Care.

Meier and Minirth's Freudian views on early life development can also be seen in what they say about child care. On one of the broadcasts a woman asked about going back to college. She said she was married and had a six-month-old. Meier's response was:

> If you went back to college right now that baby would be neglected. If that baby got taken care of by somebody else full-time the baby would be neglected. If you put that baby in day care forty hours a week that baby would be neglected and according to psychiatric research he would have permanent psychological damage.[19]

A similar statement was said on another broadcast.[20] And, in *Introduction to Psychology and Counseling*, Meier and Minirth refer to the possibility of "some degree of permanent emotional and intellectual damage."[21]

Before we discuss the statement above and the problems

associated with it, we want to make it clear that we believe that the best possible arrangement for an infant is to have a mother home with the child at least during the first two or three years of life. We believe this for biblical reasons which we shall not discuss here. In addition, we think that the research in the area of child development on the one hand and the availability of quality substitute care on the other hand would support our position, not only because it is clear that good quality, affordable child care is difficult to obtain, but also because there is a need to develop a healthy parent-infant relationship. Our strong counsel to mothers is to be home to care for their own babies during the early years of life.

There is also another factor to consider before responding to Meier's remark about full-time child care leading to "neglect" and "permanent psychological damage." Yale University's Edward Ziegler says, "In modern America mothers work for the same reasons fathers do—economic necessity."[22] Most of the jobs today do not provide enough pay to support a family.[23] It is not surprising then that men with low salaries are much more likely to have a working wife.[24] *Insight* magazine reports that "68 percent of two-parent households now have both parents on the job and in most cases need two incomes to make ends meet."[25]

Economist Eli Ginzberg calls the movement of women into the labor force "the single most outstanding phenomenon of the twentieth century."[26] While the day-care call-in question was from a woman planning to attend college, Meier's answer would apply to all women who would resort to full-time child care. It would apply to intact families with both working parents, as we just discussed, but it would also apply to single-parent (almost all of whom are women) families with infants.

Probably at least equal to the movement of women into the labor force as "the single most outstanding phenomenon of the twentieth century" is the growth in female-headed single-parent families. This explosion in numbers of female-headed single-parent families in the last fifty years has left large numbers of women with no choice about work or child care. According to *The Parental Leave Crisis*, "Experts predict that one out of every three families, possibly even one out of two will be headed by a single parent in 1990."[27]

With almost half of the marriages ending in divorce, numerous women do not receive enough child and spousal support to run a household. If two-parent families often cannot make it on one salary and need to make ends meet, it is even more true that single-parent families with infants are even more affected. The answer Meier gave literally affects millions and primarily it affects women who, even in intact families, bear the responsibility for child care.

The first problem we have with Meier's answer to the child care question is its categorical sound. It has an ecclesiastical, pontifical ring to it. He says that the "baby **would be neglected** and according to psychological research he would have **permanent psychological damage**."[28] (Emphasis ours.) In cases such as this, where there are numerous variables involved, an extreme categorical statement such as the one just quoted is bound to be wrong even though it may have some truth behind it. Day care is a dramatic fact in America. To imply that "neglect" and "permanent psychological damage" are certainties is a gross over-interpretation of the research.

Child care is not a simple matter. It involves many factors, including the type of day-care environment, the care giver(s), the child, the child's home environment, involvement of the parents, involvement of relatives and friends, just to name a few. The day-care could be given in the child's home by a relative, friend or other person or in the home of a relative, friend or other person. Or it could be family day-care in the home of a woman who may or may not care for her own children at the same time; parent co-ops; day-care centers and so on. Another variable is the age at which a child receives child care (infant or older child) and the length of time. If we enumerated all of the factors, sub-factors and related factors, it would be clear how enormously complex the situation is. It is a complexity undeserving of a glib, extreme categorical statement such as the one quoted.

There are some studies which indicate good results for

children in day care. Fredelle Maynard, in summarizing the
effects of day care on intellectual development says, "In
general, studies agree that day care of average quality has no
apparent ill effects on children's intellectual development."[29]
Researcher Jerome Kagan compared day care and home care
of children during the first three years of life. He concluded
that "day care and home-reared children developed similarly
with respect to cognitive, social and affective qualities during
the first three years of life." However, he qualified his
statement with certain provisions, such as a good ratio of
children to adults, nurturant and capable care givers, similar
values between family and care giver, and other conditions of
good child care.[30]

Dr. Harold Hodgkinson, former director of the National
Institute of Education says:

> Some of the most encouraging data in education
> come from studies done on Head Start by the
> High/Scope Educational Research Foundation of
> Ypsilanti, Michigan. Basically, the High/Scope
> research shows that every dollar spent on Head
> Start saves us $7 - in prisons that don't have to be
> built, in detoxification centers that don't have to be
> run, and in psychiatrists and counselors who don't
> have to be hired. Children who have been through a
> good Head Start program go to college far more
> often than those in the control groups. They get jobs
> more often, and they end up in jail less often.[31]

These brief examples should refute Meier's categorical
statement about the effect of day care, dogmatic accusation of
"neglect," and prediction of "permanent psychological
damage."

There are studies that support both sides of the child
care issue. Dr. Thomas Gamble and Dr. Edward Zigler
discuss "Effects of Infant Day Care: Another Look at the
Evidence." They say:

> Some prominent workers have highlighted the

potentially damaging effects of infant day care, while equally prominent workers have asserted that such care is essentially benign.[32]

The prestigious Merrill-Palmer Institute concludes: "According to our preliminary findings, day care is not necessarily harmful. But some day care programs might produce harm."[33] We think that a fair reading of the research will give a variety of results, but none so drastic as the categorical "neglect. . . permanent psychological damage" remarks expressed on Meier and Minirth's radio program.

Meier and Minirth's position on child care is based on their Freudian bias rather than on any solid research. Dr. Louise Bates Ames, co-director of the famed Gesell Institute of Child Development, says:

> I am afraid that the whole environmental school which has dominated child care in America in the last twenty-five years has made parents too anxious, too insecure and too guilty. . . . They created the attitude that the child's psyche is fragile, which it is not. Most of the damage we have seen in child rearing is the fault of the Freudian and neo-Freudians who have dominated the field. They have frightened parents and kept the truth from them. **In child care I would say that Freudianism has been the psychological crime of the century.**[34] (Emphasis added.)

Martin Gross says, "This environmental system is based on the psychodynamic theory in which the unknowing parent forces the child to repress its unconscious drives."[35] Gross concludes, *"Modern research indicates that the skeptics have been right all along: that environmental or Freudian theory is false."*[36] (Emphasis his.) Gross also says:

> In the raising of children the parent is generally the most knowledgeable guide. This reassuring philoso-phy is repeated by no less an expert than Dr. Spock

himself. "The more people have studied different methods of bringing up children the more they have come to the conclusion that what good mothers and fathers instinctively feel like doing for their babies is usually best after all."[37]

Gross concludes by saying:

The modern sin of parenting has not been one of psychological ignorance. It has been quite the opposite. By absorbing the half-truths, shibboleths and outright fallacies of the Psychological Society, the parents of the last thirty-five years have unfortunately put into massive practice an idea whose time should not have come.[38]

A writer to the editor in *Science News* says:

Our culture is obsessed with redefining all natural developmental processes, making them look like a laundry list of pathologies. Normal childhood fears have become phobias, temper outbursts are now oppositional disorders, worry is overanxious disorder and wanting one's mama around is separation anxiety.

Next come the statistical horror stories, followed by political sanction of more "health" care and treatment facilities.[39]

In conclusion, because Meier and Minirth's categorical, extreme statement of "neglect" and "permanent psychological damage" primarily affects millions of women, we see that Freudian psychology with its anti-woman and particularly anti-mother bias is the basis for their advice, rather than psychiatric research, as they maintain. A number of examples of the Freudian anti-parents and particularly anti-mother bias come through in *Happiness Is a Choice*. Meier and Minirth speak of "A child with a cold, rejecting mother and a passive or absent father."[40] The strong mother/weak father theme is found in their other books as well.[41] In one case they refer to "his mother's rejection."[42]

In another case they refer to the mother who "was extremely Victorian" and the maternal grandmother as the "boss of the family" and "very domineering."[43] In Appendix 2 of *Happiness Is a Choice*, the mother or step-mother is implicated in the problem in all eleven cases.[44] Those cases are repeated in *Introduction to Psychology and Counseling*.[45] In their book *Taking Control* , a comment is made by Meier in a section on teenage addicts. One element in Meier's formula of what he calls "cure" is to get the addict away from his mother.[46]

Almost like a refrain from the Garden of Eden, Freudian theory from the beginning pinned blame on women and has been particularly hard on mothers. Meier and Minirth's type of advice only amplifies the difficulties women encounter in the world and fuels the fires of feminism.

Sexual Identity.

Meier and Minirth's Freudian bias also affects their notions about the development of sexual identity. From their Freudian vantage point, they promote a theory of how boys become homosexuals and girls become lesbians. Their formula, reduced to its simplest, is that homosexuality is the result of an absent father and lesbianism is the result of significant separation from the mother, and all, of course, by Freudian necessity, before the the age of six.

On a radio program a male caller asked about a situation with his ex-wife. He had joint custody of his three-year-old boy. The boy spends one week with his father and three with his mother and grandmother. After further description of the situation, the following response was given about the boy:

> . . . his sexual identity will be formed from about two to six. And so if he lived with her [the boy's mother] and with the grandma and not with you he would almost for sure become a homosexual. And he

> needs to spend a lot of time with you so he'll identify
> with you, pattern his life after you, walk like you,
> talk like you and act like you. . . . I wish he was with
> you three weeks and with her for a weekend a
> month or something.[47]

The daddy, absent through work or divorce during the first
six years of life, leading to homosexuality or homosexual
tendencies, is a repeated theme on their broadcasts.[48] In
Introduction to Psychology and Counseling they put part of
the blame on the mother. They say:

> An early history characterized by an overprotective
> mother who forms an alliance with her son against
> a   hostile   detached   father   does   make   male
> individuals   more   prone   to   temptation   in   the
> homosexual direction.[49]

In *Happiness Is a Choice*   they   describe   a   hypothetical
obsessive-compulsive who is at work and absent from the
household. They say:

> He is the medical researcher who spends seven days
> (and nights) a week in the lab in order to save
> mankind from various diseases while his wife
> suffers   from   loneliness   and   his   sons   become
> homosexuals and eventually commit suicide.[50]

This is another reiteration of their formula of a father's
absence leading to his son becoming a homosexual and
another pathetic pontifical pathological prediction (suicide),
unsubstantiated by the research.

While   for   Meier   and   Minirth   the   basic   factor   in
homosexuality is an absent father, their basic factor in
lesbianism is an absent mother, or a hostile one. In reference
to the absent mother factor, these words were said on one of
their broadcasts:

> Now a little girl needs to spend a lot of time with

her mom so that she won't develop a mother vacuum later on in life. And if she doesn't spend very much time with her mother, if she's stuck in day care centers and things of that nature and doesn't spend very much time with her mother or with significant females to identify with, stable significant females, I mean the same person throughout many years, not multiple care, then she will develop lesbian tendencies when she gets older. Satan will use that mother vacuum to tempt her to meet it in a sexual way with other females.[51]

In reference to a hostile mother they say: "Females with a hostile, competitive mother and a passive father are more prone to be tempted in the lesbian direction."[52]

In addition to Meier and Minirth's predictive formulas for homosexuality and lesbianism are their formulas for male and female promiscuity. They are the flip side of the formulas for homosexuality and lesbianism. While for homosexuality the absent father is the important ingredient, for male promiscuity it is the absent mother. They say on one broadcast:

The little boy who doesn't get much time with mom when he's growing up will be more sexually promiscuous. He'll have a mother vacuum. Even though he may develop a good male sexual identity, he may become very sexually promiscuous and look down on women and be a womanizer and a male chauvinist pig, because he has a mother vacuum that was never met. He'll turn to sex to meet that vacuum even though it never really satisfies that vacuum.[53]

Now the flip side of the formula for lesbianism is the absent father. On one broadcast they say that "a girl that doesn't spend time with her dad . . . will become very promiscuous sexually later on in life, if she doesn't get enough time with daddy."[54] On another broadcast they say:

> If a little girl grows up being close to her mom but
> dad is gone all the time, then that little girl will
> crave her father's affection and not get it. She'll
> have a father vacuum and she'll end up becoming a
> hysterical female later on and she'll probably
> become sexually promiscuous.[55]

In the Freudian theory of heterosexual development the
boy ends up by identifying with the father and yet retains the
mother as the primary love object. As Freudian Theodore
Lidz says, the girl ends up identifying with the mother and
yet "must shift her basic love object from the mother to the
father."[56] According to Freud, even though the girl must shift
her love object she does not need to shift the parent with
whom she identifies. Like-parent identification and unlike-
parent as love object are supposedly the end result of properly
navigating the rough waters of the Oedipus complex.
However, according to Freudian theory, failure to accomplish
the changes required can lead to homosexuality or
lesbianism.

Martin Gross explains the Freudian view of homosexuality very simply. He says:

> Freud and many of his modern successors saw
> homosexuality as the penalty for the boy child's
> failure to win the Oedipal battle against a seductive,
> overbearing, over-affectionate mother—the classic
> Mrs. Portnoy. Instead of finally identifying with the
> hated father at the resolution of the Oedipal rivalry,
> the child identifies with the mother. Thereafter, the
> now homosexual male seeks other men as his love
> object.[57]

Gross goes on to say:

> In the Freudian homosexual model, the *penis-
> adoring child also shows disgust for the penisless
> woman*. This is coupled with his castration fear at

the hands of an angry father-rival.[58] (Emphasis his.)

Dr. Irving Bieber, another Freudian, says in the *Comprehensive Textbook of Psychiatry*:

> Thus, the parental constellation most likely to produce a homosexual or heterosexual with severe homosexual problems was a detached, hostile father and a close-binding, overly intimate, seductive mother who dominated and minimized her husband.[59]

Dr. Ronald Bayer, in his book *Homosexuality and American Psychiatry*, presents another facet of Freud's idea. He says:

> Later, Freud asserted that homosexuality was linked to the profound frustration experienced during the oedipal phase by those boys who had developed especially intense attachments to their mothers. Denied the sexual gratification for which they yearned, these boys regressed to an earlier stage of development, and identified with the woman they could not have. They then sought as sexual partners young men who resembled themselves and loved them in the way they would have had their mothers love them.[60]

It is difficult to tell if Meier and Minirth accept the entire classical Freudian theory. However there is enough similarity to conclude that they are at the very least utilizing a slight variation of the Freudian theory. Their belief that sexual identity is established before age six, that a boy needs a father present with whom to identify, and that the sole presence of a mother will move a boy to homosexuality are all variations of the Freudian formula. During his lifetime, Freud developed several versions or explanations for homosexuality. However, the basis for each explanation was always the same, that is, the unconscious Oedipal conflict occurring before age six. Meier and Minirth's explanation can certainly be traced to the same source.

With the prior information given about Freudian theory and the added information given in this section, it should be easy to fill in the details of the earlier formulas for lesbianism and promiscuity. Because a girl is unable to navigate the troubled waters of the Oedipal conflict and has not been able to make the proper parental love object/identification, she may end up a lesbian. The promiscuity formulas arise out of the same Oedipal cauldron of "castration anxiety," "penis envy," parental love object and parental identification. Following the Freudian formula, failure can result in later life promiscuity for either a boy or a girl, though the psychodynamics are different for each.

In discussing sexual identity on one of their broadcasts, Meier said:

> Patients will come in and they're thirty years old and let's say its a young man. It's a young man who was brought up by his mom and his grandmom and had two older sisters and he had no father in the home and then he went off to church and had female Sunday school teachers. He went to elementary school and had female teachers. . . . I've had many of them say, "I'm a woman who's locked into a man's body." And it really isn't their fault that they have a female sexual identity. He didn't choose it. It was sort of forced on him. . . . It's not your fault that you're a woman locked into a man's body, not your fault at all, and I sympathize with you like crazy.[61]

Please notice the words "not your fault at all." When one begins with the Freudian early determinants and adds the Freudian psychosexual stages of development, and then adds the Freudian formation of sexual identity, the equation will naturally result in "not your fault at all." This not only contradicts the Bible; it is an unsubstantiated leap from theory to unbiblical dogma to state, "not your fault at all."

On one of Meier and Minirth's programs, *The Person* by

Theodore Lidz (a Freudian) was recommended. Lidz's chapter on "The Oedipal Period" gives additional information about Freud's view of this early period of life that (without meaning to) illustrates both the degeneracy and creativity of Freud's mind. But while Meier, Minirth, and Lidz give credence to Freud's Oedipal notion, Gross says it is about as true as "the correlation between human personality and the Zodiac chart."[62]

We do not necessarily concur with any of the views quoted earlier. We are providing information in opposition to the Freudian view and its variations, including Meier and Minirth's, because we believe that the only truthful approach to problems of living is biblical, not psychoanalytical or even psychological. And we believe that there are biblical explanations for homosexuality and lesbianism to occur. However, Meier and Minirth have chosen psychoanalytical explanations.

In conclusion, as one studies Meier and Minirth with respect to their teachings on early life determinants (eighty-five percent factor), child care ("neglect" and "permanent psychological damage"), and homosexuality/lesbian/promiscuity (absent father/absent mother), it is transparent that Freud should be given much credit for what they say. Their continued failure to credit and compliment Freud is puzzling and disconcerting. Puzzling because it is only fair that Freud be given credit for their ideas. And, it is disconcerting because it should be morally mandatory to give credit where it is due, especially when Freud's opinions are spoken as facts and alluded to as research. We realize that their ideas are not completely congruent with Freud's, but that they originated with Freud is without question.

21

CLAIMS, CURES
AND QUESTIONS

Meier and Minirth's writing and speaking are periodical-
ly punctuated with claims for improvements and cures. Even
beyond their Freudian bias is their confidence for cure and/or
relief for a variety of problems. But, their claims are not
supported by the literature and research. We shall discuss
some of what they say, compare and contrast it with the
literature, and then make some general comments.

Insight Therapy.

Meier and Minirth repeatedly proclaim that insight
therapy is dramatically effective in treating all sorts of
problems. When they discuss such problems as depression,
fear of flying, multiple personalities, early life traumas,
bulimia and phobias, they recommend insight therapy. They
sometimes use extreme words such as *cures* and *you will get
over it* through the use of insight therapy.[1]

Because of their repeated endorsement and use of insight
therapy, as well as their claim for its effectiveness, it would
be helpful to know what it is. Dr. Michael McGuire in the
Psychotherapy Handbook says, "The history of Insight
Psychotherapy can be traced to Freud."[2] Because insight
therapy originated with Freud, it has to do with the activity

of exposing the contents of the so-called unconscious. Therefore, Freud archivist Dr. Jeffrey Masson precedes his definition of *insight* with definitions of *repression* and *interpretation*:

> *Repression* is the activity that permits something to remain in the unconscious. It is one of the defense mechanisms; others are denial, undoing, reaction formation. It is not a willed activity. *Interpretation* is the activity the therapist engages in when something unconscious is made conscious to the patient or when a truth is declared. *Insight* refers to the intellectual and emotional recognition of the truth of an interpretation, whereby something that has been, until then, repressed is made conscious.[3]

Masson's definitions coincide very well with Meier and Minirth's statements about insight therapy.

From this and evidence stated earlier, we can conclude that Meier and Minirth recommend and utilize a therapeutic approach that is Freudian. Three examples of mental-emotional-behavioral problems and Meier and Minirth's claim for cures with insight therapy are those of bulimia, multiple personalities, and agoraphobia.

Bulimia.

The first example is that of bulimia. Bulimia is a food related problem of binge eating and vomiting, which is usually practiced by a female. In response to a caller, Meier tells her that if she is "not in danger of any kind of physical threat," she should see "a really good insight oriented counselor who can get in touch with those repressed emotions." He goes on to say, "You will get over that symptom of bulimia when you deal with the root problem." The root problem, of course, is repressed emotions; the treatment is insight therapy; and the result is she will get over it.[4]

In searching the literature on the eating disorders of

anorexia and bulimia, we find that while much research is going on, there are no definite solutions to those problems. Direct or implied promises, such as the one above, are not given for any one particular therapeutic approach by people in touch with the research.[5] In her book on eating disorders, Dr. Hilde Bruch indicates that patients with eating disorders "appear singularly unresponsive to traditional psychoanalysis."[6] Psychoanalysis, of course, is Freudian insight therapy, which is fixated upon unconscious repressions, as in the case above.

Multiple Personalities.

A second example related to Meier and Minirth's claims for insight therapy is that of multiple personalities. The DSM-III describes the multiple personality this way: "The essential feature is the existence within the individual of two or more distinct personalities, each of which is dominant at a particular time."[7] Probably the best-known example is in the book *The Three Faces of Eve*.

On one of their programs Meier said, "**Only** insight oriented therapy" helps or cures multiple personalities.[8] (Emphasis added.) However, Dr. Richard Kluft, in his keynote address at the First International Conference on Multiple Personality/Dissociative States, says, "There is no real 'right' way to treat multiple personality."[9] Note the contrast between Meier's word *only* and Kluft's words *no real "right" way*. In a research volume on multiple personalities, Kluft says:

> The scientific study of the treatment of multiple personality disorder (MPD) has barely begun. Several treatment approaches have been described, but none has been assessed with rigorous methodologies or along objective dimensions. There are no studies comparing the efficacy of one approach with that of another. Furthermore, it is difficult to measure the impact of treatment against a cohort of untreated cases. There is no potential control population of

treated or untreated cases in the literature. The fol-
low-up of a limited number of cases and a small
number of autobiographic accounts offer tantalizing
clues but hardly constitute a data base.[10]

The literature demonstrates that those who work with
multiples disagree as to the desired end result of treatment.
Some are in favor of a complete integration of the multiples
into a single self (fusion). Others work towards a "peaceful
coexistence" of the parts. Some even question whether fusion
is possible or even necessary.[11] Dr. David Caul says, "It seems
to me that after treatment you want to end up with a functional unit, be it a corporation, a partnership, or a one-owner
business."[12] One specialist claims that "what is needed for
resolution is that the patient make clear-cut moral choices."
This individual "considers it imperative that all multiple
personalities and their equivalents make a moral choice of ex-
istential proportions between good and evil."[13]

A multiple personality disorder is a severe problem and
is recognized as such by the various researchers and
practitioners. We did not find the word *cure* in the numerous
volumes we checked, except that once, out of the numerous
volumes we checked, *cure* was used with quotation marks.[14]
No one used the word *only* in relation to a single treatment
methodology.

Agoraphobia.

The third example is a panic attack disorder. The anxiety
that becomes a panic attack when people leave home is
referred to as agoraphobia. According to one textbook:

Agoraphobics are defined not only by fears of public
places and conveyances but also by their fear of
being away from home and familiarity—places and
people that provide psychological security. Indeed,
agoraphobics tend to fear any situation where an
easy retreat to safe territory is not possible.[15]

Meier has some very definite opinions about agoraphobia. He says, "People that get it usually are the first born in their family."[16] Meier asserts that the reason is that parents "expect too much out of their first child."[17] In describing the type of counseling he does and recommends, Meier says that "they dig and probe and dig and probe and work your way through the childhood issues, adult issues and look at the repressed anger at/toward mom and dad, look at the obsessive compulsive thinking. . . ."[18] Meier speaks of either psychotherapy over a three-year period of time or hospitalization with psychotherapy for a considerably shorter period of time. He says,

> For agoraphobia we recommend hospitalization because it's so painful to go through for three years. Why stay locked up in your house three years? If you can check into a hospital unit where they do know what they're doing and where they can dig and probe, and almost all the cases we've treated, nearly all of them have gotten over their agoraphobia within about six to eight weeks in the hospital. So instead of two or three years of out-patient counseling by digging and probing, doing the same thing but doing it seven days a week, getting group therapy seven days a week, individual therapy four days a week, by digging and probing and looking at these insights daily, it usually takes longer than it does for depression. Depression usually takes one month to get over in the hospital but agoraphobia usually takes two months, sometimes even three months, once in a while even four months but usually about six weeks to sixteen weeks, somewhere in that period. And a lot of that depends on childhood factors, but by working on these things day by day a person can get totally over it for life in a couple of months in the hospital.[19]

There are several questions that need to be addressed. First, is agoraphobia associated with the first born in the family? Second, is insight therapy, the "dig and probe and dig and probe" type, usually a real deliverance from agoraphobia? And third, is it usual that "nearly all of them have gotten over their agoraphobia within six to eight weeks in the hospital"?

In all the literature we read, we found no one identifying the first born in the family as the most vulnerable to agoraphobia. Nor did we find any research which related agoraphobia to parents expecting "too much out of their first child." We did learn that "the tendency to have panic attacks runs in families."[20] We also learned about other theories that had been proposed and examined.[21-23] However, we found no pattern of the agoraphobic typically being the first born child nor any relationship to parental expectations.

We wrote to Dr. Dianne Chambless, a well-known researcher in the area of agoraphobia and asked:

1. Is the agoraphobic typically the first born in the family?

2. Is there any research to support the idea that agoraphobia is the result of parents who expect too much from their children?

She replied, "To my knowledge there are no studies of birth order or of parents' expectations."[24]

Related to birth order of children and later problems of living, Meier says:

> We're probably treating a thousand people for alcohol and drug addiction right now currently at our clinic. Nearly all of them come from families with certain dynamics that produce the alcoholism. Most of them are the youngest child in their family.[25]

Again we searched the research literature and found no support for Meier's statement. In addition, we called Dr. Herbert Fingarette, author of *Heavy Drinking: The Myth of*

Alcoholism as a Disease, and asked if he was aware of such a relationship. He said, "No."

In their latest book, Meier and Minirth claim, "Research has proven that birth order has an impact on personality development. . . ."[26] Meier and Minirth are enamored with the idea of birth order and often see it related to certain mental disorders such as agoraphobia and alcoholism. However, contrary to what they say, the research has **not** "proven that birth order has an impact on personality development." *Science* magazine featured a special report by John Tierney on "The Myth of the Firstborn." Tierney says, "Birth order theory makes an appealing neat way to categorize human beings—like astrology, but with scientific trappings." In reference to the research findings he says:

> After reviewing 35 years of research—some 1,500 studies—Cécile Ernst and Jules Angst of the University of Zurich reach a simple conclusion: On a scale of importance, the effects of birth order fall somewhere between negligible and nonexistent.[27]

The second question relates to Meier and Minirth's use of insight therapy, and especially their intense use of it. They recommend "six to eight weeks in the hospital" of "digging and probing." Because of Meier's reference to "repressed anger" and since repressed anger is their key dynamic of depression, one gets the distinct impression that Meier views agoraphobia as a form of depression. But, agoraphobia researcher Chambless says:

> Because agoraphobics begin to experience problems with their relationships and feel a general demoralization as the phobia progresses and endures, it is not surprising that most of them are also mildly to moderately depressed. For a time, this was confusing to mental health professionals, who thought that agoraphobia might be a special case of depression. Occasionally, agoraphobics are still told this. People who are severely depressed do some-

times become phobic for the duration of the depression and lose the phobias when the depression lifts. In the great majority of cases, however, agoraphobia is the primary problem, and the depression improves when the agoraphobia is successfully treated.[28]

In describing the treatment of agoraphobia, Dr. Andrew Mathews et al say:

> The central idea in the psychoanalytic view of phobias is that symptoms are the result of two processes: the repression of an emotionally charged idea and the displacement of this internal conflict to an object or situation in the outside world. . . . The repressed impulses presumably vary from patient to patient, but sexual and aggressive impulses are thought to be those most commonly involved . . . . The first requirement of analytic treatment is to uncover the repressed mental contents that account for the agoraphobia. The second is to enable the patient to deal with these directly so that the defenses of repression and displacement can be given up.[29]

In discussing the varieties of treatment for agoraphobia, Chambless says:

> Until the 1970s, agoraphobics were treated with standard (usually Freudian) psychotherapy. . . . The assumption was that with insight the phobias would improve. . . on the whole this approach did little for the phobias. . . unfortunately, most practitioners still use the ineffective method of "talk therapy."[30]

In discussing "Treatment for Fear," Chambless says:

> Considerable research has shown that a person who has a specific phobia is no more or less psychologi-

cally healthy than the average person. For this reason it is completely inappropriate for such people to be in talk therapies to overcome their problem.[31]

Thus according to the research, insight therapy, with its digging and probing, is not considered effective for either agoraphobia or specific phobias. Therefore, it seems that the issue of "six to eight weeks in the hospital" of "digging and probing" would be an overdose of what the research indicates to be the wrong treatment. It may be that "nearly all of them have gotten over their agoraphobia within about six to eight weeks in the hospital" at the Minirth-Meier Clinic. However, the research does not seem to support insight therapy with its "digging and probing" to be a primary effective method of treatment. In addition, Meier's statement that "nearly all of them have gotten over their agoraphobia within about six to eight weeks in the hospital" with "digging and probing" therapy seems enormously contrary to the usual success/ failure/relapse reported in the literature. But unless there are outside researchers examining their results, it is very difficult to obtain an objective view of their treatment.

Other Claims.

The following sections contain examples of other claims made by Meier and Minirth. The previous sections and the following contain neither unique or atypical examples of what they say. An exhaustive search of Meier and Minirth's writing and speaking for other such claims, which are not substantiated by research, would take much more space than this present section.

Schizophrenia.

On a radio broadcast, Meier said that schizophrenia comes "from severe inferiority feelings and genetic predisposition and a bunch of different factors and it's curable if you catch it early." Then he said, "If you don't get medical help for about six months it becomes incurable; the biochemical pathways become permanent." In reference to schizophrenia, he also said, "If they go six months without medication they're going to spend the rest of their lives that way and we see hundreds of them and if you catch them right away, within a week or two, they're totally curable."[32]

In *Introduction to Psychology and Counseling,* Meier and Minirth say, "Without proper management, a schizophrenic individual could be doomed to a life of insanity."[33] On the radio, Meier told of a young seminary student whom they were treating. In the course of the treatment the young man was checked out of their care. Meier said, "That was years ago and that guy is still insane today and will be the rest of his life. He would have been totally normal if he would have gotten a little bit of medication to restore him to normal."[34] In their tape series *Happiness Is a Choice* they make some of the same comments.[35]

We raise the question whether or not it is appropriate to speak of either a cause or a cure for schizophrenia. Is it appropriate for them to say that schizophrenia results "from severe inferiority feelings and genetic predisposition and a bunch of different factors"? In addition, is it appropriate to say that "it's curable"? The first issue we will address is the involvement of "inferiority feelings" in the onset of schizophrenia. According to research psychiatrist E. Fuller Torrey, schizophrenia does **not** result "from severe inferiority feelings."[36] Related to the ideas of cause and cure, the Harvard Medical School reports: "One in a hundred persons will at some time suffer from schizophrenia. **Its causes are obscure, and no way is known to prevent or cure it**."[37] (Emphasis added.)

In his book *Surviving Schizophrenia,* Torrey says:

> Contrary to the popular stereotype, schizophrenia is an eminently treatable disease. That is not to say it is a curable disease, and the two should not be confused. Successful treatment means the control of symptoms, whereas cure means the permanent removal of their causes. Curing schizophrenia will not become possible until we understand its causes;

in the meantime we must continue improving its treatment.[38]

In addition, he says:

> Drugs are the most important treatment for schizophrenia, just as they are the most important treatment for many physical diseases of the human body. Drugs do not *cure*, but rather *control*.[39] (Emphasis his.)

If, according to Harvard Medical School, "no way is known to prevent or cure" schizophrenia, then the statement by Meier that "it's curable if you catch it early" must be false. Repeatedly we see in the research literature that "not all cases of schizophrenia respond to drug therapy."[40] Furthermore, there is no early detection assuring early cure for schizophrenia. In addition, Meier's statement, "If you don't get medical help for about six months it becomes incurable," must be false. Even if they were referring to control rather than cure being limited to those diagnosed within six months, the evidence indicates that control is not limited to early diagnosis or early treatment.

Torrey mentions "twenty-five studies in which schizophrenic patients had all been followed for an average of at least ten years."[41] He says that "over 4,400 patients were followed up in these studies."[42] Then he summarizes:

> Based on the patients followed in the twenty-five studies, it seems reasonable to conclude that *one-third* of all patients hospitalized and diagnosed with schizophrenia will be found to be completely recovered when followed up ten years later.[43] (Emphasis his.)

At the "other end of the spectrum" are one-third of the patients who are unimproved. Torrey goes on to say, "This leaves the remaining one-third in the middle category of improved but not completely recovered."[44]

The Vermont Longitudinal Study would seem to contradict Meier's after "six months it becomes incurable" and "that guy is still insane today and will be the rest of his life" statements. This study of chronic schizophrenia revealed that one-half to two-thirds of former patients "had achieved considerable improvement or recovery."[45] The study showed that "forty-five percent of the sample displayed no psychiatric symptoms at all," and half of them used no medication.[46] This longitudinal, well-documented project certainly repudiates Meier's statement, "If they go six months without medication they're going to spend the rest of their lives that way."[47]

Meier refers to a six-month period of time to medicate and also refers to the pathology as schizophrenia. However, Torrey says:

> . . . schizophrenia is a serious diagnosis and should not be applied indiscriminately to anyone who has any schizophreniclike symptom, however, brief.[48]

Torrey recommends that for such individuals with schizophreniclike symptoms of less than six months duration, they should use schizophreniform disorder as the diagnosis rather than schizophrenia. Thus, according to Torrey, Meier's reference to someone with schizophreniclike symptoms prior to six months as having schizophrenia is inappropriate.

In *Happiness Is a Choice*, Meier and Minirth say that someone "might be predisposed toward schizophrenia under similar stresses because of an alteration of dopamine in the brain."[49] In *Introduction to Psychology and Counseling*, they say, "Schizophrenia is another mental illness in which inheritance may predispose toward a potential weakness."[50] They also say:

> The dopamine imbalance is possibly precipitated by too much acute stress in an individual with a genetic weakness with regard to neurotransmitters, after a difficult early environment.[51]

By *predisposed*, it seems they mean *genetically predisposed*. Torrey refers to this "genetic predisposition (diathesis) in addition to stress" as "the so-called diathesis-stress theory."[52] Torrey says:

> The main trouble with stress theories of schizophrenia is that there are no supporting data. When studies have been done ascertaining the stresses in patients' lives prior to their schizophrenic breakdown, the stresses are found to be no greater than those in a random sample of a general population.[53]

Torrey concludes that "stress theories leave many important questions unanswered."[54]

In addition to their implicating stress, Meier and Minirth also mention dopamine. Dopamine is a brain neurotransmitter. Note the following statement from Torrey:

> Finally, it is now known that drugs which are effective in schizophrenia block dopamine action. For all of these reasons many researchers **suspect** that an excess of dopamine is one of the causes of schizophrenia.[55] (Emphasis added.)

Notice the word *suspect*. In this very complex, rapidly changing field of the brain and its neurotransmitters, it is better to use moderate language. It is better to use such phrases as "it seems as if," "it appears to be," and "it may be." And yet, Meier and Minirth make definitive statements that are questionable at the very least.

Insomnia.

Meier and Minirth were being interviewed on a radio program and Meier said, "Insomnia is a one-hundred percent curable problem."[56] We have researched the literature and contacted two well-known researcher/practitioners. The two individuals are Dr. F. Grant Buckle, Medical Director, Sleep Disorders Center, The Hospital of the Good Samaritan, and Dr. German Nino-Murcia, Stanford Sleep Disorders Clinic. Based upon what we have learned, it seems obvious that Meier and Minirth's promise is another claim completely without support in the sleep disorder literature or from information received from the two sleep disorder centers contacted.

Depression.

In *Happiness Is a Choice* Meier and Minirth say, "Scientific research indicates that 85 percent of significant depressions are precipitated by life stresses."[57] Again the use of a percent such as 85 communicates a simplicity that is difficult to support from the research. The studies that do take the simplistic approach and report a percentage generally report a significantly lower one than Meier and Minirth report. However, any percentage associated with the expression "precipitated by life stresses" is too simple to be acceptable. Dr. E. S. Paykel, whom they quote, says, ". . . there is often an amalgam of recent life stresses, chronic stressful social situations and absence of social support, genetic elements suggested by a family history, and probable biochemical factors."[58] These factors create a complexity that a simple numeral followed by a percent sign will obscure. In addition, it is obvious from the research that no single factor such as "life stresses" is generally enough to explain the depression.

In her book *The Broken Brain*, Dr. Nancy Andreasen says:

> We do not fully understand how depressions are triggered. Sometimes they have obvious precipitants, as was the case with Conrad Jarrett in *Ordinary People*, who became depressed when his brother, Buck, died in a boating accident that he survived. Other depressions appear out of the blue, as did Sylvia Plath's first episode, which began after

her sophomore year at Smith while she was in New York on a coveted *Mademoiselle* guest editorship. Some patients have clear precipitants for some episodes, but not for others. . . . Sometimes depressions begin after a physical stress. . . but sometimes they begin when the patient has not experienced any kind of unusual event.[59]

She goes on to explain "endogenous" depression and then says:

Depressions occurring after a stress were called "reactive" and considered to be purely psychological. More-recent research suggests that this view is an oversimplification.[60]

Drs. Ted and Renate Rosenthal speak of "Depression as a 'Final Common Pathway.'" They say:

. . . such affective illnesses as pronounced, melancholic depressions are assumed to occur when a threshold is crossed by a combination of biological, psychological, and situational strains acting conjointly.[61]

Dr. Myrna Weissman, in discussing depression, presents evidence that "the reasons are biologic as well as psychosocial."[62]

The following quotes will illustrate the extent of the promise for cure for depression that Meier and Minirth offer. They say:

Depression is one-hundred percent curable.[63]

We have treated over two thousand patients for depression, both Christians and non-Christians, and *all* of them get over their depression.[64] (Emphasis theirs.)

But even now, by applying the contents of this book

[*Happiness Is a Choice*], depression is 100 percent treatable. In fact, depression (over a period of weeks or months) is 100 percent curable.[65]

Even the subtitle of *Happiness Is a Choice* implies the promise for cure. It is: *A Manual on the Symptoms, Causes and Cures of Depression.* Note the word *cures.*

In reviewing Meier and Minirth's book *Introduction to Psychology and Counseling* in the *Journal of Psychology and Theology*, Stanton Jones notes that "this book contains many factual errors" and then gives examples. Jones also says:

> An area of grave concern for this volume is the tendency of the authors to use empirical research to illustrate points they are advocating rather than seriously struggling with the frequently contradictory evidence of our field. Their assertions are presented as unequivocal, with evidence contradicting their positions rarely cited.[66]

The strongest point that Jones makes is that they make several "poorly qualified clinical assertions which are quite misleading, the most obvious of which was that in the treatment of the clinically depressed person."[67] Jones discusses the claim and then says, "Such claims are overstated and have no place in professional publications." In conclusion Jones says, "Overall, I cannot recommend this book as an introduction to psychology, nor as an introduction to counseling, nor as an introduction to Christian counseling."[68]

And Still Other Claims.

In their publication *Christian Psychology for Today*, Meier and Minirth list a number of problems: "panic attacks, agoraphobia (fear of open places—they can't leave their home), multiple personalities, psychoses, bedwetting and hyperactivity (in children), or sexual dysfunctions." They go on to say: "If people with such problems are to be helped, they will probably need the assistance of a trained psychologist or psychiatrist. These problems are curable. . . ."[69] There is no qualifier used. They declare very simply and very directly, "These problems are curable."

On one of their radio broadcasts Meier mentioned almost the same list and said, "They're easily curable."[70] If taken literally, this is a fantastic claim! It is a claim we have not seen supported in any of the literature; a claim we have not seen supported in any of the research; a claim which no other clinic we are aware of has made or would probably dare to make; and a claim that requires substantiation because it is in such contrast to what is known about those individual problems. We have never read nor heard of such an extreme claim in all the years we have been reading the professional journals, books, and research in these various fields.

Any statement to the effect that depression or any other such broad category of problems is one-hundred percent curable is likely to be spurious and promote false hope and grave disappointment. In *The Broken Brain*, Andreasen cautions:

> The word *cure* is used much too liberally today. We need to learn to distinguish between cure and care. People have been too often taught by both physicians and journalists to hope for "a cure" when in fact they should be hoping for care instead.[71]

We believe that by any reasonable standard, Meier and Minirth's comments made about schizophrenia, "panic attacks, agoraphobia. . . multiple personalities, psychoses, bed wetting and hyperactivity. . . sexual dysfunctions," and depression are overstatements, to say the least. The word *cure* is rarely, if ever, used for extreme disorders and we find no one who uses it as glibly as Meier and Minirth.

It is unfortunate that the major Freudian ideas that have not withstood the test of research are staunchly held and promoted by Meier and Minirth. Their continued use of the Freudian fallacies of the past, repression, the unconscious, defense mechanisms, the early psychosexual stages of development, and so on are startling in light of the current indictments against Freudian mythologies. More and more researchers and scholars are criticizing Freudian theories and presuppositions, and secular theorists are using them less and less. But Meier and Minirth continue to treat Freud's unfounded opinions as facts.

22

SAPPINESS IS A CHOICE

In their book *Introduction to Psychology and Counseling*, Meier and Minirth say:

> The science of psychology not only embraces a diversity of subjects and interests but also has the ability to provide practical knowledge for everyday living. The fact that both psychology and the Bible provide information for daily living as well as information about how human beings can be expected to think and behave in various environments has sometimes produced tension. As Christians and as responsible members of the scientific community, the authors hope that this book will help to reduce any antagonism Christians may have experienced toward psychology.[1]

We have addressed the issue of whether or not this kind of psychology is science earlier in the section on Collins as well as in our previous books. The kind of psychology that purports to understand why man is the way he is and how he changes is not science.

An even more serious error in what Meier and Minirth say is:

> The fact that both psychology and the Bible provide
> information for daily living as well as information
> about how human beings can be expected to think
> and behave in various environments has sometimes
> produced tension.[2]

They set this forth as an axiom of their faith in psychology,
but it is a false axiom. The Bible and psychology do not
provide such information. In fact, equating the two in this
manner demeans God's Word and exalts psychology. The
Bible does not merely "provide information." It is God's truth
to humanity! And psychology does not "provide information"
in a scientific sense. As we have repeatedly demonstrated,
this kind of psychology is merely a collection of the opinions of
men. By grammatically equating the Bible and psychology,
Meier and Minirth have dramatically presented a new
theology. In their new theology, God's truth and men's
opinions are presented on the same plane.

Meier and Minirth further state:

> A basic concept underlying this book is that all
> truth is God's truth, no matter where one finds it. A
> further concept is that God intends for us to learn
> truth from many sources in addition to the Bible.
> Physicians do not expect to find the treatment for a
> case of tuberculosis contained within the pages of
> the Holy Scriptures, although many principles for
> good health are found there. Geologists do not
> expect to find there a description of the sand
> containing oil reserves.[3]

We have discussed the errors of this reasoning earlier in the
Collins' section. Numerous philosophers and medical writers
have debunked this type of reasoning. The fact that
"Physicians do not expect to find the treatment for a case of
tuberculosis contained within the pages of the Holy
Scriptures" is not even remotely related to the issue of
psychology and the Bible. As Szasz has pointed out, this type
of ill-logic equates "brain and mind, nerves and

nervousness."[4]

Meier and Minirth's   constant use of the discredited medical-model rationale for the use of psychology is tragic. They apparently honestly believe in it or they would not repeatedly resort to it. In their latest book they say, "Mental health disorders are illnesses just as surely as heart disease, diabetes and pneumonia."[5] But, Dr. Ronald Leifer in his book *In the Name of Mental Health* says:

> If we grant that in its paradigmatic cognitive use in medicine the term "disease" refers to the body, to modify it with the word "mental" is at worst a mixture of logical levels called a category error, and at best it is a radical redefinition of the word "disease." A category error is an error in the use of language that, in turn, produces errors in thinking. . . . Whatever the mind may be, it is not a thing like muscles, bones, and blood.[6]

Leifer discusses the arguments for the medical model (similar to those used by Meier and Minirth) and then the defects of such arguments. He concludes by saying:

> The principle advantages of this argument are therefore neither scientific nor intellectual. They are social. They prejudice the lay public to see psychiatric practices as more like medical treatment than like social control, socialization, education, and religious consolation. It bids them to presume that the psychiatrist, like other physicians, always serves the individual in his pursuit of life, health, and happiness.[7]

Dr. E. Fuller Torrey also discusses the medical model in his book *The Death of Psychiatry*. His entire book is "an attack upon the medical model"[8] when used in the way that Meier and Minirth use it. Torrey says that "the medical model of human behavior, when carried to its logical conclusions, is both nonsensical and nonfunctional."[9]

Meier and Minirth's statement that "all truth is God's truth, no matter where one finds it"[10] is the chant of the inte-grationists. But, to what "truth" are they referring? What have the Freudian pronouncements of the Oedipus complex to do with God's truth? Or, what do Freudian determinants of behavior or Carl Jung's mythological archetypes have to do with God's truth? Or what about Roger's unconditional self-regard? Or the behaviorism of B. F. Skinner? The lack of conformity in the community of professional psychological practitioners who profess the Christian faith demonstrates more confusion than it does "God's truth."

The enticement of the "all truth is God's truth" fallacy is that there is some similarity between biblical teachings and psychological ideas. But similarities do not make psychology compatible with Christianity. They only emphasize the fact that the systems of psychological counseling are religious rather than scientific. Just as the various world religions include glimpses or elements of truth and just as Satan's words to Eve in the Garden contained some truth, so do psychological opinions of men. But we certainly would not recommend a person to search for truth in other religions. Nor would we suggest that a person seek out Satan in his search for truth about mankind.

Those who cry, "All truth is God's truth," want the free-dom to incorporate any psychological ideas or techniques that appeal to them even though the ideas and techniques are part of a godless system. The vast preponderance of what Christian therapists attempt to integrate with the Bible is based upon those theories which in turn are based upon un-biblical presuppositions. The systems of psychological coun-seling from which they borrow are based upon theories de-vised by non-Christians. And, the presuppositions upon which those theories are based include evolutionism, secular humanism, atheism, psychic determinism, environmental de-terminism, and various forms of non-Christian religions.

Because many in the church believe that theories and techniques of counseling psychology are based upon empirical evidence, they put them on the same level of authority as the Bible. In so doing, the subjective observations and biased opinions of mere mortals are placed on the same authoritative level as the inspired Word of God. But those psychological theories give no more substantive, authoritative insight into understanding the intricacies of the human psyche than literature, mythology, world religions, sociology, or philosophy. Although they may seem to reveal truth, they are clouded by subjectivity and based upon secular presuppositions.

Furthermore, attempting to syncretize psychology with Christianity denies the sufficiency of the Word of God and the sufficiency of the Spirit of God in all matters of life and conduct. It suggests that the Bible needs substantiation, confirmation, expansion, and assistance in matters of life and godliness. And, it regards the distorted, limited glimpses of human perception and understanding as necessary additions to what the Bible has to say about the human condition and conduct.

The title of this chapter is obviously a one-letter variation of Meier and Minirth's popular book *Happiness Is a Choice* . The dictionary slang definition of *sappy* is "foolish; silly; fatuous"[11] and we believe that this type of psychology is worse than "foolish; silly; fatuous." Hopefully the evidence and arguments presented in this volume reveal that this is indeed so.

We have shown throughout this section that Meier and Minirth are heavily dependent upon Freud, that at times they inaccurately use Scripture to support their personal psychological opinions, that they unjustifiably claim research support for their conclusions, and that some of their major therapeutic claims are in clear contradiction to what the research reveals.

Unfortunately, in their attempts to biblicize psychology, Meier and Minirth have ended up psychologizing the Bible. And further, they have demeaned the Word of God by sometimes twisting the Bible to make it fit their preconceived, unproven psychoanalytic opinions. They have confused the issue even more by using the defunct medical model of human behavior and justifying their psychology with "all truth is God's truth." For those individuals who want fellowship with Freud with a biblical facade, Meier and

Minirth would be a good choice.

PSYCHOHERESY

Psychology is burdened with a scrap heap of empirical results that have contributed nothing to our field except to increase the number of publications and to justify academic promotions.

Howard Kendler in *Autobiographies in Experimental Psychology.*[1]

The psychological way provides numerous theories about dealing with problems of living. The fact that the theories are not scientific seems to bother few people. The added fact that none of these often conflicting, nonscientific theories has been shown to be clearly superior to any of the others seems of little concern. No matter what psychological approach one develops, it will seem as valid as any other.[2] Anyone can do just about anything he wishes in the midst of the confusion of psychological theories and techniques. One look at the multitudinous contradictory psychological approaches with the competing claims of success should cause even the most ardent supporter of the psychological way to throw up his hands in despair.

For the Christian, the point is not simply whether or not psychotherapy works, but whether it works better than biblical counseling. The question for the church is this: Does psychological counseling have something better to offer on the average than the cure of souls? To begin with, no one really knows if psychotherapy conducted by highly trained and long experienced therapists does any better than that done by untrained and inexperienced nonprofessionals. Additionally, no one even knows if professional psychotherapy does any better than hundreds of other promises for help, such as meditation, dog-fish-or-parakeet "therapy," laughter "therapy," or just plain blowing bubbles every day to overcome depression.[3]

The research has not advanced much beyond **attempting** to prove that psychotherapy works better than no treatment, probably because it has not even proven this very well. It is still not certain from a research standpoint whether or not psychotherapy works, and if it does, how well it works. It seems logical to conclude that, if researched, the use of biblical counseling would be shown to be as effective as the over 250 present systems of promises for help. One professor of psychology reports:

> During the first half of the nineteenth century, when moral treatment was at its peak, at least 70 percent of the patients who had been ill for a year or less were released as recovered or improved. . . . Moral treatment did all this without tranquilizers, antidepressants, shock treatment, psychosurgery, psychoanalysis, or any other kind of psychotherapy.

He adds:

> The use of moral treatment declined during the second half of the nineteenth century. The results were disastrous. Recovery and discharge rates went down as moral treatment gave way to the medical approach.[4]

In its present state of confusion over its questionable successes and unquestionable failures, it seems appropriate to recommend that the church minister to people with needs rather than turning them away to a costly, often prolonged process of dubious value. People are suffering from anxiety, shyness, marital discord, drug abuse, alcoholism, sexual disorders, depression, and a host of other problems and fears. Regardless of what claims psychotherapists may make, no one has ever shown that psychological counseling is superior to unadulterated biblical counseling.

No one really knows whether psychological counseling is

superior to biblical counseling. There is only a massive, but mistaken, assumption that it is. And, it is this false assumption which has caused the church to abandon its ministry to the suffering soul. Mental illness is a myth and psychological counseling is not science.

Christians need not be submerged in this sea of confusion. Unfortunately psychotherapy has become entrenched in our society. It is a stronghold of the enemy to turn believers to another gospel—the gospel of "mental illness" and "mental health," the gospel of self and a myriad of other religious philosophies.

Our primary objection to the use of psychotherapy, however, is not based merely upon its confused state of self-contradiction, nor upon its phony scientific facade, nor on its use of the misnomer of mental illness. Our primary objection is not even based upon the attempts to explain human behavior through personal opinion presented as scientific theory. Our greatest objection to psychotherapy is that it has displaced the Word of God, the power of the cross, and the work of the Holy Spirit among Christians without proof or justification.

The frustrating part of all this is that there is absolutely no scientific justification for the integration of psychological opinions of men and therapeutic techniques into the nonphysical realm of the soul and spirit of man. Such an intrusion violates the intention of Scripture and undermines the holy work of the Spirit in the lives of Christians. And yet, the path from the church to the couch has become so well-worn that few self-respecting clergymen will resist the temptation to send an ailing parishioner down that broad way, in spite of the questionable results and expense of the effort. And, moving the psychological theories and therapies into the church is even worse.

Just because the world utilizes psychological counseling, it does not follow that the church has been wise in following the trend. The Bible warns us about using the world's systems and about trying to combine the world's ways with God's ways.

> Be ye not unequally yoked together with unbe-
> lievers: for what fellowship hath righteousness with
> unrighteousness? And what communion hath light
> with darkness? And what concord hath Christ with
> Belial? or what part hath he that believeth with an
> infidel? And what agreement hath the temple of God
> with idols? For ye are the temple of the living God;
> as God hath said, I will dwell in them, and walk in
> them; and I will be their God, and they shall be my
> people. Wherefore come out from among them, and
> be ye separate, saith the Lord, and touch not the
> unclean thing; and I will receive you. And I will be a
> Father unto you, and ye shall be my sons and
> daughters, saith the Lord Almighty. (2 Corinthians
> 6:14-18)

It is unnecessary to add psychology to the Word of God or
to use psychology in place of the Word of God. Even those
psychologies which seem to have elements of truth in them
are unnecessary because the essential elements are already
in Scripture. The way the theory is described may entice
believers into thinking that psychology has something more
than the Bible. However, if stripped down to the core, each
theory has some element of truth and just enough error to
lead people away from God and into the ways of self and
Satan.

It is extraordinary that so many people have spent so
much money for so many years on a system which has so little to give. About all that may be proven eventually through
the herculean effort of all the psychotherapies offered, pur-
chased, and evaluated (and all the billions of dollars that
have changed hands) is this: On the average, given any problem (psychological or otherwise) doing something about it is
better than doing nothing at all." (Baboyan's Law.)

In an article titled "What is Vulgar? in *The American
Scholar*, the writer says:

> Psychology seems to me vulgar because it is too
> often overbearing in its confidence. Instead of say-
> ing, "I don't know," it readily says, "unresolved

Oedipus complex" or "manic-depressive syndrome" or "identity crisis." As with other intellectual discoveries. . . psychology acts as if it is holding all the theoretical keys, but then in practice reveals that it doesn't even know where the doors are. As an old *Punch* cartoon once put it, "It's worse than wicked, my dear, it's vulgar."[5]

Because the efficacy of psychotherapy has not been demonstrated, Alexander Astin contends that "psychotherapy should have died out. But it did not. It did not even waver. Psychotherapy had, it appeared, achieved *functional autonomy*."[6] (Emphasis his.) Functional autonomy occurs when a practice continues after the circumstances which supported it are gone. Astin is suggesting that psychotherapy has become self perpetuating because there is no support for its efficacy. Astin concludes his comments with the following dismal note:

> If nothing else, we can be sure that the principle of functional autonomy will permit psychotherapy to survive long after it has outlived its usefulness as a personality laboratory.[7]

Psychotherapy has not been affirmed by scientific scrutiny and only remains because of the usual inertia that results when a movement becomes established and then entrenched.

With the questionability of the results of psychotherapy and the certainty that damage sometimes occurs, it is difficult for many critics of psychotherapy to understand either the glib pronouncements of its practitioners or the confidence of those who refer individuals to this treatment. The suspicions of psychotherapy **are** justifiable and the sensitivities of psychotherapists to criticisms are unfortunate.

Because of our familiarity with the research, we keep certain things in mind when we read and listen to the professional psychologizers of Christianity. The following assumptions do not all apply to all of the psychologizers. However, we find that the following should be considered when reading what they have written or listening to what they say.

1. What the psychologizer says about human relationships and problems of living is personal opinion rather than scientific fact.

2. Degrees, licenses, experience, and education in the field of counseling do not make the psychologizers experts on human behavior.

3. The psychologizer generally knows less about the Word and its application to problems of living than a pastor.

4. When the psychologizer mentions God or His Word, he may be doing it more to give credibility to his opinions than to promote biblical understanding.

5. The psychologizer may be interpreting Scripture from a psychological perspective rather than evaluating psychology from a biblical perspective.

6. What the psychologizer is saying is contrary to what numerous other psychologizers would say.

7. Case histories or examples used are not generally representative of what normally happens.

8. The successes claimed may have had less to do with the counselor's psychological training, licenses, and experience than with factors in the counselee's own life.

9. Successes claimed in counseling could be matched by persons not receiving psychological counseling.

10. For every success mentioned there are many failures and check to see if any are mentioned.

11. Successes in psychological counseling are often short-term.

12. If someone is improved or delivered from his problems, competent biblical counseling could have done even better.

13. For every psychological solution suggested there is a better biblical solution available.

14. There is definitely a potential harm rate for every seemingly wonderful idea from the psychological systems of men.

15. There is almost no psychological idea that cannot be made to sound biblical.

16. What the psychologizer believes to be psychologically true may dictate what is theologically true for him, rather

than the other way around.

After reviewing all of the research, one could conclude that psychotherapy is one of the biggest and most vicious ripoffs that has ever been perpetrated on the American public and that it is one of the greatest deceptions in the church today.

The largest of the four branches of psychotherapy is the humanistic one. The Association for Humanistic Psychology is the professional association of humanistic psychologists. Its president, Dr. Lawrence LeShan, says, "Psychotherapy may be known in the future as the greatest hoax of the twentieth century."[8] It may also be known as the greatest heresy of twentieth-century Christianity.

In *The Emperor's New Clothes* after the little boy cried out, "He has no clothes!" the people knew that what the boy said was true. But, the greatest tragedy was not the discovery (no clothes), but the continuation of the deception by the Emperor. The story goes on:

> The Emperor squirmed. All at once he knew that what the people said was right. "All the same," he said to himself, "I must go on as long as the procession lasts." So the Emperor kept on walking, his head held higher than ever. And the faithful minister kept on carrying the train that wasn't there.[9]

And so, like the naked Emperor, psychotherapy and all its psychologies will "go on as long as the procession lasts." For many of us the procession is over. The cure of minds (psychotherapy) never was and never will be a satisfactory replacement for or an addition to the cure of souls (biblical counseling).

NOTES

Prophets of PsychoHeresy:
1. *New World Dictionary of the American Language.* New York: Simon and Schuster, 1984, p. 1139.
2. Martin and Deidre Bobgan. *PsychoHeresy: The Psychological Seduction of Christianity.* Santa Barbara: EastGate Publishers, 1987, pp. 4, 7.
3. Bernie Zilbergeld. *The Shrinking of America.* Boston: Little, Brown and Company, 1983, p. 121.
4. *Ibid.*, p. 122.
5. *Ibid.*, p. 123.
6. Dorothy Tennov. *Psychotherapy: The Hazardous Cure.* New York: Abelard-Schuman, 1975, p. 71.
7. Bernie Zilbergeld, "Psychabuse," *Science '86,* June 1986, p. 52.
8. Letter on file.

Part One: Can You Really Trust Psychology?
1. Gary R. Collins. *Can You Trust Psychology?* Downers Grove: InterVarsity Press, 1988, p. 129.

Chapter 1: The Scientific Posture.
1. Gary R. Collins. *Can You Trust Psychology?* Downers Grove: InterVarsity Press, 1988, p. 139.
2. *Ibid.*, pp. 139-140.
3. Hillel J. Einhorn and Robin M. Hogarth, "Confidence in Judgment: Persistence of the Illusion of Validity." *Psychological Review,* Vol. 85, No. 5, 1978, p. 395.
4. American Psychiatric Association, *Amicus Curiae* brief, *Tarasoff* v. *Regents of University of California,* $_{55}$1 P.2d $_{334}$ (Cal. 1976).
5. Arthur Janov. *The Primal Scream.* New York: Dell Publishing Co., Inc. 1970, p. 19.
6. Collins, *op. cit.*, p. 154.
7. *Ibid.*, p. 155.
8. *Ibid.*, p. 141.
9. Sigmund Koch, ed. *Psychology: A Study of a Science.* New York:McGraw-Hill, 1959-1963.
10. Sigmund Koch, "The Image of Man in Encounter Groups," *The American Scholar,* Autumn 1973, p. 636.
11. Sigmund Koch, "Psychology Cannot Be a Coherent Science," *Psychology Today,* September 1969, p. 66.
12. Mary Stewart Van Leeuwen. *The Sorcerer's Apprentice.* Downers Grove: InterVarsity Press, 1982, p. 91.
13. Lee Coleman. *The Reign of Error.* Boston: Beacon Press, 1984, p. xii.
14. *Ibid.*, p. xv.
15. Jerome Frank, "Mental Health in a Fragmented Society," *American Journal of Orthopsychiatry,* July 1979, p. 404.
16. Karl Popper, "Scientific Theory and Falsifiability," *Perspectives in Philosophy.* Robert N. Beck, ed. New York: Holt, Rinehart, Winston, 1975, pp. 343, 346.
17. Carol Tavris, "The Freedom to Change," *Prime Time,* October 1980, p. 28.
18 Jerome Frank, "Therapeutic Factors in Psychotherapy," *American Journal of Psychotherapy,* Vol. 25, 1971, p. 356.
19. Lewis Thomas, "Medicine Without Science," *The Atlantic Monthly,* April 1981, p. 40.
20. *Webster's New Collegiate Dictionary.* Springfield: G. & C. Merriam Company, 1974.
21. Jonas Robitscher. *The Powers of Psychiatry.* Boston: Houghton Mifflin Company, 1980, p. 8.
22. *Ibid.*, p. 183.
23. E. Fuller Torrey. *The Mind Game.* New York: Emerson Hall Publishers, Inc., p. 8.
24. E. Fuller Torrey, "The Protection of Ezra Pound," *Psychology Today,* November 1981, p. 66.
25. Walter Reich, "Psychiatry's Second Coming," *Encounter,* August 1981, p.68.
26. *Ibid.*, p. 70.
27. Dave Hunt. *Beyond Seduction.* Eugene: Harvest House, 1987, p. 96.
28. Collins, *op. cit.*, p. 124.

Chapter 2: Truth or Confusion?
1. Gary R. Collins. *Can You Trust Psychology?* Downers Grove: InterVarsity Press, 1988, p. 28.
2. *Ibid.*, p. 121.
3. Roger Mills, "Psychology Goes Insane, Botches Role as Science," *The National Educator,* July 1980, p. 14.
4. Joseph Wolpe quoted by Ann Japenga, "Great Minds on the Mind Assemble for Conference," *Los Angeles Times,* 18 December 1985, Part V, p. 16.
5. Collins, *op. cit.*, p. 94.

6. *Ibid.*, p. 90.
7. *Ibid.*, p. 89.
8. *Ibid.*, pp. 89-90.
9. *Ibid.*
10. *Ibid.*, p. 94.
11. *Ibid.*
12. *Ibid.*, p. 72.
13. *Ibid.*, pp. 72, 90, 94.
14. Thomas Szasz. *The Myth of Psychotherapy.* Garden City: Doubleday/Anchor Press, 1978, pp.182-183.
15. Franklin D. Chu and Sharland Trotter. *The Madness Establishment.* New York: Grossman Publishers, 1974, p. 4.
16. Collins, *op. cit.*, p. 135.
17. *Ibid.*
18. Szasz, *op. cit.*, p. 7.
19. Collins, *op. cit.*, p. 114.
20. Barbara Brown. *Supermind.* New York: Harper & Row, Publishers, 1980, p. 8.
21. *Ibid.*, p. 6.
22. Louisa E. Rhine. *Mind Over Matter: Psychokinesis.* New York: MacMillan, 1970, pp. 389-390.
23. Collins, *op. cit.*, p. 115.
24. *Ibid.*, p. 114.
25. Aaron T. Beck and Jeffrey E. Young, "Depression." *Clinical Handbook of Psychological Disorders.* David H. Barlow, ed. New York: The Guilford Press, 1985, p. 207.

Chapter 3: Psychological Cults.
1. Gary R. Collins. *Can You Trust Psychology?* Downers Grove: InterVarsity Press, 1988, p. 101.
2. Paul C. Vitz. *Psychology as Religion: The Cult of Self Worship.* Grand Rapids: Wm. B. Eerdmans Publishing Co., 1977.
3. Collins, *op. cit.*, p. 31.
4. *Ibid.*, p. 30.
5. *Ibid.*, p. 33.
6. *Ibid.*, p. 32.
7. Allen E. Bergin, "Psychotherapy and Religious Values," *Journal of Consulting and Clinical Psychology*, Vol. 48, No. 1, 1980, p. 97.
8. Allen E.Bergin, "Psychotherapeutic Change and Humanistic Versus Religious Values," BMA Audio Cassette, #T-301. New York: The Guilford Press, 1979.
9. Bergin, "Psychotherapy and Religious Values," *op. cit.*, pp. 101-2.
10. Allen E. Bergin, "Behavior Therapy and Ethical Relativism: Time for Clarity," *Journal of Consulting and Clinical Psychology.* Vol. 48, No. 1, 1980, p. 11.
11. Hans Strupp, "Some Observations on the Fallacy of Value-free Therapy and the Empty Organism," in *Psychotherapies: A Comparative Casebook.* Steven Morse and Robert Watson, eds. New York: Holt, Rinehart, and Winston, 1977, p. 313.
12. Perry London. *The Modes and Morals of Psychotherapy.* New York: Holt, Rinehart, and Winston, 1964, pp. 1-40, 6.
13. *Ibid.*, p. 5.
14. Steven Morse and Robert Watson. *Psychotherapies: A Comparative Casebook.* New York: Holt, Rinehart, and Winston, 1977, p. 3.
15. Collins, *op. cit.*, p. 29.
16. *Ibid.*, p. 74.
17. *Ibid.*
18. *Ibid.*, pp. 74-75.
19. *Ibid.*, p. 75.
20. *Ibid.*
21. *Ibid.*
22. Daniel Goleman. *The Meditative Mind.* Los Angeles: Jeremy P. Tarcher, Inc., 1988.
23. Collins, *op. cit.*, p. 118.
24. Jonathan Adolph, "What is the New Age?" *The 1988 Guide to New Age Living*, published by *New Age Journal*, 1988, pp. 11-12.
25. Abraham Maslow. *Toward a Psychology of Being.* Princeton: Van Nostrand Reinhold, 1968, pp. iii-iv.

Chapter 4: Integration or Separation?
1. Gary R. Collins. *Can You Trust Psychology?* Downers Grove: InterVarsity Press, 1988, p. 52.
2. *Ibid.*, p. 19.
3. *Ibid.*
4. Martin and Deidre Bobgan, "Psychotherapeutic Methods of CAPS Members," *Christian Association for Psychological Studies Bulletin* 6, No. 1, 1980, p. 13.
5. Morris Parloff, "Psychotherapy and Research: An Anaclitic Depression," *Psychiatry*, Vol. 43, November 1980, p. 291.
6. Carl Rogers, "Some Personal Learnings about Interpersonal Relationships," 16mm film developed by Dr. Charles K. Ferguson. University of California Extension Media Center, Berkeley, CA, film

#6785.
7. Collins, *op. cit.*, p. 19.
8. *Ibid.*
9. Linda Riebel, "Theory as Self-Portrait and the Ideal of Objectivity," *Journal of Humanistic Psychology*, Spring1982, pp. 91, 92.
10. Harvey Mindess. *Makers of Psychology: The Personal Factor*. New York: Insight Books, 1988, p. 15.
11. *Ibid.*, pp. 15-16.
12. *Ibid.*, p. 16.
13. *Ibid.*, p. 46.
14. *Ibid.*, p. 169.
15. Collins, *op. cit.*, p. 19.
16. *Ibid.*, p. 20.
17. *Ibid.*, p. 62.
18. *Ibid.*
19. *Ibid.*, p. 63.
20. *Ibid.*, p. 91.
21. *Ibid.*, p. 96.
22. *Ibid.*
23. *Ibid.*, p. 95.
24. *Ibid.*, pp. 95-96.
25. *Ibid.*, p. 96.
26. *Ibid.*
27. *Ibid.*, p. 127.
28. *Ibid.*, p. 17.
29. *Ibid.*, p. 128.
30. *Ibid.*
31. *Ibid.*
32. P. Sutherland and P. Poelstra, "Aspects of Integration." Paper presented at the meeting of the Western association of Christians for Psychological studies, Santa Barbara, CA, June 1976.
33. Collins, *op. cit.*, p. 129.
34. *Ibid.*
35. *Ibid.*
36. *Ibid.*
37. *Ibid.*, p. 58.
38. *Ibid.*
39. *Ibid.*, pp. 72-73.
40. *Ibid.*, p. 72.
41. John D. Carter and Bruce Narramore. *The Integration of Psychology and Theology*. Grand Rapids: Zondervan Publishing House, 1979, p. 15.
42. Charles Tart. *Transpersonal Psychologies*. New York: Harper & Row, Publishers, 1975, p. 4.
43. James D. Foster et al, "The Popularity of Integration Models, 1980-1985." *Journal of Psychology and Theology*, Vol. 16, No. 1, 1988, p. 4, 8.
44. *Ibid.*, p. 8.
45. *Ibid.*
46. E. E. Griffeth quoted by Everett L. Worthington, Jr., "Religious Counseling: A Review of Published Empirical Research." *Journal of Counseling and Development*, Vol. 64, March 1986, p. 427.
47. Collins, *op. cit.*, p. 59.
48. *Ibid.*, p. 130.

Chapter 5: Effectiveness.
1. Hans Strupp, Suzanne Hadley, Beverly Gomes-Schwartz. *Psychotherapy for Better or Worse*. New York: Jason Aronson, Inc., 1977, pp. 115-116.
2. American Psychiatric Association Commission on Psychotherapies. *Psychotherapy Research: Methodological and Efficacy Issues*, 1982, p. 228.
3. "Ambiguity Pervades Research on Effectiveness of Psychotherapy," *Brain-Mind Bulletin*, 4 October 1982, p. 2.
4. Allen E.Bergin, "Therapist-Induced Deterioration in Psychotherapy," BMA Audio Cassette #T-302. New York: Guilford Publishers, Inc., 1979.
5. Judd Marmor, "Foreword." *Psychotherapy Versus Behavior Therapy* by R. Bruce Sloan et al. Cambridge: Harvard University Press, 1975, p. xv.
6. David Gelman and Mary Hager, "Psychotherapy in the '80's," *Newsweek*, 30 November 1981, p. 73.
7. Sol L. Garfield and Allen E. Bergin, eds. *Handbook of Psychotherapy and Behavior Change*. New York: John Wiley & sons, 1978.
8. Hans J. Eysenck, "The Effects of Psychotherapy: An Evaluation," *Journal of Consulting Psychology*, Vol. 16, 1952, p.322.
9. *Ibid.*, pp. 322-323.
10. Hans J. Eysenck, "Psychotherapy, Behavior Therapy, and the Outcome Problem," BMA Audio Cassette #T-308. New York: Guilford Publications, inc., 1979.

11. Hans J. Eysenck, letter to editor, *American Psychologist*, January 1980, p. 114.
12. Hans J. Eysenck, "The Effectiveness of Psychotherapy: The Specter at the Feast," *The Behavioral and Brain Sciences*, June 1983, p. 290.
13. Gary R. Collins. *Can You Trust Psychology?* Downers Grove: InterVarsity Press, 1988, p. 28.
14. Allen E. Bergin and Michael J. Lambert, "The Evaluation of Therapeutic Outcomes," *Handbook of Psychotherapy and Behavior Change*, 2nd Ed. Sol Garfield and Allen E. Bergin, eds. New York: John Wiley & Sons, 1978, p. 145.
15. Sol Garfield, "Psychotherapy: Efficacy, Generality, and Specificity," *Psychotherapy Research: Where Are We and Where Should We Go?* Janet B. W. Williams and Robert L. Spitzer, eds. New York: The Guilford Press, 1983, p. 296.
16. Morris Parloff, "Psychotherapy and Research: Anaclitic Depression." *Psychiatry*, Vol. 43, November 1980, p. 287.
17. Allen E. Bergin and Michael J. Lambert, "The Evaluation of Therapeutic Outcomes," in *Handbook of Psychotherapy and Behavior Change*. Sol L. Garfield and Allen E. Bergin, eds. New York: John Wiley & Sons, 1978, p. 180.
18. Allen E. Bergin, "Psychotherapy and Religious Values." *Journal of Consulting and Clinical Psychology*, Vol. 48, p. 98.
19. Parloff, *op. cit.*, p. 288.
20. Jerome Frank, "Mental Health in a Fragmented Society: The Shattered Crystal Ball." *American Journal of Orthopsychiatry*, Vol. 49, No. 3, July 1979, p. 406.
21. Leslie Prioleau, Martha Murdock, and Nathan Brody, "An Analysis of Psychotherapy Versus Placebo Studies," *The Behavioral and Brain Sciences*, June 1983, p. 284.
22. D. Patrick Miller, "An Interview on Shamanism with Leslie Gray." *The Sun*, Issue 148, pp. 6-7.
23. Everett L. Worthington, Jr., "Religious Counseling: A Review of Published Empirical Research," *Journal of Counseling and Development*, Vol. 64, March 1986, p. 429.
24. Garfield, "Psychotherapy: Efficacy . . .," *op. cit.*, p. 295.
25. *Ibid.*, p. 303.
26. S. J. Rachman and G. T. Wilson. *The Effects of Psychological Therapy*, 2nd Enlarged Edition. New York: Pergamon Press, 1980, p. 251.
27. Eysenck, "Psychotherapy, Behavior Therapy, and the Outcome Problem," *op. cit.*
28. P. London and G. L. Klerman, "Evaluating Psychotherapy," *American Journal of Psychiatry* 139:709-17, 1982, p. 715.
29. Donald Klein statement in "Proposals to Expand Coverage of Mental Health under Medicare-Medicaid." Hearing before the subcommittee on Health of the Committee on Finance, Ninety-Fifth Congress, Second Session, 18 August 1978, p. 45.
30. Jay B. Constantine letter, printed in *Blue Sheet*, Vol. 22 (50), 12 December, 1979, pp. 8-9.
31. Nathan Epstein and Louis Vlok, "Research on the Results of Psychotherapy: A Summary of Evidence," *American Journal of Psychiatry*, August 1981, p. 1033.
32. Rachman and Wilson, *op. cit.*, p. 77.
33. *Ibid.*, p. 259.
34. Michael Shepherd, "Psychotherapy Outcome Research and Parloff's Pony," *The Behavioral and Brain Sciences*, June 1983, p. 301.
35. Collins, *op. cit.*, p. 28.
36. Carin Rubenstein, "A Consumer's Guide to Psychotherapy." *EveryWoman's Emotional Well-Being*. Carol Tavris, ed. Garden City: Doubleday and Company, Inc., 1986, p. 447.
37. Richard Stuart. *Trick or Treatment*. Champaign: Research Press, 1970, p. i.
38. Strupp, Hadley, Gomes-Schwartz, *op. cit.*, pp. 51, 83
39. Allen E. Bergin and Michael J. Lambert, "The Evaluation of Therapeutic Outcomes," *Handbook of Psychotherapy and Behavior Change*, 2nd Ed. Sol Garfield and Allen E. Bergin, eds. New York: John Wiley & Sons, 1978, p. 145.
40. Parloff, *op. cit.*, p. 284.
41. Carol Tavris, "You Are What You Do," *Prime Time*, November 1980, p. 47.
42. Bergin, "Therapist-Induced Deterioration in Psychotherapy," *op. cit.*
43. Michael Scriven quoted by Allen E. Bergin, "Psychotherapy Can Be Dangerous," *Psychology Today*, November 1975, p. 96.
44. Michael Scriven letter on file.
45. Martin and Deidre Bobgan. *The Psychological Way/The Spiritual Way*. Bethany House Publishers, 1979, pp. 21-23.
46. Dorothy Tennov. *Psychotherapy: The Hazardous Cure*. New York: Abelard-Schuman, 1975, p. 83.
47. Allen E. Bergin, "Negative Effects Revisited: A Reply," *Professional Psychology*, February 1980, p. 97.
48. Collins, *op. cit.*, p. 47.
49. Joseph Durlak, "Comparative Effectiveness of Paraprofessional and Professional Helpers," *Psychological Bulletin* 86, 1979, pp. 80-92.
50. Daniel Hogan. *The Regulation of Psychotherapists*. Cambridge: Ballinger Publishers, 1979.
51. James Fallows, "The Case Against Credentialism," *The Atlantic Monthly*, December 1985, p. 65.
52. Frank, *op. cit.*, p. 406.
53. Eysenck, "The Effectiveness of Psychotherapy: The Specter at the Feast," *op.cit.*, p. 290.
54. Donald Klein, "Specificity and Strategy in Psychotherapy," *Psychotherapy Research*. Janet B. W. Williams and Robert L. Spitzer, eds. New York: The Guilford Press, 1984, p. 308.
55. *Ibid.*, p. 313.

56. Joseph Wortis, "General Discussion." *Psychotherapy Research*. Janet B. W. Williams and Robert L. Spitzer, eds. New York: The Guilford Press, 1984, p. 394.
57. James Pennebaker quoted by Kimberly French, "Truth's Healthy Consequences," *New Age Journal*, November 1985, p. 60.
58. Robert Spitzer, "General Discussion," *Psychotherapy Research, op. cit.*, p. 396.
59. Collins, *op. cit.*, pp. 46-47.
60. Bobgan, *op. cit.*, p. 60.
61. Hugh Drummond, "Dr. D. Is Mad As Hell," *Mother Jones*, December 1979, p. 52.
62. Bobgan, *op. cit.*, pp. 61-62.
63. George Albee, "The Answer Is Prevention," *Psychology Today*, February 1985, p. 60.
64. Collins, *op. cit.*, p. 47.
65. *Ibid.*
66. Martin and Deidre Bobgan. *PsychoHeresy: The Psychological Seduction of Christianity.* Santa Barbara: EastGate Publishers, 1987.

Chapter 6: The Self-Centered Gospel.
1. L. Berkhof. *Systematic Theology.* Grand Rapids: Wm. B. Eerdmans Publishing Co., 1941, p. 20.
2. Paul Brownback. *The Danger of Self-Love.* Chicago: Moody Press, 1982, p. 33.
3. Gary R. Collins. *The Magnificent Mind.* Waco: Word Books, 1985, p. 143.
4. Gary R. Collins. *Can You Trust Psychology?* Downers Grove: InterVarsity Press, 1988, p. 86.
5. Don Matzat, "The Great Psychology Debate." *The Christian News*, June 20, 1988, p. 6.
6. Collins, *Can You Trust Psychology? op. cit.*, p. 144, quoting Nathaniel Brandon, "Restraints May Allow Fulfillment," *APA Monitor*, October 1984, p. 5.
7. Carl Rogers, Graduation Address, Sonoma state College, quoted by William Kirk Kilpatrick in *The Emperor's New Clothes.* Westchester: Crossway Books, 1985, p. 162.
8. Kilpatrick, *ibid.*
9. Adrianne Aron, "Maslow's Other Child." Rollo May et al, eds. *Politics and Innocence: A Humanistic Debate.* Dallas: Saybrook Publishers, 1986, p. 96.
10. Daniel Yankelovich. *New Rules: Searching for Self-Fulfillment in a World Turned Upside Down.* New York: Random House, 1981, p. xx.
11. *Ibid.*, xviii.
12. *Ibid.*, jacket cover.
13. Rollo May, "The Problem with Evil." *Politics and Innocence, op. cit.*, p. 22.
14. John D. McCarthy and Dean R. Hoge, "The Dynamics of Self-Esteem and Delinquency." *American Journal of Sociology*, Vol. 90, No. 2, p. 407.
15. *Ibid.*
16. David Myers. *The Inflated Self.* New York: Seabury, 1984, p. 24.
17. Patricia McCormack, "Good News for the Underdog," *Santa Barbara News-Press*, 8 November 1981, p. D-10.
18. Larry Scherwitz, Lewis E. Graham, II and Dean Ornish, "Self-Involvement and the Risk Factors for Coronary Heart Disease," *Advances, Institute for the Advancement of Health*, Vol. 2, No. 2, Spring 1985, p. 16.
19. *Ibid.*, p. 17.
20. Collins, *Can You Trust Psychology? op. cit.*, pp. 145-146.
21. *Ibid.*, p. 145.
22. *Ibid.*

Chapter 7: Where Do We Go from Here?
1. Gary R. Collins. *Can You Trust Psychology?* Downers Grove: InterVarsity Press, 1988, pp. 94-95.
2. Don Matzat, "The Great Psychology Debate." *The Christian News*, June 20, 1988, p. 6.
3. Collins, *op. cit.*, p. 125.
4. Looney et al, cited in James D. Guy and Gary P. Liaboe, "The Impact of Conducting Psychotherapy on Psychotherapists' Interpersonal Functioning." *Professional Psychology: Research and Practice*, Vol. 17, No. 2, 1986, p. 111.
5. Guy and Liaboe, *op. cit.*, p. 111.
6. *Ibid.*, pp. 111-112, and Bernie Zilbergeld. *The Shrinking of America: Myths of Psychological Change.* Boston: Little, Brown and Company, p. 164.
7. Guy and Liaboe, *op. cit.* p. 112.
8. Ruth G. Matarazzo, "Research on the Teaching and Learning of Psychotherapeutic Skills." *Handbook of Psychotherapy and Behavior Change: An Empirical Analysis.* Allen E. Bergin and Sol Garfield, eds. New York: Wiley, 1971, p. 910.
9. Collins, *op. cit.*, p. 104.
10. *Ibid.*, p. 79.
11. *Ibid.*, p. 82.
12. *Ibid.*, p. 101.
13. Joseph Palotta. *The Robot Psychiatrist.* Metairie: Revelation House Publishers, Inc., 1981, p. 400.
14. Collins, *op. cit.*, pp. 120-121.
15. *Ibid.*, p. 90.
16. *Ibid.*, p. 57.
17. Thomas Szasz. *The Myth of Psychotherapy.* Garden City: Anchor/Doubleday, 1978, p. xxii.

348 **Prophets of PsychoHeresy**

18. Martin and Deidre Bogan. *The Psychological Way/The Spiritual Way.* Minneapolis: Bethany House Publishers, 1979, back cover.
19. Bernie Zilbergeld. *The Shrinking of America.* Boston: Little, Brown and Company, 1983.
20. Bernie Zilbergeld quoted by Don Stanley, "OK, So Maybe You Don't Need to See a Therapist." *Sacramento Bee,* 24 May 1983, p. B-4.
21. Bogban, *op. cit,* back cover,
22. D. E. Orlinsky and K. E. Howard, "The Relation of Process to Outcome in Psychotherapy" in *Handbook of Psychotherapy and Behavior change,* 2nd Ed. Sol Garfield and Allen E. Bergin, eds. New York: Wiley & Sons, 1978, p. 288.
23. J. Vernon McGee, "Psycho-Religion—The New Pied Piper," *Thru the Bible Radio Newsletter,* November 1986.
24. J. Vernon McGee letter on file, 18 September 1986.
25. Collins, *op. cit.,* p. 165.

Part Two: Inside-Out Theology.

Chapter 8: Integration.
1. Lawrence J. Crabb, Jr. *Effective Biblical Counseling.* Grand Rapids: Zondervan Publishing House, 1977, p. 15.
2. *Ibid.,* p. 15.
3. Lawrence J. Crabb, Jr. *Understanding People.* Grand Rapids: Zondervan Publishing House, 1987, pp. 66-72.
4. Crabb, *Effective Biblical Counseling, op. cit.,* pp. 47-56.
5. *Ibid.,* p. 48.
6. *Ibid.,* pp. 35-46.
7. *Ibid.,* p. 52.
8. Crabb, *Understanding People, op. cit.,* pp. 66-67.
9. *Ibid.,* p. 63.
10. *Ibid.,* pp, 54, 56-57.
11. *Ibid.,* p. 56.
12. *Ibid.,* pp. 63, 70ff.
13. *Ibid.,* p. 69.
14. *Ibid.,* p. 56.
15. *Ibid.,* pp. 57-58.
16. *Ibid.,* pp. 50-53, 56-57, 64-65, 68-69.
17. *Ibid.,* p. 58.
18. *Ibid.,* p. 57.
19. *Ibid.*
20. *Ibid.,* pp. 55-58.
21. *Ibid.*
22. *Ibid.,* p. 58.
23. *Ibid.,* p. 57.
24. *Ibid.,* p. 58.

Chapter 9: The Use and Praise of Psychology.
1. Lawrence J. Crabb, Jr. *Understanding People.* Grand Rapids: Zondervan Publishing House, 1987, 15.
2. Lawrence J. Crabb, Jr. *Effective Biblical Counseling.* Grand Rapids: Zondervan Publishing House, 1977, p. 52ff.
3. *Ibid.,* p. 56.
4. *Ibid.,* p. 15.
5. *Ibid.,* p. 37.
6. Lawrence J. Crabb, Jr. *Basic Principles of Biblical Counseling.* Grand Rapids: Zondervan Publishing House, 1975, p. 77.
7. J. P. Chaplin. *Dictionary of Psychology,* Revised Edition. New York: Dell Publishing Company, 1968, pp. 555-556.
8. Crabb, *Understanding People, op. cit.,* p. 59.
9. *Ibid.,* p. 61.
10. *Ibid.,* pp. 215-216.
11. Lawrence J. Crabb, Jr. *Inside Out.* Colorado Springs: NavPress, 1988, pp. 14-15, 32, 44-49, 73, 119, 122, 128.
12. *Ibid.,* pp. 44, 52-53, 182ff.
13. Crabb, *Understanding People, op. cit.,* p. 142ff.
14. *Ibid.,* pp. 143-144.
15. *Ibid.,* p. 144.
16. *Ibid.,* pp. 48-58, 144ff.
17. *Ibid.,* pp. 144-145.
18. *Ibid.,* pp. 126-130.
19. *Ibid.,* p. 129.
20. *Ibid.*
21. Ernest R. Hilgard, Rita L. Atkinson, Richard C. Atkinson. *Introduction to Psychology,* 7th Edition.

New York: Harcourt, Brace, Janovich, Inc., 1979, p. 389.
22. Jeffrey Masson. *Against Therapy*. New York: Atheneum, 1988, p. 45ff.
23. Crabb, *Inside Out, op. cit.*, pp. 44, 182.
24. Crabb, *Understanding People, op. cit.*, p. 142.
25. *Ibid.*, pp. 44, 182.
26. *Ibid.*, p. 129.
27. *Ibid.*
28. *Ibid.*
29. Thomas Szasz. *The Myth of Psychotherapy*. Garden City: Doubleday/Anchor Press, 1978, p. 146.
30. Crabb, *Effective Biblical Counseling, op. cit.*, p. 43.
31. B. H. Shulman, "Adlerian Psychotherapy." *Encyclopedia of Psychology*. Raymond J. Corsini, ed. New York: John Wiley and Sons, 1984, p. 18.
32. Alfred Adler. *The Practice of Individual Psychology*. New York: Harcourt, Brace & Company, Inc., 1929, p. 10.
33. *Ibid.*, p. 21.
34. Crabb, *Inside Out, op. cit.*, pp. 167-170.
35. Crabb, *Effective Biblical Counseling, op. cit.*, p. 152; Crabb, *Understanding People, op. cit.*, p. 203.
36. Shulman, *op. cit.*, p. 19.
37. *Ibid.*, p. 20.
38. *Ibid.*
39. H. H. Mosak, "Adlerian Psychology." *Encyclopedia of Psychology*. Raymond J. Corsini, ed. New York: John Wiley and Sons, 1984, p. 18.
40. Albert Ellis, "Is Religiosity Pathological?" *Free Inquiry*, Spring 1988(927-32), p. 27.
41. *Ibid.*, p. 31.
42. *Ibid.*
43. Crabb, *Effective Biblical Counseling, op. cit.*, p. 56.

Chapter 10: Need Theology.
1. Lawrence J. Crabb, Jr. *Basic Principles of Biblical Counseling*. Grand Rapids: Zondervan Publishing House, 1975, p. 53.
2. Lawrence J. Crabb, Jr. *Effective Biblical Counseling*. Grand Rapids: Zondervan Publishing House, 1977, p. 61.
3. *Ibid.*, pp. 60-61.
4. *Ibid.*, pp. 91-96.
5. Lawrence J. Crabb, Jr. *Understanding People*. Grand Rapids: Zondervan Publishing House, 1987, p. 146ff.
6. Lawrence J. Crabb, Jr. *Inside Out*. Colorado Springs: NavPress, 1988, pp. 52-56.
7. *Ibid.*, p. 125.
8. *Ibid.*, p. 127.
9. Crabb, *Understanding People*, op. cit., p. 188.
10. *Ibid.*, p. 114.
11. Crabb, *Basic Principles of Biblical Counseling, op. cit.*, p. 53.
12. Lawrence J. Crabb, Jr. and Dan B. Allender. *Encouragement*. Grand Rapids: Zondervan Publishing House, 1984, pp. 31-36; Crabb, *Effective Biblical Counseling, op. cit.*, p. 61.
13. Crabb, *Effective Biblical Counseling, op. cit.*, p. 71.
14. Crabb, *Understanding People*, op. cit., pp. 130-138.
15. *Ibid.*, p. 129.
16. *Ibid.*, pp. 148-152.
17. *Ibid.*, p. 165.
18. *Ibid.*, pp. 158-168.
19. *Ibid.*, pp. 171-189.
20. Tony Walter. *Need: The New Religion* . Downers Grove: InterVarsity Press,1985, Preface.
21. *Ibid.*, p. 5.
22. *Ibid.*, p. 13
23. *Ibid.*, p. 161.
24. *Ibid.*, p. 111.
25. Crabb, *Understanding People*, op. cit., pp. 93-96.
26. *Ibid.*, p. 93.
27. *Ibid.*, p. 15.
28. A. W. Tozer. *The Pursuit of God*. Harrisburg: Christian Publications, 1948, pp. 91-92.

Chapter 11: The Unconscious: A Key to Understanding People?
1. Lawrence J. Crabb, Jr. *Understanding People*. Grand Rapids: Zondervan Publishing House, 1987, pp. 126ff., 142ff., and Lawrence J. Crabb, Jr. *Effective Biblical Counseling*. Grand Rapids: Zondervan Publishing House, 1977, p. 91ff.
2. Crabb, *Effective Biblical Counseling, op. cit.*, p. 91.
3. *Ibid.*, p. 92.
4. Lawrence J. Crabb, Jr. and Dan B. Allender. *Encouragement*. Grand Rapids: Zondervan Publishing House, 1984, p. 95.
5. Crabb, *Understanding People*, op. cit., p. 148.
6. *Ibid.*, p. 148.

7. Lawrence J. Crabb, Jr. *The Marriage Builder*. Grand Rapids: Zondervan Publishing House,1982, p. 49.
8. Crabb, *Understanding People*, op. cit., p. 144.
9. *Ibid.*, pp. 144-145.
10. Karl Popper, "Scientific Theory and Falsifiability." *Perspectives in Philosophy*. Robert N. Beck, ed. New York: Holt, Rinehart, Winston, 1975, p. 343.
11. *Ibid.*, pp. 344-345.
12. *Ibid.*, p. 344.
13. *Ibid.*, p. 343.
14. Carol Tavris, "Freedom to Change," *Prime Time*, October 1980, p. 28.
15. Jerome Frank, "Therapeutic Factors in Psychotherapy," *American Journal of Psychotherapy*, Vol. 25, 1971, p. 356.
16. Crabb, *Understanding People*, op. cit., p. 146.
17. *Ibid.*
18. *Ibid.*
19. *Ibid.*
20. Lawrence J. Crabb, Jr. *Inside Out*. Colorado Springs: NavPress, 1988, pp. 54, 64, 93.
21. *Ibid.*, pp. 44, 54, 80-81, 92, etc.
22. *Ibid.*, pp. 64.
23. *Ibid.*, p. 57.
24. Crabb, *Effective Biblical Counseling, op. cit.*, p. 91.
25. *Ibid.*, p. 91.
26. *Ibid.*, pp. 47-49.
27. W. E. Vine. *The Expanded Vine's Expository Dictionary of New Testament Words.* John Kohlenberger III, ed. Minneapolis: Bethany House Publishers, 1984, pp. 741-742.
28. Crabb, *Understanding People*, op. cit., p. 129.
29. *Ibid.*, p. 129ff.; Crabb, *Effective Biblical Counseling, op. cit.*, p. 78; Crabb, *Basic Principles of Biblical Counseling, op, cit.*, p. 80.
30. Crabb, *Understanding People*, op. cit., pp. 142-143.
31. Houston Smith. *The Religions of Man*. New York: Harper & Row, 1965, p. 52.
32. *Ibid.*, pp. 52-53.

Chapter 12: Personal Circle: Unconscious Motivators of Behavior.
1. Lawrence J. Crabb, Jr. *Understanding People*. Grand Rapids: Zondervan Publishing House, 1987, p. 15.
2. Lawrence J. Crabb, Jr. *Effective Biblical Counseling*. Grand Rapids: Zondervan Publishing House, 1977, pp. 60-61.
3. Lawrence J. Crabb, Jr. *Inside Out*. Colorado Springs: NavPress, 1988, p. 83.
4. Lawrence J. Crabb, Jr. *The Marriage Builder*. Grand Rapids: Zondervan Publishing House,1982, p. 29.
5. Crabb, *Effective Biblical Counseling, op. cit.*, p. 139.
6. *Ibid.*, p. 74ff.
7. Crabb, *Understanding People*, op. cit., p. 93-96.
8. Crabb, *Basic Principles of Biblical Counseling*, op. cit., p. 74; Crabb, *Effective Biblical Counseling*, op. cit., pp. 60-61, 116, 118, etc.; Crabb, *Understanding People*, op. cit., pp. 146-148; Crabb, *Inside Out, op. cit.*, p. 54.
9. Crabb, *Effective Biblical Counseling, op. cit.*, p. 76.
10. Crabb, *Understanding People*, op. cit., p. 93ff.
11. Crabb, *Effective Biblical Counseling, op. cit.*, p. 76.
12. *Ibid.*
13. *Ibid.*
14. Crabb, *Inside Out, op. cit.*, pp. 15, 16, 18.
15. Crabb, *Effective Biblical Counseling, op. cit.*, pp. 76-77.
16. *Ibid.*, pp. 77-78.
17. *Ibid.*, p. 74ff.
18. A. H. Maslow. *Motivation and Personality*. New York:Harper & Brothers Publishers, 1954, p. 90.
19. *Ibid.*, p. 91.
20. *Ibid.*, p. 105.
21. Crabb, *The Marriage Builder, op. cit.*, p. 29.
22. *Ibid.*
23. Crabb, *Understanding People*, op. cit., p. 134.
24. *Ibid.*, p. 109.
25. *Ibid.*
26. *Ibid.*
27. Crabb, *Inside Out, op. cit.*, p. 64.
28. Crabb, *Understanding People*, op. cit., p. 111.
29. *Ibid.*, p. 15.
30. Crabb, *Effective Biblical Counseling, op. cit.*, p. 61.
31. *New American Standard Bible*. La Habra: The Lockman Faoundation, 1960, 1962, 1963, 1968, 1971, 1973, 1977.
32. Crabb, *Understanding People*, op. cit., p. 105.

33. *Ibid.*
34. *Ibid.*, p. 106.
35. *Ibid.*, p. 105.
36. *Ibid.*
37. *Ibid.*, p. 106.
38. Crabb, *Inside Out, op. cit.*, p. 69.
39. *Ibid.*, p. 92.
40. Crabb, *Understanding People*, op. cit., p. 105.
41. *Ibid.*, p. 107ff.
42. *Ibid.*, p. 105.
43. *Ibid.*, pp. 104-107 with 142-152.
44. *Ibid.*, p. 111.
45. Crabb, *Inside Out, op. cit.*, p. 68.
46. *Ibid.*, p. 71.
47. *Ibid.*, p. 54.
48. *Ibid.*, pp. 55-56.
49. Crabb, *The Marriage Builder, op. cit.*, p. 29.
50. Crabb, *Understanding People*, op. cit., p. 111.
51. *Ibid.*, p. 217.
52. *Ibid.*, p. 134.
53. Crabb, *Inside Out, op. cit.*, pp. 53-57.
54. Crabb, *Understanding People*, op. cit., p. 111.

Chapter 13: The Rational Circle: Guiding Fictions and Wrong Strategies.
1. Lawrence J. Crabb, Jr. *Effective Biblical Counseling*. Grand Rapids: Zondervan Publishing House, 1977, p. 91ff.
2. *Ibid.*, pp. 91-96.
3. Lawrence J. Crabb, Jr. *Inside Out*. Colorado Springs: NavPress, 1988, pp. 52ff.
4. Lawrence J. Crabb, Jr. *Understanding People*. Grand Rapids: Zondervan Publishing House, 1987, p. 147ff.
5. Crabb, *Effective Biblical Counseling, op. cit.*, pp. 76ff., 91-96; Crabb, *Understanding People*, op. cit. pp. 130, 146ff.; Crabb, *Inside Out, op. cit.*, pp. 44ff., 182ff.
6. Crabb, *Understanding People*, op. cit., p. 145.
7. Crabb, *Effective Biblical Counseling, op. cit.*, p. 69.
8. Lawrence J. Crabb, Jr. *Basic Principles of Biblical Counseling*. Grand Rapids: Zondervan Publishing House, 1975, p. 87.
9. Crabb, *Effective Biblical Counseling, op. cit.*, p. 91.
10. *Ibid.*
11. *Ibid.*, p. 92.
12. Lawrence J. Crabb, Jr. *The Marriage Builder*. Grand Rapids: Zondervan Publishing House,1982, p. 48.
13. *Ibid.*
14. Crabb, *Understanding People, op. cit.*, p. 147.
15. *Ibid.*, p. 143.
16. *Ibid.*, p. 148.
17. Crabb, *Inside Out, op. cit.*, p. 54.
18. *Ibid.*, pp. 44ff., 182ff.
19. Crabb, *Basic Principles of Biblical Counseling, op. cit.*, pp. 56-57, 74; Crabb, *Effective Biblical Counseling, op. cit.*, pp. 69, 105, 116.
20. Crabb, *Understanding People, op. cit.*, pp. 129-130.
21. *Ibid.*, p. 129.
22. *Ibid.*
23. *Ibid.*, p. 130.
24. Crabb, *Effective Biblical Counseling, op. cit.*, pp. 77ff., 94, 120ff., 130ff., 139ff., 153ff.; Crabb, *Understanding People, op. cit.*, pp. 94, 126ff., 137ff., 142-152, 162ff., 177ff.; Crabb, *Inside Out, op. cit.*, pp. 116ff., 156ff., 182ff.
25. Lawrence J. Crabb, Jr. and Dan B. Allender. *Encouragement*. Grand Rapids: Zondervan Publishing House, 1984, pp. 86-89.
26. *Ibid.*, p. 87.
27. *Ibid.*
28. Crabb, *Inside Out, op. cit.*, p. 121ff.
29. Carol Tavris. *Anger: The Misunderstood Emotion*. New York: Simon and Schuster, 1982, p. 36.
30. Crabb, *Encouragement, op. cit.*, p. 33.
31. Crabb, *Understanding People, op. cit.*, p. 115.
32. *Ibid.*, p. 67.
33. *Ibid.*
34. Crabb, *Inside Out, op. cit.*, pp. 15, 16, 18.
35. *Ibid.*, p. 29.
36. *Ibid.*, p. 99.
37. Crabb, *Understanding People, op. cit.*, p. 149ff.; Crabb, *Inside Out, op. cit.*, p. 116ff.
38. Crabb, *Understanding People, op. cit.*, p. 144.

39. *Ibid.*, p. 144.
40. *Ibid.*
41. Crabb, *Inside Out, op. cit.*, p. 119.
42. *Ibid.*, p. 120.
43. *Ibid.*, pp. 119-120.
44. Crabb, *Understanding People, op. cit.*, pp. 149-152.
45. *Ibid.*, pp. 149-150.
46. Crabb, *Inside Out, op. cit.*, p. 184.
47. *Ibid.*
48. *Ibid.*, pp. 196-200.

Chapter 14: Volitional and Emotional Circles and the Process of Change.
1. Lawrence J. Crabb, Jr. *Effective Biblical Counseling.* Grand Rapids: Zondervan Publishing House, 1977, p. 90.
2. *Ibid.*, pp. 91-94.
3. *Ibid.*, p. 94.
4. Lawrence J. Crabb, Jr. *Understanding People.* Grand Rapids: Zondervan Publishing House, 1987, pp. 94, 158-165.
5. *Ibid.*, p. 159.
6. Alfred Adler. *The Practice of Individual Psychology.* New York: Harcourt, Brace & Company, Inc., 1929, p. 4.
7. Crabb, *Understanding People, op. cit.*, p. 161.
8. *Ibid.*, p. 95, 188-189.
9. *Ibid.*, p. 144.
10. Crabb, *Effective Biblical Counseling, op. cit.*, p. 95.
11. Lawrence J. Crabb, Jr. *Inside Out.* Colorado Springs: NavPress, 1988, p. 89.
12. Crabb, *Understanding People, op. cit.*, pp. 13ff., 67ff., 101ff., 146ff.; Crabb, *Inside Out, op. cit.*, pp. 14ff., 32ff., 74ff., 90ff., 116ff, 156ff.
13. Crabb, *Effective Biblical Counseling, op. cit.*, p. 46.
14. Crabb, *Inside Out, op. cit.*, p. 170.
15. *Ibid.*, p. 167.
16. Crabb, *Effective Biblical Counseling, op. cit.*, p. 46.
17. John Rowan, "Nine Humanistic Heresies." *Journal of Humanistic Psychology*, Vol. 27, No. 2, Spring 1987 (141-157), pp. 143-144.
18. Crabb, *Understanding People, op. cit.*, p. 130.
19. Crabb, *Inside Out, op. cit.*, p. 186.
20. J. P. Chaplin. *Dictionary of Psychology*, New Revised Version. New York: Dell Publishing Co., Inc., 1968, p. 2.
21. Sol Garfield and Allen E. Bergin, eds. *Handbook of Psychotherapy and Behavior Change*, 2nd Ed. New York: John Wiley and Sons, 1978, p. 180.
22. David A. Shapiro, "Comparative Credibility of Treatment Rationales." *British Journal of Clinical Psychology*, 1981, Vol. 20 (111-122), p. 112.
23. Crabb, *Inside Out, op. cit.*, p. 165.
24. *Ibid.*, p. 185.
25. *Ibid.*, p. 186.
26. *Ibid.*
27. *Ibid.*, p. 165.
28. *Ibid.*, p. 210.
29. *Ibid.*, p. 211.
30. *Ibid.*
31. *Ibid.*
32. Crabb, *Inside Out Film Series,* Film 2. Colorado Springs: NavPress, 1988.
33. Crabb, *Inside Out, op. cit.*, p. 64.
34. *Ibid.*, p. 163.
35. *Ibid.*, p. 161.

Chapter 15: Enslaving the Gospel to Psychology.
1. Everett F. Harrison, ed. *Baker's Dictionary of Theology.* Grand Rapids: Baker Book House, 1960, p. 205.
2. Lawrence J. Crabb, Jr. *Understanding People.* Grand Rapids: Zondervan Publishing House, 1987, p. 211.
3. Lawrence J. Crabb, Jr. *Inside Out.* Colorado Springs: NavPress, 1988, pp. 189-200.
4. Lawrence J. Crabb, Jr. *The Marriage Builder.* Grand Rapids: Zondervan Publishing House,1982, pp. 21, 27, 34-36, 40-43, 46-47, 53, 57, 59, 71, 77, 90, 91, 94-96, 98.
5. Letter on file.
6. Lawrence J. Crabb, Jr. *Effective Biblical Counseling.* Grand Rapids: Zondervan Publishing House, 1977, p. 48.

Part Three: Fellowship with Freud.
1. Frank B. Minirth and Paul D. Meier. *Happiness Is a Choice.* Grand Rapids: Baker Book House, 1978.

2. Frank B. Minirth and Paul D. Meier. *Happiness Is a Choice*, Way to Grow Cassettes. Waco, TX: Word, Inc., November 15, 1986.

Chapter 16: Freudian Foundations.
1. "The Minirth-Meier Clinic" Radio Program, P. O. Box 1925, Richardson, TX, 75085, April 29, 1987.
2. *Ibid.*, September 16, 1987.
3. Frank Minirth, Paul Meier, and Don Hawkins, "Christianity and Psychology: Like Mixing Oil and Water?" *Christian Psychology for Today*, Spring 1987, p. 4.
4. Frank B. Minirth and Paul D. Meier. *Happiness Is a Choice*. Grand Rapids: Baker Book House, 1978, pp. 49, 54, 108, 215.
5. Paul Meier, Frank Minirth, and Frank Wichern. *Introduction to Psychology and Counseling.* Grand Rapids: Baker Book House, 1982, p. 282.
6. Frank B. Minirth, Paul D. Meier, and Don Hawkins. *Worry-Free Living*. Nashville: Thomas Nelson Publishers, 1989, p. 99.
7. *Hippocrates*, May-June, 1989, p. 12.
8. Nancy Andreasen. *The Broken Brain*. New York: Harper and Row, 1984, p. 231ff.
9. Minirth, Meier, Hawkins, "Christianity and Psychology: Like Mixing Oil and Water?" *op. cit.*, p. 4.
10. Andreasen, *op. cit.*, p. 231.
11. *Mayo Clinic Health Letter*, Dec. 1985, p. 4.
12. Athanasios P. Zis and Frederick K. Goodwin, "The Amine Hypothesis." *Handbook of Affective Disorders*. E. S. Paykel, ed. New York: The Guilford Press, 1982, p. 186.
13. Joseph J. Schildkraut, Alan I. Green, John J. Mooney, "Affective Disorders: Biochemical Aspects." *Comprehensive Textbook of Psychiatry/IV*, 4th ed., 2 vols. Harold I. Kaplan and Benjamin J. Sadock, eds. Baltimore: Williams & Wilkins, 1985, p. 77.
14. "The Minirth-Meier Clinic," *op. cit.*, February 24, 1988.
15. Minirth and Meier, *Happiness Is a Choice, op. cit.*, p. 36.
16. *Ibid.*
17. *Ibid.*, pp. 115, 118, 169.
18. *Ibid.*, p. 37.
19. *Ibid.*, p. p. 39.
20. *Ibid.*, pp. 37, 50, 54, 69, 106, 108.
21. "The Nature and Causes of Depression-III." *Harvard Medical School Mental Health Letter*, March 1988, p. 3.
22. *Ibid.*
23. Minirth and Meier, *Happiness Is a Choice, op. cit.*, p. 168.
24. Frank Minirth. *Christian Psychiatry*. Old Tappan: Fleming H. Revell Company, 1977, p. 180.
25. E. S. Paykel, "Life Events and Early Environment." *Handbook of Affective Disorders*. New York: The Guilford Press, 1982, p.148.
26. *Ibid.*, p. 154.
27. *Ibid.*, p. 156.
28. "The Nature and Causes of Depression-III," *op. cit.*, p. 3.
29. Minirth and Meier, *Happiness Is a Choice, op. cit.*, p. 69.
30. Sigmund Freud, "Mourning and Melancholia." (1917) *The Standard Edition of the Complete Psychological Works of Sigmund Freud*, trans. and ed. James Strachey, Anna Freud, et al., 24 vols. London: Hogarth Press, 1953-1974, Vol. 14, p. 248.
31. "The Nature and Causes of Depression-III," *op. cit.*, p. 3.
32. Minirth and Meier, *Happiness Is a Choice, op. cit.*, p. 106.
33. Philip Harriman. *Dictionary of Psychology*. New York: Philosophical Library, 1947, p. 289.
34. Minirth and Meier, *Happiness Is a Choice, op. cit.*, p. 246.
35. Myer Mendelson, "Psychodynamics of Depression." *Handbook of Affective Disorders*. E. S. Paykel, ed. New York: The Guilford Press, 1982, p. 162.
36. Adolf Grunbaum. *The Foundations of Psychoanalysis*. Berkeley: University of California Press, 1984, p. 3.
37. *Ibid.*, back cover flap.
38. David Holmes, "Investigations of Repression." *Psychological Bulletin*, Vol. 81, 1974, p. 649.
39. *Ibid.*, p. 650.
40. "The Nature and Causes of Depression-III," *op. cit.*, p. 3.
41. "The Minirth-Meier Clinic," *op. cit.*, September 3, 1987.
42. Minirth and Meier, *Happiness Is a Choice, op. cit.*, p. 169; Meier, Minirth, and Wichern, *Introduction to Psychology and Counseling, op. cit.*, pp. 202-203.
43. Minirth and Meier, *Happiness Is a Choice, op. cit.*, p. 47.
44. "The Nature and Causes of Depression-III," *op. cit.*, p. 2.
45. Minirth, Meier, and Hawkins, "Christianity and Psychology: Like Mixing Oil and Water?" *op. cit.*, p. 4.
46. Minirth and Meier, *Happiness Is a Choice, op. cit.*, p. 37.
47. *Ibid.*, p. 50.
48. *Webster's New World Dictionary of the America Language*, Second College Edition. New York: Simon and Schuster, 1984.
49. Minirth and Meier, *Happiness Is a Choice, op. cit.*, p. 157.
50. *Ibid.*, p. 97.

51. *Ibid.*, p. 69.
52. "The Minirth-Meier Clinic," *op. cit.*, March 2, 1988.
53. Letter on file.
54. Judy Eidelson, "Depression: Theories and Therapies." *EveryWoman's Emotional Wellbeing*, Carol Tavris, ed. Garden City: Doubleday and Company, Inc., 1986, p. 397.
55. *Ibid.*, p. 396.
56. "Depression." Medical Essay, *Mayo Clinic Health Letter*, February 1989, p. 4.
57. Eidelson, *op. cit.*, p. 396.
58. *Ibid.*, pp. 396-397.
59. Andreasen, *op. cit.*, p. 41.
60. Robert Hirschfeld, "That Old Let-Down Feeling." *New York Times Book Review*, April 5, 1987, p. 32.
61. *Ibid.*

Chapter 17: Freudian Fallacies.
1. "The Minirth-Meier Clinic" Radio Program, P. O. Box 1925, Richardson, TX, 75085, February 3, 1988.
2. *Ibid.*, September 3, 1987.
3. *Ibid.*, April 7, 1988.
4. *Ibid.*, April 27, 1988.
5. Minirth, Frank B. and Paul D. Meier. *Happiness Is a Choice.* Grand Rapids; Baker Book House, 1978, pp. 153ff., 177.
6. "The Minirth-Meier Clinic," *op. cit.*, Febraury 3, 1988.
7. Frank Minirth. *Christian Psychiatry.* Old Tappan: Fleming H. Revell Company, 1977, p. 142.
8. Frank Minirth, Paul Meier, and Don Hawkins. *Worry-Free Living*, Nashville: Thomas Nelson Publishers, 1989, pp. 67, 112, 113.
9. Carol Tavris. *Anger: The Misunderstood Emotion.* New York: Simon and Schuster, 1982, p. 37.
10. *Ibid.*, p. 38.
11. *Ibid.*, p. 21.
12. Carol Tavris, "Anger Diffused." *Psychology Today*, November 1982, p. 29.
13. Leonard Berkowitz, "The Case for Bottling Up Rage," Psychology Today, July 1973, p. 31.
14. Tavris, "Anger Diffused," *op. cit.*, p. 33.
15. Redford Williams. *The Trusting Heart.* New York: Times Books, 1989, p. 186.
16. Tavris, "Anger Diffused," *op. cit.*, p. 25.
17. "The Minirth-Meier Clinic," *op. cit.*, September 3, 1987; October 4, 1988; January 31, 1989.
18. Minirth and Meier, *Happiness Is a Choice, op. cit.*, p. 153.
19. Frank Minirth, Don Hawkins, Paul Meier, and Richard Flournoy. *How to Beat Burnout.* Chicago: Moody, 1986, p. 44.
20. Minirth and Meier, *Happiness Is a Choice, op. cit.*, p. 137.
21. *Ibid.*, p. 216.
22. Frank B. Minirth, Paul D. Meier, and Don Hawkins. *Worry-Free Living.* Nashville: Thomas Nelson Publishers, 1989, p. 32.
23. Minirth and Meier, *Happiness Is a Choice, op. cit.*, p. 15.
24. John Searle. "Minds, Brains and Science." The 1984 Reith Lectures. London: British Broadcasting Corporation, 1984, pp. 44, 55-56.
25. Edmund Bolles. *Remembering and Forgetting.* New York: Walker and Company, 1988, p. 139.
26. *Ibid.*, p. xi.
27. *Ibid.*, p. 165.
28. Nancy Andreasen. *The Broken Brain.* New York: Harper and Row, 1984, p. 90.
29. "The Minirth-Meier Clinic," *op. cit.*, September 16, 1987; October 4, 1988.
30. Minirth and Meier, *Happiness Is a Choice, op. cit.*, p. 137.
31. *Ibid.*, p. 169.
32. Paul Meier, Frank Minirth, and Frank Wichern. *Introduction to Psychology and Counseling.* Grand Rapids: Baker Book House, 1982, p. 299.
33. *Ibid.*, p. 298.
34. Minirth, *Christian Psychiatry*, op. cit., p. 194.
35. J. P. Chaplin. *Dictionary of Psychology*, New Revised Edition. New York: Dell Publishing Co., Inc., 1968, 1975, pp. 245-246.
36. Minirth, *Christian Psychiatry*, op. cit., p. 194.
37. Chaplin, *op. cit.*, p. 26.
38. *Today's Dictionary of the Bible.* Compiled by T. A. Bryant. Minneapolis: Bethany House Publishers, 1982, p. 270.
39. Minirth and Meier, *Happiness Is a Choice, op. cit.*, p. 69.
40. Frank Sulloway. *Freud: Biologist of the Mind: Beyond the Psychoanalytic Legend.* New York: Basic Books, 1979.
41. Frank J. Sulloway, "Grunbaum on Freud: Flawed Methodologist or Serendipitous Scientist?" *Free Inquiry*, Vol. 5, No. 4, Fall 1985, p. 27.
42. Hans Eysenck, "The Death Knell of Psychoanalysis." *Free Inquiry*, Fall, 1985, p. 32.
43. Frederick Crews, "The Future of an Illusion." *The New Republic*, June 21, 1985, p. 32.
44. *Ibid.*, p. 33.
45. *Ibid.*, p. 28.

46. E. Fuller Torrey. *The Death of Psychiatry.* Radnor: Chilton Book Company, 1974, p. 5.
47. Thomas Szasz. *The Myth of Psychotherapy.* Garden City: Doubleday/Anchor Press, 1978, p. 101.
48. Adolf Grunbaum quoted by Daniel Goleman, "Pressure Mounts for Analysts to Prove Theory Is Scientific," *New York Times,* 15 January 1985, p. C-1.
49. Peter Medawar. *Pluto's Republic.* New York: Oxford University Press, 1982, pp. 71-72.
50. Garth Wood. *The Myth of Neurosis.* New York: Harper & Row, 1986, p. 264ff.
51. *Ibid.,* p. 265.
52. *Ibid.,* p. 285.
53. *Ibid.,* p. 291.
54. Szasz, *op. cit.,* p. 146.

Chapter 18: Personality Disorders.
1. Paul Meier, Frank Minirth, and Frank Wichern. *Introduction to Psychology and Counseling.* Grand Rapids: Baker Book House, 1982, p. 403.
2. *Christian Psychology Today,* Vol. 3, No. 3, Summer 1988.
3. "The Minirth-Meier Clinic," Radio Program, P. O. Box 1925, Richardson, TX, 75085, April 29, 1987; May 26, 1987; February 2, 1988; March 2, 1988; March 16, 1988.
4. *Ibid.,* May 26, 1987.
5. *Brain / Mind Bulletin,* September 1987, Vol. 12, No. 12, p. 1.
6. "Japan's Success? It's in the Blood," *Newsweek,* 1 April 1985, p. 45.
7. "Vision Training Provides Window to Brain Change," *Brain / Mind Bulletin,* October 25, 1982, p. 1.
8. "Auditory Perspective Enlarges Realm of Hearing," Brain/Mind Bulletin, Nov. 22, 1982, p. 1.
9. Ernest Hilgard, Richard Atkinson, Rita Atkinson.*Introduction to Psychology.* New York: Harcourt, Brace, Jovanovich, Inc., 1975, p. 368.
10. Peter Glick, "Stars in Our Eyes." *Psychology Today,* August 1987, p. 6.
11. Calvin W. Hall and Gardner Lindzey. *Theories of Personality.* New York: John Wiley & Sons, Inc., 1957, p.359.
12. Robitscher, Jonas. *The Powers of Psychiatry.* Boston: Houghton Mifflin Company, 1980, p. 167.
13. *Diagnostic and Statistical Manual of Mental Disorders, DSM-III-R,* Third Edition - Revised. Washington: American Psychiatric Association, 1987.
14. J. Katz. In *U. S. v. Torniero,* 570 F. Supp. 721 (D.C. Conn, 1983); quoted in R. Slovenko, "The Meaning of Mental Illness in Criminal Responsibility," *Journal of Legal Medicine,* Vol. 5, March 1984 (1-61).
15. Robitscher, *op. cit.,* p. 166.
16. "The Minirth-Meier Clinic," *op. cit.,* May 26, 1987; *Christian Psychology Today,* Vol. 4, No. 3, Summer 1988.
17. Meier, Minirth, and Wichern, *Introduction to Psychology and Counseling, op. cit.,* p. 178.
18. Herb Kutchins and Stuart A. Kirk, "The Future of DSM: Scientific and Professional Issues." *The Harvard Medical School Mental Health Letter,* Vol. 5, No. 7, January 1989, p. 4.
19. *Ibid.,* p. 5.
20. *Ibid.*
21. *Ibid.,* p. 6.
22. *Ibid.*
23. *Ibid.*
24. "AAPL and DSM-III," *Newsletter of the American Academy of Psychiatry and the Law,* Summer 1976, p. 11.
25. "Current DSM-III Outline," *Psychiatric News,* 17 November 1978, p. 17.
26. Thomas Szasz. *Insanity: The Idea and Its Consequences.* New York: John Wiley & Sons, 1987, p. 80.
27. Alfred Freedman, Harold Kaplan, and Benjamin Sadock. *Modern Synopsis of Comprehensive Textbook of Psychiatry,* 2nd Ed. Baltimore: Williams & Wilkins, 1976, p. 407.
28. Szasz, *op. cit.,* p. 80.
29. David Faust and Jay Ziskin, "The Expert Witness in Psychology and Psychiatry," *Science,* Vol. 241, 1 July 1988, p. 32.
30. Frank B. Minirth and Paul D. Meier. *Happiness Is a Choice.* Grand Rapids: Baker Book House, 1978, p. 59.
31. "The Minirth-Meier Clinic," *op. cit.,* April 29, 1987; March 16, 1988; Frank Minirth. *Christian Psychiatry.* Old Tappan: Fleming H. Revell Company, 1977, pp. 99, 102.
32. "The Minirth-Meier Clinic," *op. cit.,* May 26, 1987; *Christian Psychology Today,* Vol. 4, No. 3, Summer 1988.
33. Minirth and Meier, *Happiness Is a Choice, op. cit.,* p. 108.
34. "The Minirth-Meier Clinic," *op. cit.,* March 2, 1988.
35. Minirth and Meier, *Happiness Is a Choice, op. cit.,* p. 85.
36. *Ibid.,* p. 87.
37. Martin and Deidre Bobgan. *The Psychological Way / The Spiritual Way.* Minneapolis: Bethany House Publishers, 1979, p. 68ff.
38. Meier, Minirth, and Wichern, *Introduction to Psychology and Counseling, op. cit.,* pp. 110-111.
39. Minirth and Meier, *Happiness Is a Choice, op. cit.,* p. 79.
40. *Ibid.,* p. 80.
41. *Diagnostic and Statistical Manual of Mental Disorder, DSM-III-R, op. cit.,* p. 348.
42. *Ibid.,* p. 349.

43. Minirth and Meier, *Happiness Is a Choice, op. cit.*, p. 84.
44. Theodore Lidz. *The Person.* New York: Basic Books, Inc., Publishers, 1968, p. 226.
45. *Ibid.*, p. 230.
46. E. M. Thornton. *The Freudian Fallacy.* Garden City: The Dial Press, Doubleday & Company, Inc., 1984, p. 146.
47. Sigmund Freud. *The Standard Edition of the Complete Psychological Works of Sigmund Freud*, trans. and ed. James Strachey, Anna Freud, et al., 24 vols. London: Hogarth Press, 1953-1974, Vol. 7, p. 78.
48. Jim Swan, "Mater and Nannie. . . ." *American Imago*, Spring 1974, p. 10.
49. Minirth and Meier, *Happiness Is a Choice, op. cit.*, pp. 114-115.
50 Ernest Hilgard, Richard Atkinson, Rita Atkinson. *Introduction to Psychology*, 7th Ed. New York: Harcourt, Brace, Jovanovich, Inc., 1979, p. 168.
51. Terence Hines. *Pseudoscience and the Paranormal.* New York: Prometheus Books, 1988, p. 111.
52. Meier, Minirth, and Wichern, *Introduction to Psychology and Counseling, op. cit.*, p. 154.
53. J. Allan Hobson, "Dream Theory: A New View of the Brain-Mind," The Harvard Medical School Mental Health Letter, Feb. 1989, p. 4.
54. *Ibid.*
55. *Ibid.*
56. *Ibid.*, p. 5.
57. Meier, Minirth, and Wichern, *Introduction to Psychology and Counseling, op. cit.*, p. 248.
58. Lenore E. Walker, "Battered Women." *Women and Psychotherapy : An Assessment of Research and Practice.* Annette M. Brodsky and Rachel T. Hare-Mustin, eds. New York: The Guilford Press, 1980, p. 340.
59. *Ibid.*, p. 341.
60. Irene Hanson Frieze and Maureen C. McHugh, "When Disaster Strikes." *EveryWoman's Emotional Well-Being.* Carol Tavris, ed. Garden City: Doubleday & Company, Inc., 1986, p. 356.
61. *Ibid.*, p. 358.
62. Minirth and Meier, *Happiness Is a Choice, op. cit.*, pp. 96-97.
63. J. P. Chaplin. *Dictionary of Psychology*, Revised Edition. New York: Dell Publishing Co., Inc., 1968, 1975, p. 302.
64. Irene S. Gillman, "An Object-Relations Approach to the Phenomenon and Treatment of Battered Women." *Psychiatry*, Vol. 43, November 1980, p. 346.
65. Walker, *op. cit.*, p. 343.
66. Paula Caplan. *The Myth of Women's Masochism.* New York: E. P. Dutton, 1985.
67. Richard Gelles and Murray A. Straus . *Intimate Violence.* New York: Simon and Schuster, 1988.
68. Harriet Lerner. *The Dance of Anger.* New York: Harper & Row, Publishers, 1985.
69. Jeffrey M. Masson. *The Assault on Truth: Freud's Suppression of the Seduction Theory. New York: Viking Penguin, 1984, 1985.*
70. Florence Rush. *The Best Kept Secret: Sexual Abuse of Children.* Inglewood Cliff: Prentice-Hall, 1980.
71. Gelles and Straus, *op. cit.*
72. Caplan, *op. cit.*, p. 1.
73. *Ibid.*, pp. 1-2.
74. *Ibid.*, p. 2.
75. Letter on file.
76. Theodor Reik. *Masochism in Modern Man.* New York: Farrar, Straus and Company, 1941, p. 214.
77. *Ibid.*, p. 197.
78. *Ibid.*, p. 203.
79. Caplan, *op. cit.*, p. 164.
80. *Ibid.*, p. 165.
81. Gelles and Straus, *op. cit.*, p. 5.
82. *Ibid.*, p. 49.
83. *Ibid.*, p. 146.
84. Jeffrey M. Masson. *Against Therapy: Emotional Tyranny and the Myth of Psychological Healing.* New York: Atheneum, 1988, p. x.
85. *Ibid.*, p. 7.
86. *Ibid.*, p. 65.
87. Anna Freud, quoted by Jeffrey Masson. *The Assault on Truth, op. cit.*, p. 113.
88. Thomas Szasz. *The Myth of Psychotherapy.* Garden City: Doubleday/Anchor Press, 1978, p. 133.
89. Minirth and Meier, *Happiness Is a Choice, op. cit.*, 84.
90. *Ibid.*
91. *Diagnostic and Statistical Manual of Mental Disorders, DSM-III-R, op. cit.*, p. 349.
92. "The Minirth-Meier Clinic," *op. cit.*, March 2, 1988.
93. *Ibid.*, February 2, 1988.
94. *Ibid.*
95. Andrew M. Mathews, Michael G. Gelder, Derek W. Johnston. *Agoraphobia : Nature and Treatment.* New York: The Guilford Press, 1981, p. 7.
96. David Faust and Jay Ziskin, "The Expert Witness in Psychology and Psychiatry," *Science*, Vol. 241, 1 July 1988, p. 34.
97. Lee Coleman. *The Reign of Error.* Boston: Beacon Press, 1984, p. 21.

98. *Ibid.*, p. xv.

Chapter 19: Defense Mechanisms.
1. Paul Meier, Frank Minirth, and Frank Wichern. *Introduction to Psychology and Counseling.* Grand Rapids: Baker Book House, 1982, p. 231.
2. *Ibid.*, p. 107.
3. *Ibid.*, p. 232.
4. Ernest Hilgard, Richard Atkinson, Rita Atkinson. *Introduction to Psychology*, 7th Ed. New York: Harcourt, Brace, Jovanovich, Inc., 1979, pp. 389-390.
5. *Ibid.*, p. 390.
6. *Ibid.*, pp. 390-391.
7. *Ibid.*, p. 426.
8. *Ibid.*, p. 427.
9. Sigmund Freud, "Mourning and Melancholia." (1917) *The Standard Edition of the Complete Psychological Works of Sigmund Freud*, trans. and ed. James Strachey, Anna Freud, et al., 24 vols. London: Hogarth Press, 1953-1974, Vol. 14, p. 248.
10. Meier, Minirth, and Wichern, *Introduction to Psychology and Counseling, op. cit.*, p. 231ff.
11. "The Minirth-Meier Clinic" Radio Program, P. O. Box 1925, Richardson, TX, 75085, March 2, 1988.
12. Frank B. Minirth and Paul D. Meier. *Happiness Is a Choice.* Grand Rapids: Baker Book House, 1978, p. 61.
13. *Ibid.*, p. 89.
14. *Ibid.*, p. 127.
15. Adolf Grunbaum. *The Foundations of Psychoanalysis.* Berkeley: University of California Press, 1984, back cover flap.
16. "The Minirth-Meier Clinic," *op. cit.*, March 2, 1988.
17. Meier, Minirth, and Wichern, *Introduction to Psychology and Counseling, op. cit.*, p. 235.
18. *Ibid.*
19. *Ibid.*
20. *Ibid.*
21. *Ibid.*
22. Charles Pfeiffer and Everett F. Harrison, eds. *The Wycliffe Bible Commentary.* Chicago: Moody Press, 1962, p. 941.
23. Meier, Minirth, and Wichern, *Introduction to Psychology and Counseling, op. cit.*, p. 235.
24. *Ibid.*
25. *Ibid.*

Chapter 20: Personality Formation.
1. Frank B. Minirth and Paul D. Meier, "Counseling and the Nature of Man," in *Walvoord: A Tribute.* Donald Campbell, ed. Chicago: Moody Press, 1982, p. 306.
2. Frank B. Minirth and Paul D. Meier. *Happiness Is a Choice.* Grand Rapids: Baker Book House, 1978, p. 48.
3. Paul Meier, Frank Minirth, and Frank Wichern. *Introduction to Psychology and Counseling.* Grand Rapids: Baker Book House, 1982, p. 99.
4. Sigmund Freud. *The Ego and the Id.* Translated by Joan Riviere; revised and edited by James Strachey. New York: W. W. Norton and Company, Inc., 1960, p. 13.
5. "The Minirth-Meier Clinic" Radio Program, P. O. Box 1925, Richardson, TX, 75085, February 19, 1987.
6. Minirth and Meier, *Happiness Is a Choice, op. cit.*, 82.
7. Paul D. Meier. *Christian Child-Rearing and Personality Development.* Grand Rapids: Baker Book House, 1977, p. 99.
8. Martin Gross. *The Psychological Society.* New York: Random House, 1978, p. 254.
9. Carol Tavris, "The Freedom to Change," *Prime Time*, October 1980, p. 28.
10. *Ibid.*, p. 31.
11. *Ibid.*
12. *Ibid.*, p. 32.
13. *Ibid.*
14. Orville G. Brim, Jr. and Jerome Kagan. *Constancy and Change in Human Development.* Cambridge: Harvard University Press, p. 1980, p. 1.
15. Letter on file.
16. Letter on file.
17. Letter on file.
18. Minirth and Meier, *Happiness Is a Choice, op. cit.*, p. 48.
19. "The Minirth-Meier Clinic" Radio Program, P. O. Box 1925, Richardson, TX, 75085, May 26, 1987.
20. *Ibid.*, February 19, 1987.
21. Meier, Minirth, and Wichern, *Introduction to Psychology and Counseling, op. cit.*, p. 98.
22. Edward Ziegler quoted by Fredelle Maynard. *The Child Care Crisis.*, New York: Viking Penguin Inc., 1985, p. 10.
23. Caroline Bird. *The Two-Paycheck Marriage.* New York: Pocket books, 1980, pp. 4-5.
24. *Women and Poverty*, National Council of Welfare, October, 1979, Table 4.
25. Jeff Shear, "Baby's Angle and a Mother's Touch," *Insight*, 30 January 1989, p. 53.

26. Eli Ginzberg, quoted by Sheila B. Kamerman. *Parenting in an Unresponsive Society.* New York: Free Press, 1980, p. 8.
27. Johanna Freedman. *Parental Leave Crisis.* Edward F. Zigler and Meryl Frank, eds. New Haven: Yale University Press, 1988, p. 27.
28. "The Minirth-Meier Clinic," *op. cit.,* May 26, 1987.
29. Fredelle Maynard. *The Child Care Crisis.* New York: Viking Penguin , Inc., 1985, p. 113.
30. Jerome Kagan, quoted in Maynard, *ibid.,* p. 15.
31. Harold Hodgkinson interviewed by William Duckett, "Using Demographic Data for Long-Range Planning," *Phi Delta Kappa,* October 1988, p. 168.
32. Thomas Gamble and Edward Zigler, "Effects of Infant Day Care: Another Look at the Evidence." *The Parental Leave Crisis, op. cit.,* p. 77.
33. Greta G. Fein and Elaine R. Moorin, "Group Care Can Have Good Effects," *Day Care and Early Education,* Spring 1980, p. 17.
34. Louise Bates Ames, quoted by Martin Gross. *The Psychological Society.* New York: Random House,1978, p. 247.
35. Gross, *ibid.,* p. 250.
36. *Ibid.,* p. 251.
37. *Ibid.,* p. 269.
38. *Ibid.*
39. Eugene J. Webb, letter, *Science News,* Vol. 135, No. 5, 4 February 1989, p. 67.
40. Minirth and Meier, *Happiness Is a Choice, op. cit.,* p. 52.
41. Meier, Minirth, and Wichern, *Introduction to Psychology and Counseling, op. cit.,* pp. 383, 389; Meier, *Christian Child-Rearing and Personality Development,* op. cit., p.17.
42. Minirth and Meier, *Happiness Is a Choice, op. cit.,* p. 60.
43. *Ibid.,* p. 82.
44. *Ibid.,* pp. 209-211.
45. Meier, Minirth, and Wichern, *Introduction to Psychology and Counseling, op. cit.,* pp. 268-270.
46. Frank Minirth, Paul Meier, Seigfried Fink, Walter Byrd, and Don Hawkins. *Taking Control.* Grand Rapids: Baker Book House, 1988, pp. 127-128.
47. "The Minirth-Meier Clinic," *op. cit.,* February 17, 1987.
48. *Ibid.,* June 18, 1986; February 4, 1988; April 7, 1988.
49. Meier, Minirth, and Wichern, *Introduction to Psychology and Counseling, op. cit.,* p. 193.
50. Minirth and Meier, *Happiness Is a Choice, op. cit.,* p. 56.
51. "The Minirth-Meier Clinic," *op. cit.,* June 18, 1986.
52. Meier, Minirth, and Wichern, *Introduction to Psychology and Counseling, op. cit.,* p. 193.
53. "The Minirth-Meier Clinic," *op. cit.,* June 18, 1986.
54. *Ibid.,* February 17, 1987.
55. *Ibid.,* June 18, 1986.
56. Theodore Lidz. *The Person.* New York: Basic Books, Inc., Publishers, 1968, p. 229.
57. Gross, *op. cit.,* pp. 79-80.
58. *Ibid.,* p. 80.
59. Irving Bieber, quoted by Alfred M. Freedman and Harold I. Kaplan. *Comprehensive Textbook of Psychiatry.* Baltimore, Md: Williams & Wilkins Company, 1967, p. 968.
60. Ronald Bayer. *Homosexuality and American Psychiatry: The Politics of Diagnosis.* New York: Basic Books, Inc., Publishers, 1981, p. 24.
61. "The Minirth-Meier Clinic," *op. cit.,* June 18, 1986.
62. Gross, *op. cit.,* p. 81.

Chapter 21: Claims, Cures, and Questions
1. "The Minirth-Meier Clinic" Radio Program, P. O. Box 1925, Richardson, TX, 75085, September 3, 1987; October 22, 1987.
2. Michael T. McGuire. *The Psychotherapy Handbook.* Richie Herink, ed. New York: New American Library, 1980, p. 301.
3. Jeffrey M. Masson. *Against Therapy: Emotional Tyranny and the Myth of Psychological Healing.* New York: Atheneum, 1988, p. xx.
4. "The Minirth-Meier Clinic," *op. cit.,* October 22, 1987.
5. Susan C. Wooley and Orlando W. Wooley, "Eating Disorders." *Women and Psychotherapy : An Assessment of Research and Practice.* Annette M. Brodsky and Rachel T. Hare-Mustin, eds. New York: The Guilford Press, 1980, pp. 135-158.
6. Hilde Bruch. *Eating Disorders: Obesity, Anorexia, and the Person Within.* New York: Basic Books, 1973, p. 336.
7. *Diagnostic and Statistical Manual of Mental Disorders, DSM-III,* Third Edition. Washington: American Psychiatric Association, 1980, p. 257.
8. "The Minirth-Meier Clinic," *op. cit.,* September 3, 1987.
9. Richard Kluft, "Healing the Multiple," *Institute of Noetic Sciences,* Vol. 1, No. 3/4, p. 15.
10. Richard P. Kluft, "Treatment of Multiple Personality Disorder," *The Psychiatric Clinics of North America,* Symposium on Multiple Personality, Vol. 7, No. 1, March 1984, p. 9.
11. John Beahrs. *Unity and Multiplicity: Multilevel Consciousness of Self in Hypnosis, Psychiatric Disorder and Mental Health.* New York: Brunel/Mazel, 1982, pp. 133-134.
12. David Caul, quoted by E. Hale, "Inside the Divided Mind," *New York Times Magazine,* April 17, 1983, p. 106.

13. Beahrs, *op. cit.*, p. 132.
14. *Ibid.*, pp. 133, 156.
15. Dianne L. Chambless, "Characteristics of Agoraphobics,"*Agoraphobia: Multiple Perspectives on Theory and Treatment*. Dianne L. Chambless and Alan J. Goldstein, eds. New York: John Wiley & Sons, 1982, p. 2.
16. "The Minirth-Meier Clinic," *op. cit.*, February 2, 1988.
17. *Ibid.*
18. *Ibid.*
19. *Ibid.*
20. Dianne L. Chambless, "Fears and Anxiety." *EveryWoman's Emotional Well-Being*. Carol Tavris, ed. Garden City: Doubleday and Company, Inc., 1986, p. 424.
21. Chambless, "Characteristics of Agoraphobics," *op. cit.*, p. 10ff.
22. Andrew Mathews et al. *Agoraphobia: Nature and Treatment*. New York: The Guilford Press, 1981, pp. 38-39.
23. Dianne L. Chambless and Alan J. Goldstein, "Anxieties: Agoraphobia and Hysteria." *Women and Psychotherapy* New York: The Guilford Press, 1980, p. 122.
24. Letter on file.
25. "The Minirth-Meier Clinic," *op. cit.*, June 18, 1986.
26. Frank Minirth, Paul Meier, Don Hawkins. *Worry Free Living*. Nashville: Thomas Nelson Publishers, 1989, p. 59.
27. John Tierney, "The Myth of the Firstborn," *Science*, December 1983, p. 16.
28. Chambless, "Fears and Anxiety," *op. cit.*, p. 420.
29. Mathews, *op. cit.*, pp. 63-64.
30. Chambless, "Fears and Anxiety," *op. cit.*, p. 425.
31. *Ibid.*, p. 430.
32. Paul Meier on "Issues of the '80's," Richard Land, Moderator, KCBI, Dallas, Texas, 11 October 1985.
33. Paul Meier, Frank Minirth, and Frank Wichern. *Introduction to Psychology and Counseling*. Grand Rapids: Baker Book House, 1982, p. 335.
34. Meier on "Issues of the '80's," *op. cit.*
35. Minirth, Frank B. and Paul D. Meier. *Happiness Is a Choice*, Way to Grow Cassettes. Waco, TX: Word, Inc., November 15, 1986, Tape 4.
36. Letter on file.
37. *Harvard Medical School Mental Health Letter*, Vol. 2, No. 12, June 1986, p. 1.
38. E. Fuller Torrey. *Surviving Schizophrenia*. Harper & Row, Publishers, 1983, p. 99.
39. *Ibid.*, p. 111.
40. A. Carlsson, "The Dopamine Hypothesis of Schizophrenia 20 Years Later." *Search for the Causes of Schizophrenia*. H. Hafner, W. F. Gattaz, and W. Janzarik, eds. New York: Springer-Verlag, 1987, p. 223.
41. Torrey, *op. cit.*, p. 65.
42. *Ibid.*, p. 66.
43. *Ibid.*
44. *Ibid.*
45. "The Vermont Longitudinal Study of Persons with Severe Mental Illness I and II." *American Journal of Psychiatry*, Vol. 144, No. 6, June 1987, p. 718.
46. *Ibid.*, p. 730.
47. Meier on "Issues of the '80's," *op. cit.*
48. Torrey, *op. cit.*, p. 47.
49. Frank B. Minirth and Paul D. Meier. *Happiness Is a Choice*. Grand Rapids: Baker Book House, 1978, p. 44; Meier, Minirth, and Wichern, *Introduction to Psychology and Counseling, op. cit.*, p. 163.
50. Meier, Minirth, and Wichern, *Introduction to Psychology and Counseling, op. cit.*, p. 164.
51. *Ibid.*, p. 182.
52. Torrey, *op. cit.*, p. 96.
53. *Ibid.*
54. *Ibid.*
55. *Ibid.*, p. 85.
56. Meier on "Issues of the '80's," *op. cit.*
57. Minirth and Meier, *Happiness Is a Choice, op. cit.*, p. 98.
58. Letter on file.
59. Nancy Andreasen. *The Broken Brain*. New York: Harper and Row, 1984, p. 40
60. *Ibid.*
61. Ted L. Rosenthal and Renate H. Rosenthal, "Clinical Stress Management." *Clinical Handbook of Psychological Disorders*. New York: The Guilford Press, 1985, pp. 149-150.
62. Myrna Weissman, "Depression." *Women and Psychotherapy*. Annette M. Brodsky and Rachel Hare-Mustin, eds. New York: The Guilford Press, 1980, p. 97.
63. Meier on "Issues of the '80's," *op. cit.*
64. Minirth and Meier, *Happiness Is a Choice, op. cit.*, p. 133.
65. *Ibid.*, p. 195.
66. Stanton Jones, "The first Christian 'Introduction to Psychology and Counseling' Text?" *Journal of Psychology and Theology*, Spring 1983, Vol. 11, No. 1, p. 60.

67. *Ibid.*
68. *Ibid.*
69. Frank Minirth and Paul Meier, "How To Seek a Counselor." *Christian Psychology for Today*, Vol. 3, No. 2, Spring 1987, p. 12.
70. "The Minirth-Meier Clinic," *op. cit.*, December 16, 1986.
71. Andreasen, *op. cit.*, p. 257.

Chapter 22: Sappiness Is a Choice.
1. Paul Meier, Frank Minirth, and Frank Wichern. *Introduction to Psychology and Counseling.* Grand Rapids: Baker Book House, 1982, p. 16.
2. *Ibid.*
3. *Ibid.*
4. Thomas Szasz. *The Myth of Psychotherapy.* Garden City: Doubleday/Anchor Press, 1978, p. 7.
5. Frank B. Minirth, Paul D. Meier, and Don Hawkins. *Worry-Free Living.* Nashville: Thomas Nelson Publishers, 1989, p. 42.
6. Ronald Leifer. *In the Name of Mental Health.* New York: Science House, 1969, pp.36-37.
7. *Ibid.*, p. 38.
8. E. Fuller Torrey. *The Death of Psychiatry.* Radnor: Chilton Book Company, 1974, preface.
9. *Ibid.*, p. 24.
10. Meier, Minirth, and Wichern, *Introduction to Psychology and Counseling, op. cit.*, p. 16.
11. *Webster's New World Dictionary of the American Language*, Second College Edition. New York: Simon and Schuster, 1984.

PsychoHeresy.
1. Howard Kendler in *Autobiographies in Experimental Psychology*. Ronald Gandelman, ed. Hillsdale: Lawrence Erlbaum, 1985, p. 46.
2. Allen E. Bergin and Michael J. Lambert, "The Evaluation of Therapeutic Outcomes," *Handbook of Psychotherapy and Behavior Change*, 2nd Edition. Sol Garfield and Allen E. Bergin, eds. New York: John Wiley & Sons, 1978, p. 170.
3. Ursula Vils, "Professor Helps Play Bubble to the Surface," *Los Angeles Times*, 10 September 1981, Part V, pp. 1, 15.
4. Ronald L. Koteskey, "Abandoning the Psyche to Secular Treatment," *Christianity Today*, June 1985, p. 20.
5. Aristides, "What Is Vulgar?" *The American Scholar*, Winter 1981-1982, p. 17.
6. Alexander W. Astin, "The Functional Autonomy of Psychotherapy." *The Investigation of Psychotherapy: Commentaries and Readings.* Arnold P. Goldstein and Sanford J. Dean, eds. New York: John Wiley, 1966, p. 62.
7. *Ibid.*, p. 65.
8. Dr. Lawrence LeShan. *Association for Humanistic Psychology*, October 1984, p. 4.
9. Hans Christian Andersen. *The Emperor's New Clothes.* New York: Golden Press.

Books from EastGate

Christian Psychology's War on God's Word:
The Victimization of the Believer by Jim Owen is about the sufficiency of Christ and about how "Christian" psychology undermines believers' reliance on the Lord. Owen demonstrates how "Christian" psychology pathologizes sin and contradicts biblical doctrines of man. He further shows that "Christian" psychology treats people more as victims needing psychological intervention than sinners needing to repent. Owen beckons believers to turn to the all-sufficient Christ and to trust fully in His ever-present provisions, the power of His indwelling Holy Spirit, and the sure guidance of the inerrant Word of God.

PsychoHeresy: The Psychological Seduction of Christianity by Martin and Deidre Bobgan exposes the fallacies and failures of psychological counseling theories and therapies for one purpose: to call the church back to curing souls by means of the Word of God and the work of the Holy Spirit rather than by man-made means and opinions. Besides revealing the anti-Christian biases, internal contradictions, and documented failures of secular psychotherapy, PsychoHeresy examines various amalgamations of secular psychologies with Christianity and explodes firmly entrenched myths that undergird those unholy unions.

Prophets of PsychoHeresy I by Martin and Deidre Bobgan is a sequel to *PsychoHeresy*. It is a more detailed critique of the writings of four individuals who attempt to integrate psychological counseling theories and therapies with the Bible. They are: Dr. Gary Collins, Dr. Lawrence Crabb, Jr., Dr. Paul Meier, and Dr. Frank Minirth. The book deals with issues, not personalities.

Prophets of PsychoHeresy II by Martin and Deidre Bobgan is a critique of Dr. James Dobson's teachings on psychology and self-esteem. In addition, several chapters are devoted to self-esteem, from the perspective of the Bible, research, and historical development. As with the Bobgans' other books, this is a discussion of teachings rather than personalities. The purpose of the book is to alert Christians to the inherent dangers of turning to the psychological wisdom of men to understand why we are the way we are, why we do what we do, and how we are to change.

More Books from EastGate

12 Steps to Destruction: Codependency/Recovery Heresies by Martin and Deidre Bobgan provides essential information for Christians about codependency/recovery teachings, Alcoholics Anonymous, Twelve-Step groups, and addiction treatment programs. They are examined from a biblical, historical, and research perspective. The book urges believers to trust in the sufficiency of Christ and the Word of God instead of the Twelve Steps and codependency/recovery theories and therapies.

Four Temperaments, Astrology & Personality Testing by Martin and Deidre Bobgan answers such questions as: Do the four temperaments give true insight into people? Are there any biblically or scientifically established temperament or personality types? Are personality inventories and tests valid ways of finding out about people? How are the four temperaments, astrology, and personality testing connected? Personality types and tests are examined from a biblical, historical, and research basis.

The Grand Demonstration: A Biblical Study of the So-Called Problem of Evil by Dr. Jay E. Adams penetrates deeply into the scriptural teaching about the nature of God and the existence of evil. Nearly every Christian asks this question: "Why is there sin, rape, disease, war, pain, and death in a good God's world?" But he rarely receives a satisfactory answer. Nevertheless God has spoken clearly on this issue. Moving into territory others fear to tread, Dr. Adams maintains that a fearless acceptance of biblical truth solves the so-called problem of evil.

Lord of the Dance: The Beauty of the Disciplined Life by Deidre Bobgan is for women who desire a deeper, more meaningful, intimate walk with the Savior. From her background in classical ballet, Deidre draws unique parallels between the training of a ballet dancer and a disciplined, graceful walk with God.

For information, write to:

EastGate Publishers
4137 Primavera Road
Santa Barbara, CA 93110